Jeremy Robinson has written many critical studies, including *Steven Spielberg*, *Arthur Rimbaud*, and *The Sacred Cinema of Andrei Tarkovsky*, plus literary monographs on: William Shakespeare; Samuel Beckett; Thomas Hardy; André Gide; Robert Graves; and John Cowper Powys.

It's amazing for me to see my work treated with such passion and respect. There is nothing resembling it in the U.S. in relation to my work.

Andrea Dworkin (on *Andrea Dworkin*)

This model monograph – it is an exemplary job, and I'm very proud that he has accorded me a couple of mentions... The subject matter of his book is beautifully organised and dead on beam.

Lawrence Durrell (on *The Light Eternal: A Study of J.M.W. Turner*)

His poetry is very good deep moving stuff.

Cloud Nine magazine

Jeremy Robinson's poetry is certainly jammed with ideas, and I find it very interesting for that reason. It's certainly a strong imprint of his personality.

Colin Wilson

Sex-Magic-Poetry-Cornwall is a very rich essay... It is a very good piece... vastly stimulating and insightful.

Peter Redgrove

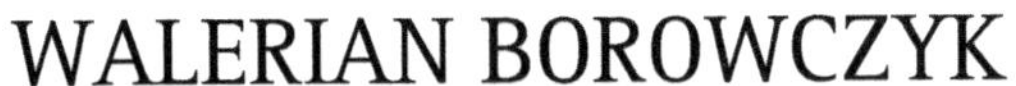

WALERIAN BOROWCZYK

WALERIAN BOROWCZYK

Cinema of Erotic Dreams

Jeremy Mark Robinson

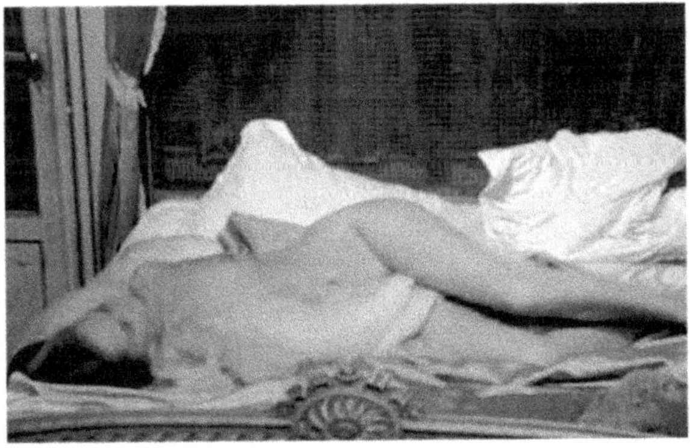

CRESCENT MOON

First published 2008. Second edition 2012.

Printed and bound in the U.S.A.
Set in Rotis Serif 10 on 14pt, and Gill Sans Light display.
Designed by Radiance Graphics.

British Library Cataloguing in Publication data available for this title.

ISBN-13 9781861713124 (Hbk)

ISBN-13 9781861713674 (Pbk)

Crescent Moon Publishing
P.O. Box 1312
Maidstone, Kent
ME14 5XU, Great Britain
www.crmoon.com

CONTENTS

ACKNOWLEDGEMENTS

To the copyright holders of the illustrations.
To authors quoted and their publishers.

PICTURE CREDITS

Argos Films. Pagan. Cult Epics. Severin Films. Naja Films. Palace Video. New Horizon. Gaumont/ Columbia. C.A.V. Distribution. Nouveaux Pictures. New Line Cinema. Sara Distribution. Jupiter Communications. CDF Films. Lisa Film. Top Video.

PART ONE

WALERIAN BOROWCZYK

Omnia vincit Amor: et nos cedamus Amori.
Love carries all before him: we too must yield to Love.

Virgil, *Aenid* (X. 69)

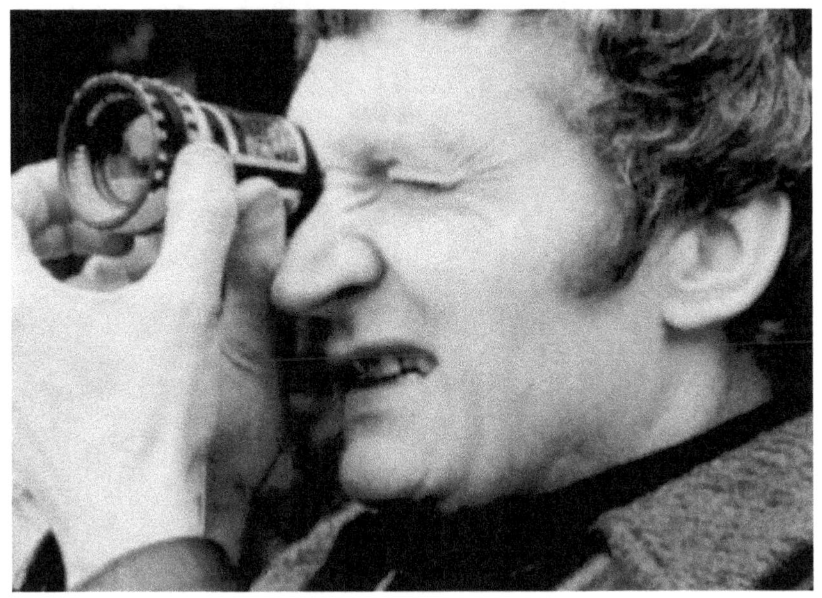

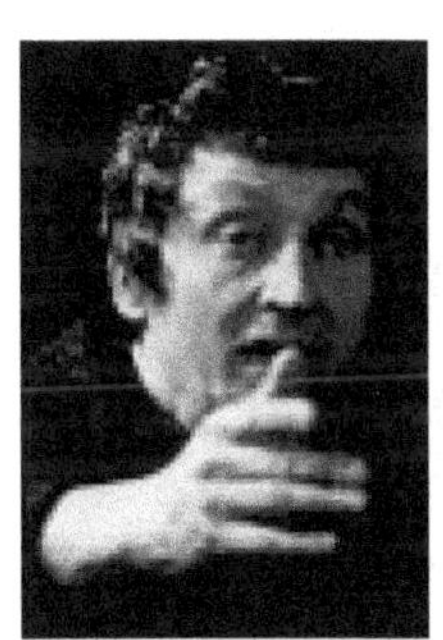

Walerian Borowczyk

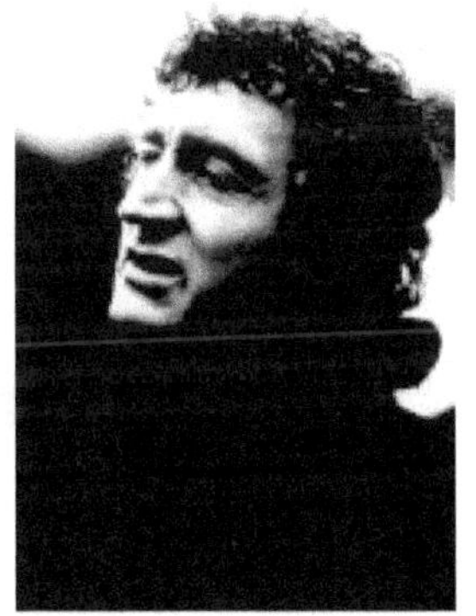

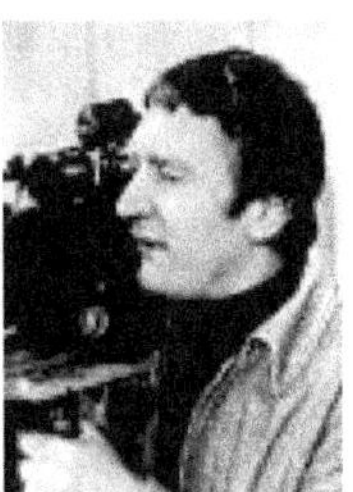

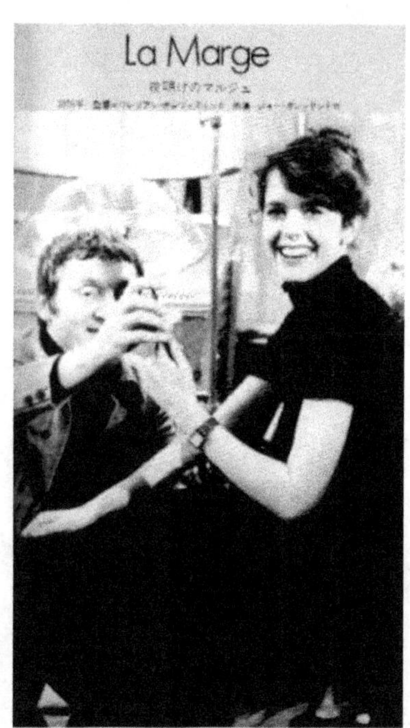
La Marge

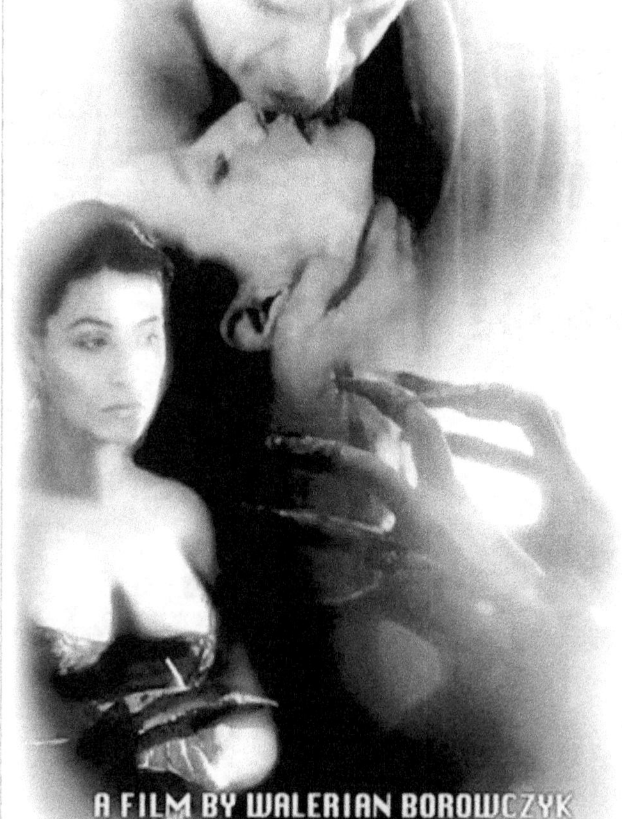
A Cult Epics Release
LOVE RITES
A FILM BY WALERIAN BOROWCZYK
THE DIRECTOR OF THE BEAST

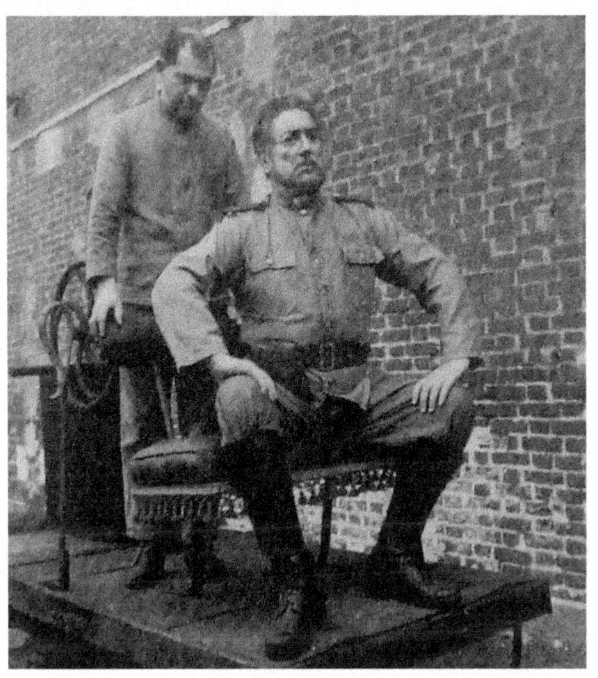

The king, Goto III, and his assassin, Grozo,
in a true masterpiece of cinema,
Walerian Borowczyk's Goto, Island of Love

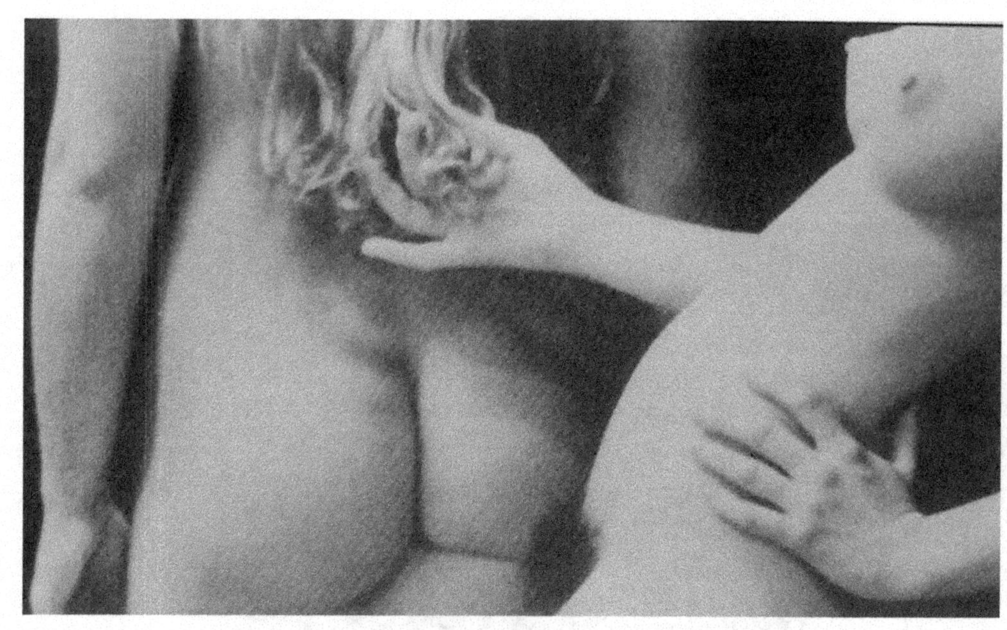

Walerian Borowczyk's Immoral Tales (1974)

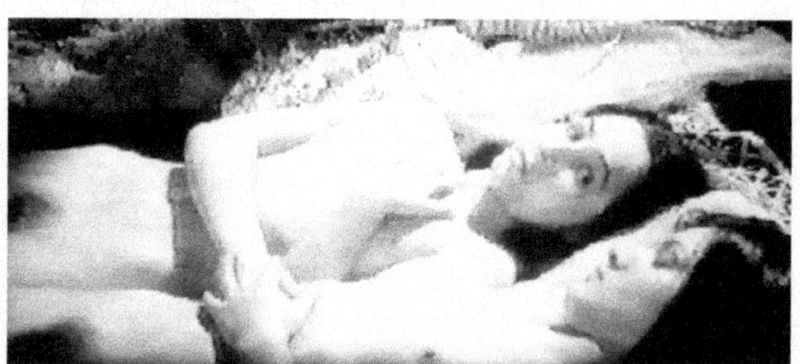

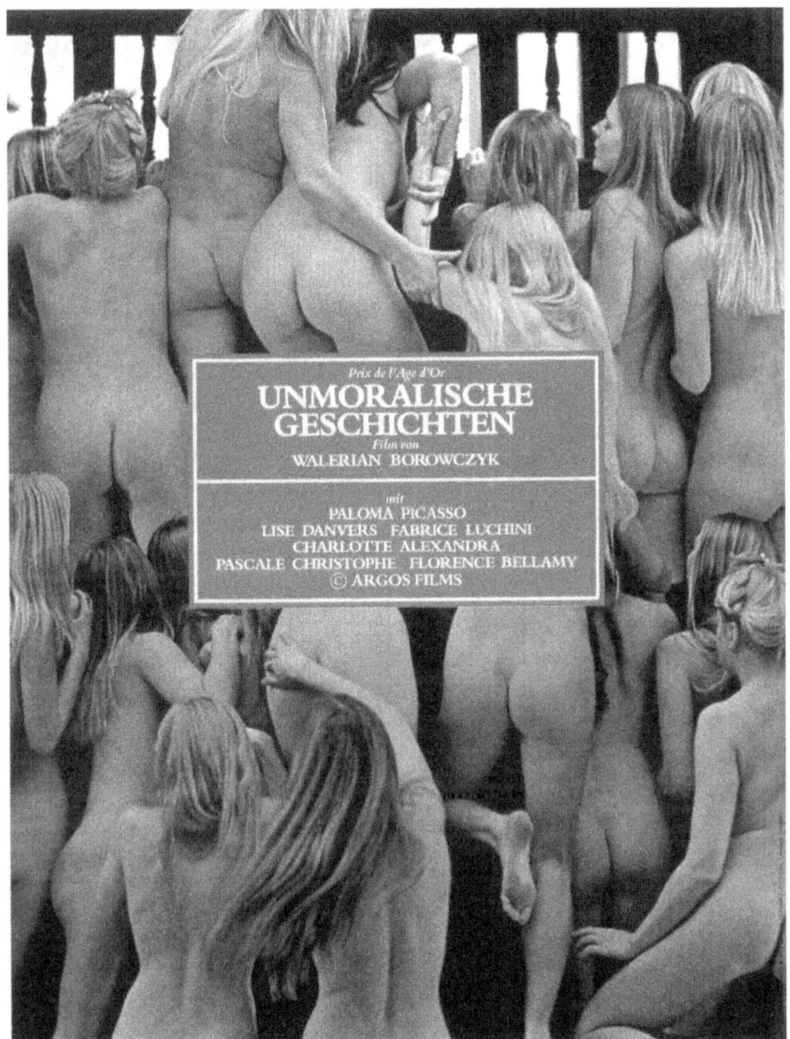

Argos Films' Immoral Tales

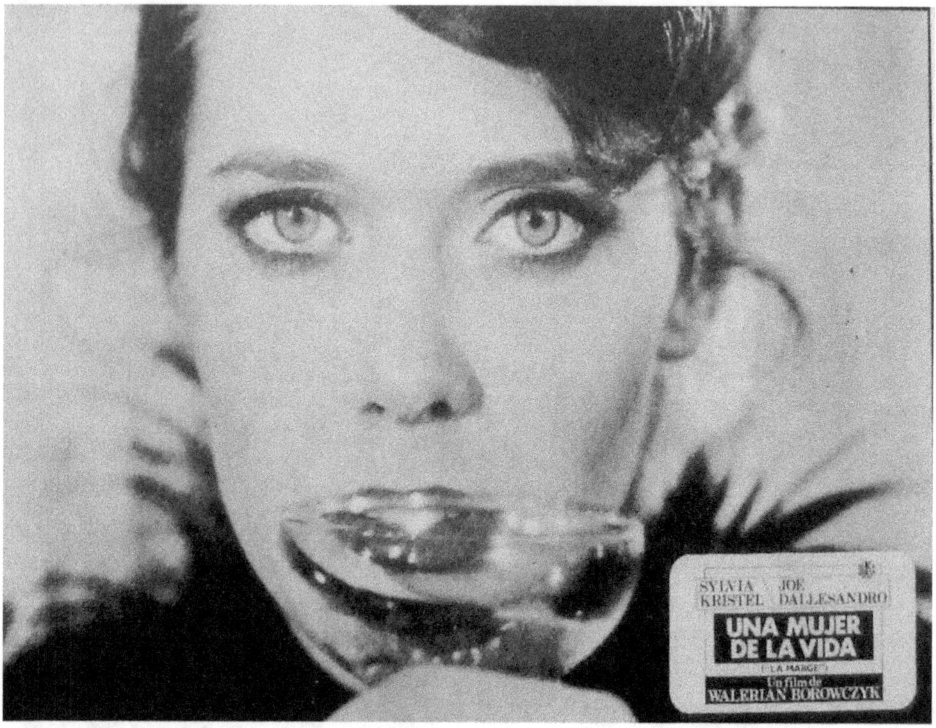

Walerian Borowczyk's La Marge

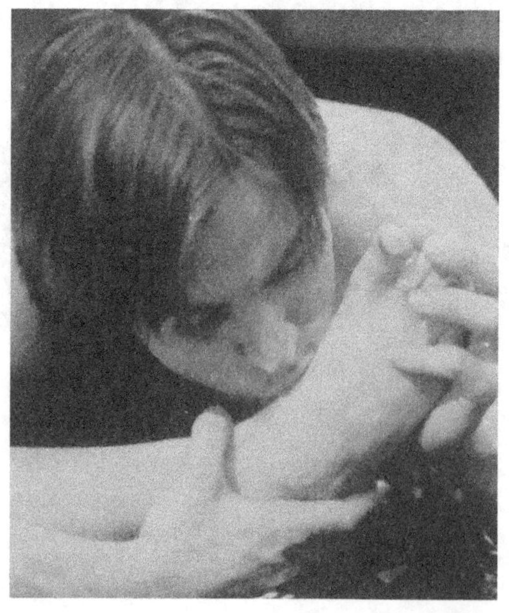

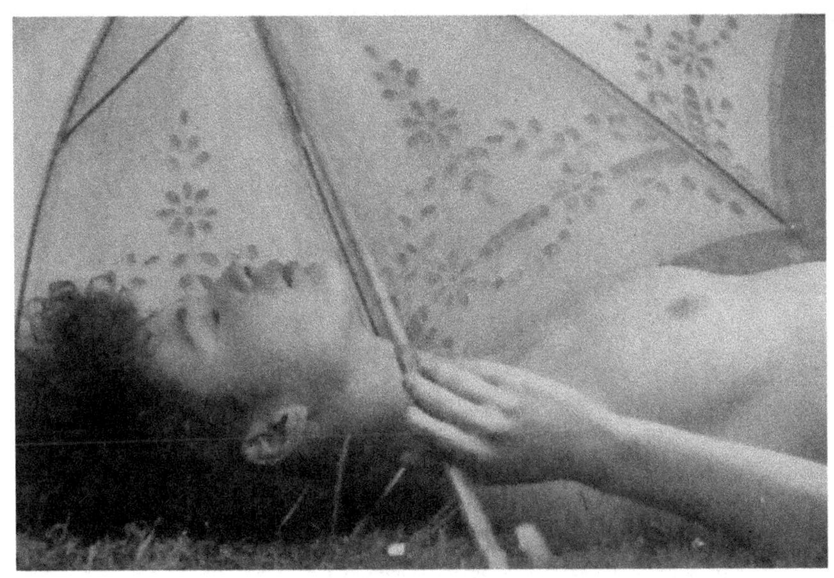

The Art of Love, below, and Three Immoral Women, above.

Marina Pierro in ancient Rome, and Gaëlle Legrand –
a girl in 19th century France playing with her rabbit.

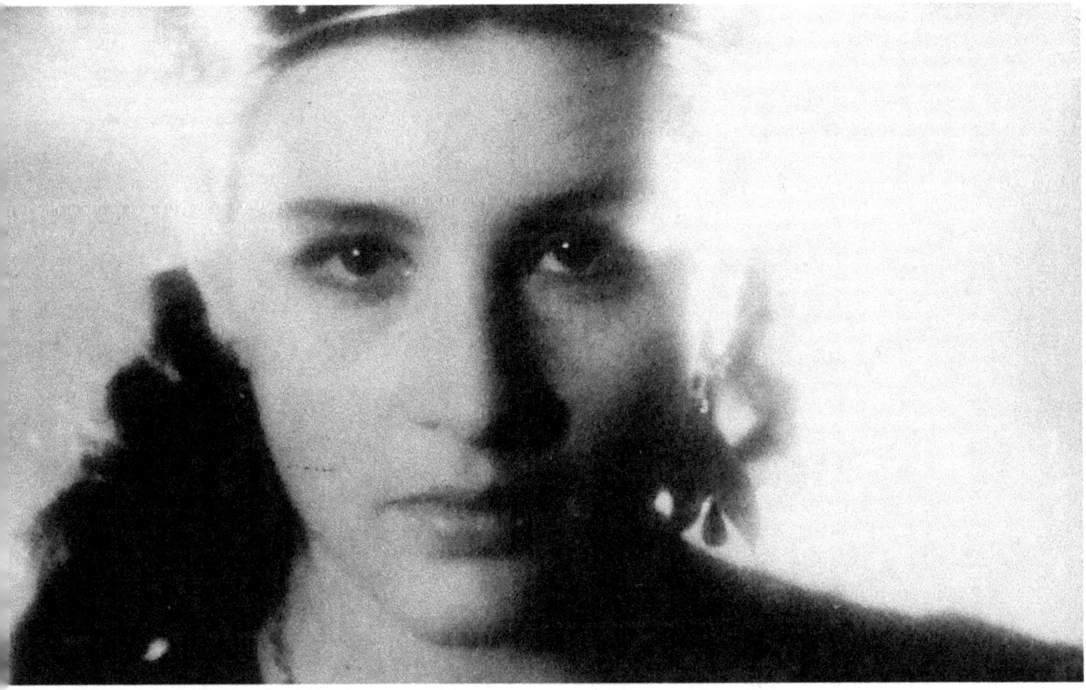

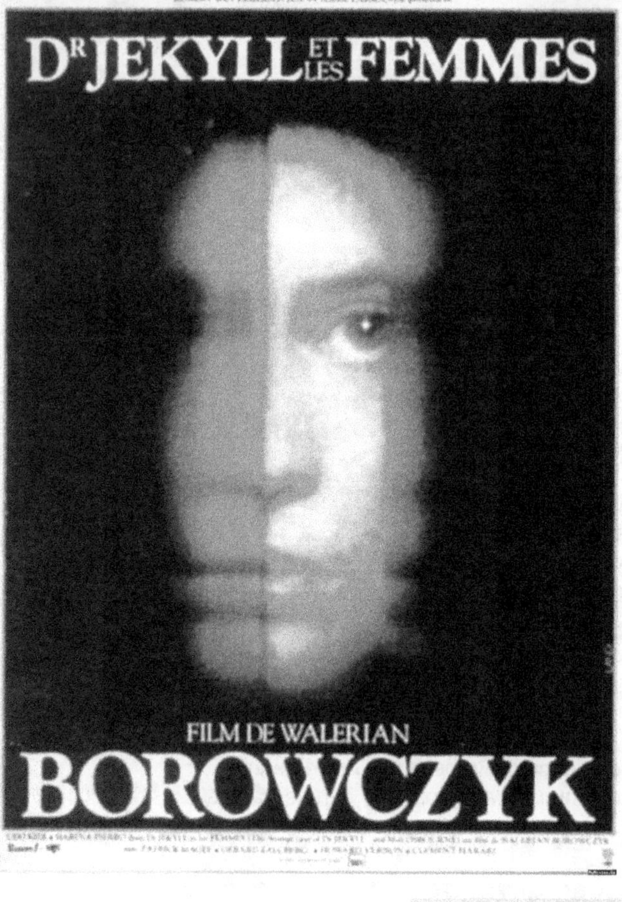

Behind Convent Walls (right).
Dr Jekyll and His Women (above).

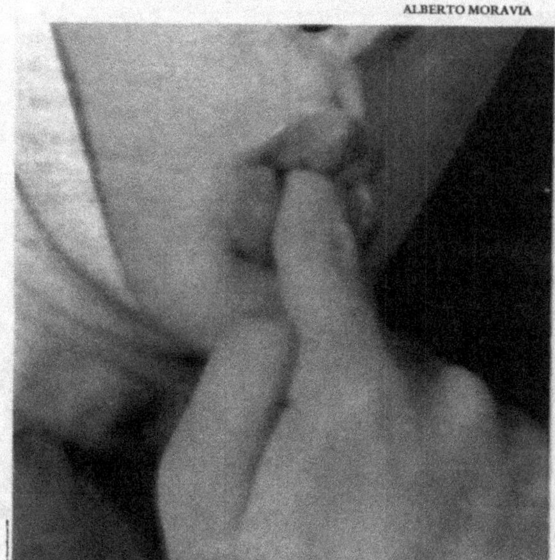

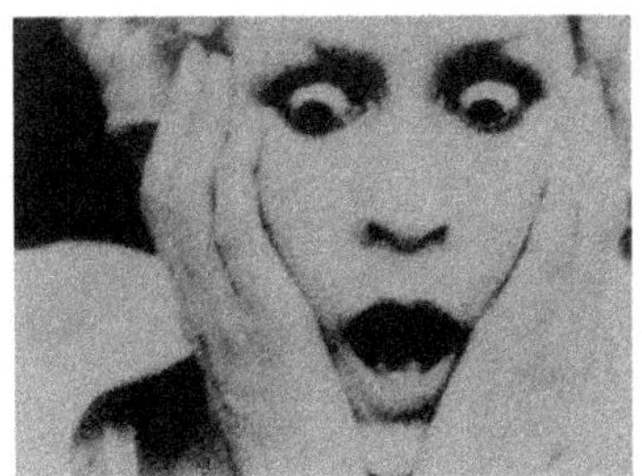

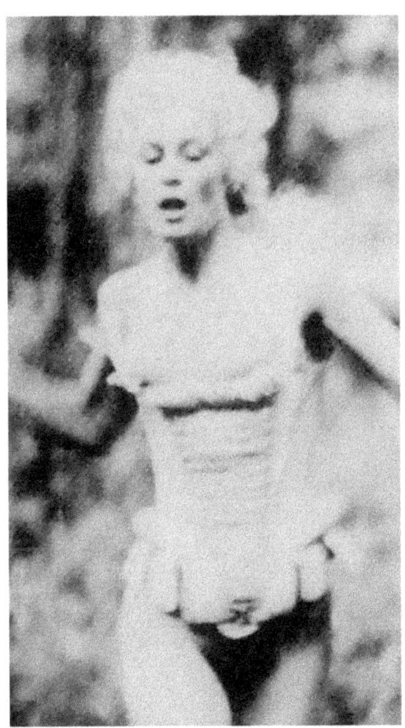

Sirpa Lane in Walerian Borowczyk's The Beast

1

THE CINEMA OF WALERIAN BOROWCZYK

Eroticism, sex, is one of the most moral parts of life. Eroticism does not kill, exterminate, encourage evil, lead to crime. On the contrary, it makes people gentler, brings joy, gives fulfilment, leads to selfless pleasure.

Walerian Borowczyk[1]

1 Interview with Andrzej Markowski, *Kino*, 4, 1975.

Walerian Borowczyk (known as 'Boro') is one of cinema's one-offs. Quite simply, there is no filmmaker quite like Borowczyk. Borowczyk's movies have an extraordinary, magical quality. They reach a place very rare in contemporary cinema, and are quite unlike the pictures of any other *auteur.* Borowczyk's films create their own space, with imagery, sounds and music of a really exceptional power.

Goto: Island of Love was the first Walerian Borowczyk film that made a big impression on audiences and critics, winning a number of prizes. I first saw *Goto: Island of Love* in 1982, at Bournemouth Film School, when we watched 16mm prints as part of our film history course. You could see there was an astonishing vision at work here. I remember above all the creation of a visceral, idiosyncratic and original world.

If I had to single out some movies, I'd cite *Blanche, Immoral Tales, Behind Convent Walls, The Beast* and *Goto*, for their painterly sense, the use of props and costumes, and the incredible attention to detail. Very stylish, mysterious, poetic. Not forgetting the acute awareness of the history of religion and literature. Walerian Borowczyk produced some of the most memorable images in European cinema, the equal of Ingmar Bergman, Sergei Paradjanov or Andrei Tarkovsky.

I reckon there's one absolute Walerian Borowczyk masterpiece, and that's *Goto: Island of Love.* That can rank alongside the great films in the history of cinema. I'd put *Immoral Tales* in the masterpiece class too. The other Borowczyk films are often as fascinating, often more grotesque – certainly more sexually explicit – but probably not as wholly satisfying as *Goto: Island of Love* – from a conventional critical standpoint. But *The Beast, Blanche, Behind Convent Walls,* and *Love Rites* would count as extraordinary films by most standards.[2] They may not be quite up there with *Persona* (Ingmar Bergman) or *8 1/2* (Federico Fellini), but taken together they form a group of works that mark Borowczyk out as a maverick original. Similarly, Borowczyk isn't a filmmaker celebrated by critics or filmmakers, like Akira Kurosawa, Ingmar Bergman, Orson Welles, Federico Fellini, Jean Renoir or Sergei Eisenstein, and his films don't make critics' top ten lists.

2 For detractors, Borowczyk's films were better when they concerned ideas rather than the senses – philosophy not sex.

You probably won't know many other people who've even heard of Walerian Borowczyk, let alone seen one of his films. His reputation as a producer of European arty porny films (art-as-porn films or porn-as-art films) is probably all that many people will have heard of him (movies with sex and nudity do seem to travel well). Needless to say, Borowczyk's films are *not* shown regularly on television (in Britain at least), even by channels which boast of their open-mindedness and international film broadcasts. I can think of maybe one occasion when *Goto: Island of Love* was shown in the U.K. in 25 years, but I may be wrong about that.

Similarly, you won't see Walerian Borowczyk's pictures at the cinema nowadays, even rep and arthouse and independent cinemas rarely screen his films. It's mainly home video releases (and, later, home DVD releases) that's enabled Borowczyk's films to reach a contemporary audience (the porny and arty elements make them perfect for niche marketing to the cognoscenti). And you'll have to hunt to find them all. You won't find *The Beast* next to *Back To the Future* and *Bad Boys* on the 'B' shelf in your local video store.[3]

Another problem with assessing Boro's work is the quality of the prints, DVDs and videos available – this is a fantastically visual film-maker, but some prints are so washed out and nasty. Then there's the aspect of the sound and dubbing: some Borowczyk movies are only available in dubbed versions, rather than the much-preferred original sound plus sub-titles.

As copies of some of Walerian Borowczyk's thirteen live action feature films aren't easily available, they won't be included in this book: *Bloodbath of Dr Jeckyll* and *Lulu.* I haven't seen *Blanche* and *La Marge* for a long time, so I have only included my notes on those films, written when I saw them. It's frustrating that so many of Borowczyk's 14 feature flicks (13 live action movies plus one animated film) are hard to find. Especially when there's so much other dreck readily available.[4]

3 Even the ten films available in the U.S.A. and the U.K. are difficult to track down – you'll have to try the usual places – amazon.com, ebay.com – but there'll be plenty more hunting around to find the rarer items.

4 You can see some of Borowczyk's short films on the excellent UbuWeb Film site (ubu.com), and also YouTube (youtube.com).

However, for a time Walerian Borowczyk's films were popular, or at least they were on general release. According to David Cook's *A History of Narrative Film* (one of the best books on cinema *ever*, a total must-have), *The Story of Sin* was the most popular film in Poland in 1975, and *Immoral Tales* was the second most popular film in France in 1974 (that means a *lot* of people saw it – the French love movies more than almost anyone in the world).[5]

They *are* an acquired taste, but once you've seen a Walerian Borowczyk film, you don't forget it. No one else makes movies quite like Borowczyk's; the word 'unique' is thrown around a lot in critical circles, about this or that writer, this or that actor, this or that dancer. But Borowczyk's films truly are unique. As soon as that classical organ music starts up, completely distinctive, you know you're entering Borowczyk Land, a very strange place. Music's a big part of the Borowczyk world: you won't hear music like this anywhere else in cinema – and certainly not in *these* contexts. Again, many filmmakers are cited as having a distinctive way of using music – Martin Scorsese, Stanley Kubrick, Robert Altman – but Borowczyk's music has carved out its own niche. I must stop using the word 'unique' to describe Borowczyk's cinema, but he really is a man of unique talents.

You probably won't recognize many of the people in Walerian Borowczyk's films. He didn't use big stars, except once: Sylvia Kristel, darling of the Euro art film/ porn scene in the mid-1970s. There are some recognizable actors in some of Borowczyk's films, though: Patrick Magee, Udo Keir, and Joe Dallesandro, but everyone else is a French, or Italian or German actor you've probably never seen before (or since).

Walerian Borowczyk's films are completely un-politically correct. But you probably already knew that. It's not that Borowczyk sets out to offend (although there is something of the trickster, the Surrealist *épater* of the bourgeoisie about Borowczyk, as with many artists). Rather, Borowczyk simply puts in his films what he wants.

5 C. Tohill, 55. Cinema admissions in 1973 were 176 million, down from 276 million in 1964.

✢

Born on September 2, 1923 in Kwilcz in Poland, Walerian Borowczyk died on February 3, 2006, in Paris. Borowczyk studied at the Cracow Academy of Fine Arts (Andrzej Wajda was a fellow student), as a painter. Borowczyk wrote as well as directed most of his films; that's a very important point: it means that Borowczyk was much closer to being the true 'author' of his films than directors for hire (and even many celebrated directors *don't* also write their own movies. It also means that Borowczyk was largely the *originator* of his films: they didn't come from some outside influence or source, like a film producer or studio. (Other well-known Polish filmmakers include: Andrzej Wajda, Andrzej Munk, Jerzy Skolimowski, Krzystzof Zanussi, Roman Polanski and Krzysztof Kieslowski).

Based in Paris for much of his life (with his films made in French),[6] after moving there from Poland in 1958, Walerian Borowczyk was a painter and illustrator who went on to make short animated films (which included *Holy Smoke* (1963), *Le Jeux des Anges* (1964), and *Le Dictionnaire de Joachim* (1965)). Borowczyk's first animations were made with Jan Lenica (1928-2001)[7] - *Dom, Love Requited,* and *Once There Was.*

Other early films (some only a few seconds long) included *L'Ėcole* (1958), *Dom* (1958), *Les Astronautes* (1959), *Le Concert de M. et Mme. Kabal* (1962), *Renaissance* (1963), *L'Encyclopédie de grand-maman* (1963), *Rosalie* (1966), *Diptque* (1967) and *Gavotte* (1967). In his animations, Walerian Borowczyk employed a variety of techniques, including pixillation, loops, collage, and painting on the film itself.

Les Astronautes was a wonderful comic adventure film (made with Chris Marker) about a man who constructs a bizarre spaceship and takes it into space, to the moon and beyond. There's visual and comic invention aplenty in *Les Astronautes*, and all manner of techniques are employed in the visual treatment, from tinted black-and-white stills, to stop motion animation, captions, smoke effects, and live action. Walerian Borowczyk and Chris Marker mix up the animation

6 Most of Borowczyk's feature films were made in French, and in France. He also shot in Italy and Poland.
7 Lenica emigrated to Paris in 1963.

techniques into a dazzling whole. And there's a typically Borowczykian moment when the man flies his rocket ship next to an apartment and spies on a half-naked woman in a window.

In *The School*, black-and-white still photographs depict a soldier being irritated by a fly, classic Surrealist Borowczyk humour. In *L'Encyclopédie de grand-maman,* Borowczyk indulges again in his love of early photographs. *House* (*Dom*) has moments of erotic intensity, which would become a staple of Borowczyk's cinema: a woman (played by Boro's wife, Ligia Branice), caresses and kisses the bust of a man. In *Renaissance*, a host of objects (such as an owl, a brass horn, a table and some books) are re-animated – putting themselves back together from a state of chaos and disrepair. *Scherzo Infernal* (1984) was a later work of animation, an outrageous, violent and comic satire on religion featuring grotesque demons.

Walerian Borowczyk's short films have a beauty, a mystery, a texture which's absolutely compelling. And the brilliant use of sound – of sound effects and music – should also be mentioned (although the visuals are so hypnotizing, coming thick and fast, it's easy to forget how much of the impact of these short films comes from sound).

Walerian Borowczyk's first feature film was the singular *Goto: Island of Love* (1968), although a feature of his collected animation was released before that: *Le Thêatre de M. et Mme. Kabal* (1967). *Goto: Island of Love* was followed by *Le Phonographie* (1969), *Blanche* (1971), *Une Collection Particulière* (1973), *Contes Immoraux* (*Immoral Tales,* 1974) and *Histoire d'un Péché* (*Story of a Sin*, 1975).

La Bête (*The Beast,* 1975) was Walerian Borowczyk's most controversial film, a mixture of French farce, surrealism, and a lot of sex (including bestiality). Borowczyk's next film, *La Marge* (1976, *The Margin,* a.k.a. *The Streetwalker* and *Emmanuelle '77*) again combined eroticism and surrealism; it was based on Borowczyk's friend André Pieyre de Mandiargues' novel, and starred Sylvia Kristel (of the *Emmanuelle* films) and Joe Dallesandro (of Andy Warhol's coterie).

Other films followed, including *Briefe von Paris* (1975), *Interieur d'un Convent* (*Behind Convent Walls,* 1977), *Belt of Fire* (1978), about the mass murderer Gilles de Rais, *Les Héroïnes du Mal* (*Three Immoral*

Women, 1979), *L'Armoire* (1979), *Collections Privées* (1979), *Lulu* (1980), taken from Frank Wedekind's two plays (which had formed the basis of *Pandora's Box*), *Bloodbath of Dr Jeckyll* (a.k.a. *Blood of Dr Jeckyll* and *The Experiment,* 1981), *Ars Amandi* (*The Art of Love,* 1983), based on Ovid, episodes of *Série Rose* (1986-1991), and 1988's *Cérémonie d'Amour* (a.k.a. *Love Rites*). *Love Rites* starred Mathieu Carrière as a man who meets a prostitute (Marina Pierro) on the Paris Métro. Pierro, who had starred in *The Art of Love,* was superb as the mysterious, eternal prostitute, a mythical figure recalling the 'holy whores' of ancient religions.

Many of these European art films contained Walerian Borowczyk's trademarks – surrealism, sex, violence and bizarre incidents. In 1986, Borowczyk made *Emmanuelle 5*, which seemed to confirm his softcore porn status for detractors. In tackling the *Emmanuelle* franchise, though, Borowczyk sent it up (there was a scene set at the Cannes film festival, with audiences clamouring to see a fictional porn film, *Love Express*).

The era of the 1960s and 1970s was a time when films with graphic sexual content, including porn films, entered the mainstream, or at least were widely distributed, and became chic. It was the era of *Deep Throat, Ai No Corrida, Last Tango In Paris* and *I am Curious, Yellow* (1997's *Boogie Nights* is a marvellous visit to the Seventies porn boom). It was a time when relaxed censorship regulations, the new permissiveness, the sexual liberation, the Pill, audiences demanding more liberal films, and other factors, enabled filmmakers to depict more sex and nudity in their movies.

As well as porn manufacturers, 'serious' filmmakers began to include 'X' rated or 'adult' material. So you have Bernardo Bertolucci showing sodomy in *Last Tango In Paris*, Nagima Oshima depicting penetration in *In the Realm of the Senses,* Pier Paolo Pasolini including erections in his 'Trilogy of Life' films, and so on. Borowczyk's pictures were very much part of this culture – or at least, they were *received* and *interpreted* within this porn/ art, art film/ porn film context.

Among the regular collaborators in Walerian Borowczyk's movies were actors such as Marina Pierro and his wife Ligia Branice, DPs Guy Durban and Bernard Daillencourt, production designer Jacques D'Ovidio, Dominique Duvergé (AD and production manager), and writer André Pieyre de Mandiargues.

Walerian Borowczyk's films, like so many European films which have a life outside their country of origin on the international market, have a bewildering number of alternative titles (only a tiny percentage of movies ever get shown outside their country of origin). *La Bête* is also known as *The Beast, The Beast in Heat* and *Death's Ecstasy. Cérémonie d'amour* (1988) was *Queen of the Night* in the U.S.A., and also *Rites of Love* or *Love Rites. Docteur Jekyll et les femmes* (1981) was titled *The Blood of Doctor Jeckyll, The Bloodbath of Doctor Jeckyll* (the British cut version), *Bloodlust, Dr. Jeckyll and His Women* (the American dubbed version), *Dr. Jeckyll and Miss Osbourne*, and *The Experiment* (the British censored version). *Les Héroïnes du mal* (1979) is variously *Heroines of Evil, Heroines of Pain, Immoral Women* and *Three Immoral Women. Behind Convent Walls* (*Interno di un convento*, 1977) is also *Sex Life in a Convent* and *Within a Cloister. La Marge* (1976) is also *The Margin, Emmanuelle '77* and *The Streetwalker.*

⚜

Walerian Borowczyk quickly gained a reputation for producing erotic and (what some people saw as) pornographic material, combined with beautiful, painterly image-making, in which objects and details were given as much weight as people ('I attach a great deal of importance to details', Borowczyk said [J. Gerber, 173]). I don't regard Borowczyk's films as 'pornographic' at all (my own views are resolutely anti-censorship and pro-erotic. If that also means pro-pornography, fine).

There *is* a lot of nudity in Walerian Borowczyk's flicks, compared to the regular Hollywood film, or mainstream flicks in Europe and Asia. But not so extreme when compared to the European art film, which does occasionally have plenty of nudity. Or porn, of course.

However, it can be historically justified in another respect: go into any major art museum around the world and you'll probably encounter hundreds of naked bodies. From the Renaissance onwards nudity has been a regular element in high art (and of course in the art of the ancient world). By the time of the 19th century, academy and classical nudes are everywhere. There's Perseus rescuing Andromeda from the serpent, and she's naked; there's Cleopatra or Aphrodite reclining in her boudoir, and she's naked; there's a bunch of nice young boys swimming in a river, and they're naked. And it's obvious that painters and their patrons were choosing mythological or historical subjects (as opposed to Christian or Biblical ones) precisely so they could depict naked men and women. You couldn't show the Virgin Mary naked, but you could show the Goddess Venus naked. There's no doubt that the fine art nude is a classy, upmarket form of lowbrow, populist tits and ass.

If you have a few million dollars to spare and fancied funding some film adaptions of classic erotic books – *Fanny Hill, Moll Flanders, The Romance of Lust, The Perfumed Garden,* and of course *The Kama Sutra* – Walerian Borowczyk is without question the filmmaker for the job, in the entire history of cinema.

✣

I've mentioned Walerian Borowczyk in relation to pornography a few times in this book, but the connection lies more in the minds of the people – critics, fans, viewers – watching and discussing Borowczyk's films, than in the films themselves. I don't think the naked human body is pornographic, or showing it is pornographic, and nearly all of so-called pornography is really erotica, designed as entertainment. Rather, the emphasis on extreme violence and suffering in, for instance, Hollywood movies, is way more 'pornographic' than Borowczyk's films. There's male rape, for example, in movies like *Pulp Fiction, The Shawshank Redemption* and *Deliverance,* and some dubious depictions of sadomasochistic acts in pictures like *Misery, Frenzy,* and *Suspiria.* But those films don't have the stigma of pornography attached to them. And the level of violence and gore in movies such as *Black Hawk Down, Sin City* and *300* is so repulsive, so extreme. There's a sickening emphasis on aggression and physical pain which I regard as psychotic. It's the kind of thing cultists and martyrs would get off on in the early Christian era – all those religious obsessives who whipped themselves or lived in holes in the ground.

⚜

Information on Walerian Borowczyk is scant, to say the least. I mean, way scanter than many other lesser-known filmmakers. You have to really hunt and dig around. Of sources that are readily available, I'd recommend David Cook's *A History of Narrative Film.* There's a useful chapter on Borowczyk in *Immoral Tales: Sex and Horror Cinema in Europe 1956-1984*, by Cathal Tohill and Pete Tombs, a really marvellous movie book. About the best introduction to Boro you'll find. J. Gerber's book on the film producer Anatole Dauman includes a section on Borowczyk. Michael Richardson has a chapter on Boro in his *Surrealism and Cinema* (details on these books are in the bibliography).

Walerian Borowczyk is often mentioned in guidebooks to European and world cinema, but the entries are usually short and not particularly useful, merely repeating the same facts. Similarly, on the internet, there is information on Borowczyk, but not much, and so websites that I would recommend are few. Imdb.com is always good, and Senses of Cinema, and the Movie Review Query Engine (mrqe.com).[8] I have included a filmography of Borowczyk, because apart from places like the Internet Movie Database, it's difficult to find.

In short, Walerian Borowczyk deserves to be much better known in film circles, and his movies deserve to be seen. But his films seem destined to be lumped with exploitation cinema, softcore porn, mondo cinema, and arthouse cinema, perpetually on the outer reaches of world cinema. (And Borowczyk's films are difficult to track down; only ten are currently available in the U.K., and you'll need to search hard to find them).

8 There's a terrific gallery of Borowczyk's art at Animation World Network: awm.com/gallery/boro/info

WALERIAN BOROWCZYK, WOMEN AND PORNOGRAPHY

Walerian Borowczyk was a *connoisseur* of erotica, as his films bear out, and had a small museum of erotic objects. Like many an erotic addict, Borowczyk was in love with the female form and sex. His movies are full of images of naked or semi-nude women, like painterly studies out of the art of J.A.D. Ingres, Titian or Peter Rubens, the camera often lingering on their pudenda and pubic hair, their breasts, or close-ups of their mouths. Often, Borowczyk's women are alone, engaging in autoerotic, narcissistic acts, like the women in high art: bathing, admiring themselves in a mirror, or, unlike in high art, caressing some object, and masturbating. Few filmmakers have as many images of masturbation, particularly female masturbation, in their works as Walerian Borowczyk.

Walerian Borowczyk favoured slim, young women in his films. At least in the lead roles. The fleshly, curvy figures of the art of Aristide Maillol or Eric Gill or Peter Rubens are much rarer in his cinema. He didn't go for the super-mammary women of Russ Meyer, either (and Borowczyk's camera lingers more over hips, asses and vulvas than breasts. But he clearly fetishized everything, and memorably mouths). If one were being socially conscious and right-on, one could also remark that Borowczyk favoured white women, not black or Asian women.

Walerian Borowczyk has never been simply a high-class eroticist, as his detractors have asserted (I don't regard him as a pornographer at all – a lover of erotica, certainly). He shoots from a finished script, and pays special attention to the set, the design, and the many unusual props and objects in the frame. (It would take a long time to find and rent/ buy all the props and furniture for a Borowczyk movie).

But Walerian Borowczyk's cinema seems to have been overshadowed by the nudity and porno elements, with viewers and critics seeing that and not much else. A pity, because there's so much more going on in Borowczyk's films than nude bodies and fucking. And there's also a feeling that Borowczyk wasted his talent on worthless films. So that his career begins strongly, with *Goto: Island of Love*, *Blanche* and *Immoral Tales*, but deteriorates to the crass level of

Emmanuelle 5. There's a feeling that Borowczyk would have done so much better if he'd concentrated on some really challenging subjects, something that was worthy of his talent.

That's one view. Fine. But the facts don't bear it out. For instance, *Love Rites*, released in 1988, is a fine Walerian Borowczyk film – the equal, I'd say, with *The Story of Sin*. So it wasn't really a 'decline' into mediocrity and dirty old man territory, because *Love Rites* shows Borowczyk enjoying himself immensely with a tale of man who gets involved with a prostitute in modern-day Paris and discovers more than he bargained for. *Love Rites* is not porn, not smut, not a dirty old man leching after acres of young naked flesh.

And since the late 1990s and early 2000s, there has been a liberalization in film censorship/ classification (in the U.K.), with a bunch of films reaching more mainstream markets which have been trumpeted for containing more sexually explicit material. Yes, you can see cocks and cunts at play in films like *Romance, Intimacy, Pola X, 9 Songs* and others, but those movies aren't a patch on even the lesser Borowczyk films.

Is Walerian Borowczyk's cinema sexist or misogynist? It's hardly worth even bothering to address the question, because most every feminist or critic who looks at Borowczyk's films will be certain of his out-and-out sexism and his blatant misogynism. A feminist would say 'is there a moment in Borowczyk's cinema when he *isn't* misogynist or sexist?' Borowczyk himself, though, clearly didn't hate women, or fear them, or whatever. But his films contain plenty of ammunition for evidence of fear, anxiety, neurosis and all the rest of it about women.

I don't like to say 'misogynism' in relation to Walerian Borowczyk: I don't think woman-hating is part of Borowczyk's cinema or philosophy at all. The opposite, in fact (but feminists counter that worshipping women can be as bad as disliking and fearing them).

What's striking, though, while we're on the subject of women and feminism, is just how many of Walerian Borowczyk's films feature women in the lead roles. *Blanche, Three Immoral Women, Immoral Tales, The Beast, The Story of Sin, The Streetwalker, Lulu, Emmanuelle 5, Behind Convent Walls, The Art of Love, Love Rites* – actually, it's *all* of Borowczyk's live-action films, apart from *Goto: Island of Love* and *Dr Jeckyll.* And that makes Borowczyk *very* unusual for a male film director, and for any major filmmaker.

For all its apparent sexism and misogynism, Walerian Borowczyk's cinema also contains some strong roles for women. Miriam in *Love Rites*, for instance, may be a sadistic prostitute, but she's also a strong, independent woman. And at the end of *La Bête* it's the two beasts that die, while the heroines survive (though damaged).

I wouldn't say that the sexism was any worse in Walerian Borowczyk's films than, say, the films of Jean-Luc Godard or Rainer Maria Fassbinder or many European art filmmakers (have a look at Godard's *Contempt* or *Prénom: Carmen*, for instance). But the sexism certainly is more overt, more obvious. Borowczyk's cinema reveals the sexism, the patriarchal laws, the social hierarchies in which women are secondary participants, much more vividly than many other European movies of the same era.

Having considered Walerian Borowczyk's films for some time, I wonder if one of the reasons that some viewers find the concentration on sex and nudity off-putting is the way that Borowczyk incorporates it. Sex scenes and nudity are regular elements in movies – at least in the Western tradition, and have been since cinema was invented. But in Borowczyk's films, the camera lingers over parts of the body far, far longer than most movies do. And Borowczyk employs not one shot of a butt or a mound, but many. Hold on anything like that for too long and some viewers get uncomfortable. It's not that they don't wanna see nude bodies, whether male, female or whatever, it's that Borowczyk's films put viewers into a particular viewing position which makes their voyeurism palpable.

⚜

Walerian Borowczyk cast beautiful women in his leading roles: Sylvia Kristel, Ligia Branice, and Marina Pierro. If you were cast in a Walerian Borowczyk film, you'd be expected to strip off – completely (no body suits, no special clothes to hide bits you don't wanna show). You'd probably have to do a sex scene, and also some homosexual sex. You might have to run through fields or woods naked (and barefoot).

But Boro and his casting assistants certainly had a knack for discovering terrific unknown actors (and performers willing to do a lot of crazy stuff).

There's more humour than one might think in Walerian Borowczyk's films. Not understanding the humour is part of the problem with viewing films with subtitles or dubbing (to test this – watch a movie in a language you don't understand with an audience that does understand it. You'll see a difference between the subtitles you don't think are particularly funny and the audience laughing).

But true eroticism, Walerian Borowczyk said, doesn't like laughter or jokes. True eroticism was a serious business, he remarked. Borowczyk though couldn't resist adding humour to sexual situations. He called *The Beast* more a comedy than an erotic film.

A film director who has employed even more nudity than Walerian Borowczyk – in terms of sheer numbers – is Peter Greenaway. There are similarities between Borowczyk and Greenaway, but not in the use of nudity and sex. In Greenaway's cinema naked bodies are presented in a cool, even cold, scientific and medical fashion. They are arranged as out of historical paintings but they look like people queuing up to be medically examined. Borowczyk's approach is much more openly erotic. He loves naked bodies (and not only women's). In Greenaway's cinema there a feeling of the filmmaker being ashamed or restrained even as he's fascinated by nudity. He wants to be a *European* filmmaker but can't quite shake off the repressed *British* side. In Borowczyk's cinema, he doesn't care about repression and such things, and is happy to linger at length over nude bodies.

MAKING A BOROWCZYK FILM

What was it like making a Walerian Borowczyk film? Here are some guesses. I don't know for sure, but I bet the hours were long on a Borowczyk shoot; I bet Borowczyk would carry on filming until he got what he wanted. I bet the actors had to rough it along with the crew (no comfy trailers, no comfy limos ferrying actors from comfy hotels miles away). I bet Borowczyk wouldn't have any time for actors who didn't want to do what they'd agreed to do (like stripping off or simulating sex).

I bet Walerian Borowczyk was meticulous to the point of driving everyone else in the crew nuts (I can imagine Borowczyk art directing scenes to the point of maddening detail – adjusting the way the folds in a dress lay on a bed, for instance, or having a painting hang on a wall in *just the right way*. The actress Grazyna Dlugolecka commented that Borowczyk moved actors around like puppets, and seemed to more concerned with how props looked). I bet Borowczyk inspired a kind of grudging respect in his cast and crew.

It seems that Walerian Borowczyk shot everything, too, and didn't hand over shooting to second unit directors or assistants. In other words, you can sense Borowczyk's presence behind every scene. Sex film producer Alain Siritsky said that Borowczyk 'can do everything: write, lighting, set design, edit and even do the poster'.[9]

I imagine that producers and crew, as with Orson Welles or Alfred Hitchcock, wouldn't interfere with Walerian Borowczyk's vision once the film had been agreed upon and was shooting. Borowczyk knew what he was doing and I bet producers and crew found it easier just to let him get on with it (film directors are well-known for not wanting to hear the word 'no' when they're shooting. All they want to hear is, 'yes, I think we can do that').

I doubt there were extensive rehearsal periods for the actors, or any rehearsal at all. Many Walerian Borowczyk scenes look as if the director has told an actor, 'OK, run along that path', 'How far?', 'I'll tell you when to stop'. And off they go.

9 Quoted in C. Tohill, 227.

And a lot of Walerian Borowczyk's scenes look as if the scene was just one take, and Borowczyk would say fine, print, let's go to the next set-up, put the camera over here by the Renoir nude, Julio. I doubt that Borowczyk asked for endless takes like Stanley Kubrick – partly because these were low budget films, and precious film stock would need to be used carefully. On the other hand, being a perfectionist would mean Borowczyk would likely keep going until it was close to being right.

BOROWCZYK IN THE INTERNATIONAL MOVIE MARKET

Remember, too, that Walerian Borowczyk's films were low budget affairs. By low budget, I mean truly *low budget*. They were shot on 35mm film stock, true (and thankfully), but Borowczyk would have been using budgets in the region of, I reckon, $200,000-400,000, and maybe even less. For comparison, Hollywood calls a film 'low budget' these days if it comes in at less than 30 million bucks. (When deciding what to spend the budget on, you can bet that Borowczyk made sure the costumes on each film looked right. And they did).

It was the same with Walerian Borowczyk's contemporaries, like Pier Paolo Pasolini or Jean-Luc Godard: their financers and distributors knew that there was an audience for the films of these *auteurs* within their country of origin. And if the subject matter was appealing (and nudity helped plenty), the films might be able to travel outside of their country of origin. One must never forget that only a *tiny fraction* of films made in Europe get released in cinemas outside their country of origin – in the 1960s and 1970s as now. You may think 1,000s of foreign language movies are widely available, but there are many thousands more that don't go beyond national borders. In other words, to get financed, the films must have been able to be sustained by the audiences of their own country (in other words, Borowczyk's films were low budget partly because they would only be seen predominantly in France or Italy).

Remember, too, that this was an era when ancillary markets were much smaller than today: no video, no DVD, no cable and satellite channels. Secondary markets of the 1960s-1970s would include television, and not much else. Only with the rise of home entertainment delivery systems in the Eighties would Walerian Borowczyk's films be able to generate revenue from areas outside of theatrical exhibition or television (and I bet quite a few of Borowczyk's films were rarely if ever shown on network TV).

But if we're talking about Walerian Borowczyk at all now, it means that his movies have had some life outside of their country of origin and their particular era. They have lived on, somehow. In itself, that's an amazing fact, because thousands of films and filmmakers have disappeared - from France, Italy, Spain, Germany, wherever in Europe, and will be remembered only by a few devotees.

In all, Walerian Borowczyk made 14 feature films, and originated the ideas for many of them. Only later did Borowczyk become a director for hire, with producers coming to him with offers. It changes things considerably when you're developing projects yourself - you have much more of yourself invested in them, for a start (but they often take much longer to get going and complete).

Only 14 films (and you'll be doing well to see them all, too). We might lament that Stanley Kubrick or Andrei Tarkovsky didn't make many pictures. But not Walerian Borowczyk, because he was making art before and after his feature film career. (One wonders, though, what Borowczyk might have done with a mega budget, with the vast resources of set construction, location shooting, extras and visual effects of a contemporary blockbuster movie. It would never happen, of course, for numerous reasons). If you want to take in the *Collected Works* of Ingmar Bergman or Jean-Luc Godard, though, you're talking about huge amounts of film, video, television, radio and theatrical work.

Another thing: thankfully, unlike some European art films one could mention, Walerian Borowczyk's films are 90 to 100 minutes long. That's just right. No need for movies running two-and-a-half hours or more. No need for the misconceived length of *Céline and Julie Go Boating* or *The Damned* (*auteur* films which outlast their welcome).

WALERIAN BOROWCZYK AND GENRE

Walerian Borowczyk stuck to particular genres in his films, and didn't venture into, say, gangster flicks, or science fiction, or Westerns. Borowczyk is not interested in America at all, like so many of his European art film contemporaries, like Jean-Luc Godard, Wim Wenders or Rainer Werner Fassbinder. He doesn't quote from American movies, doesn't use American stars in his films, and isn't using American cinematic forms in his pictures. While filmmakers such as Godard were constantly critical of America yet talked about American cinema and recreated it in their films, Borowczyk just wasn't interested.

Walerian Borowczyk's movies remain resolutely *European*, the Old World not the New World, through and through (Werner Herzog and Ingmar Bergman resemble Borowczyk in this respect). There might have been overtures to Borowczyk from American film producers or studios, but Borowczyk preferred to remain in Europe to work. He didn't, like so many of his European contemporaries, 'go Hollywood' (and like so many European filmmakers right back to the early days of cinema). And while filmmakers like Godard or Truffaut remained in Europe but used American cinematic forms and ideas (and actors), Borowczyk never did. (However, he did work for some of the big names among European producers, such as Pierre Braunberger, Anatole Dauman, Alain Sarde, and the Hakim brothers).

And when we say that Walerian Borowczyk's movies are 'European', we also mean a very old idea of Europe. Borowczyk does deal with contemporary Europe, of course (not least with Communist

Poland, his home country), and he does tackle the political and social situation in Europe from the 1950s onwards.[10] But, really, Borowczyk is interested in the idea of a Europe that stretches back into the 18th and 19th centuries, and into the Renaissance and the Middle Ages. And Borowczyk went right back to ancient Rome, with his play on the poet Ovid (Ovid was big in the Middle Ages, in the courtly love tradition).

See, one of the most striking aspects of Walerian Borowczyk's cinema is that so many of his films were *historical*: they were costume dramas and history movies (and his first film – for some his best film – *Goto: Island of Love* – was one of the strangest historical pictures ever made). That's a long tradition in the European art film, of course: every European art filmmaker has delved into history. But only a few have made historical films as their basic genre or type of movie.

There's Werner Herzog, and Pier Paolo Pasolini. And if European art filmmakers go back into the past, it's usually into the 20th century, and in particular the middle years – leading up to and during World War Two. Borowczyk, though, loves to explore older cultures than that. And if he does do something set in the 20th century, it's the period *before* the First World War, before that war changed everything in Europe. (In this sense, Borowczyk's cinema is a perpetually *fin-de-siècle* cinema, always on the bring of collapse, always showing societies in decay).

It's important, too, to remember that Walerian Borowczyk was an artist and animator for a long time before moving into live-action features. In other words, he wasn't only a filmmaker through-and-through, and wasn't a filmmaker throughout his artistic career. By the time *Goto: Island of Love* was released, for instance, Walerian Borowczyk was 45. His feature film career is actually a period of around twenty years, from 1968 to 1988 – and after that he continued to make art, write short stories and have exhibitions. (He also directed some TV, including *Série Rose*, in 1988 and 1990.)

Walerian Borowczyk said that whatever the medium – film, short

10 Politics plays a huge part in Polish cinema, of course – and includes issues such as Communism, Solidarity, socialist realism, Marxism, liberalization, and continual confrontations and dialogues between the State and the film industry.

stories, painting – his creativity was the same. Jean-Luc Godard made similar remarks: filmmaking and writing were part of the same creative activity, and if he wasn't able to make movies, Godard said, he'd write. Borowczyk said he created very swiftly. 'I conceive all my films in an instant, and only objective means prevent me from making them in that instant' (D. Thomson, 2001).

⚜

I've mentioned how exotic and weird Walerian Borowczyk's films are, but there were many pictures made in the 1960s and 1970s which were just as crazy – I mean those movies labelled 'mondo cinema', or 'exploitation cinema', or 'sexploitation', or 'underground cinema'. And spoofing Catholic themes and imagery is a big part of those European movies (understandable, being as many were made in Italy, France and Spain). There are films about vampires, Dracula, Frankenstein, monsters, occultism, horror, Satanism, the Devil, nuns, and on and on, in 100s of films made in Europe from the 1960s to the 1980s, the era when Borowczyk was active in feature filmmaking.

And Walerian Borowczyk's flicks, with their eroticized nuns, their sex scenes and nudity, their sense of the grotesque, are very much part of low budget European filmmaking of the 1960s-70s, part of the cast of horror, sex, exploitation and *fantastique* films – the vampires, aliens, serial killers, babes and freaks. (And Hollywood and American TV of course recycles vampires and horror numerous times – the *Vampire Diaries, Underworld, True Blood* and the *Twilight Saga* movie and TV franchises being recent examples).

Part of the reason is that horror, thriller and occult films are cheap to make. And that's also why so many of those movies include nudity – all you have to do is get people to take off their clothes. You don't have to build vast sets or have costly costumes. It's the same with porno films (and also why porn often takes up horror or sci-fi or occult genres). As low budget Spanish horror maestro José Larraz put it:

> When you have no money, the only guarantee for the box office is sex. How can I make a film like *The Spy Who Came In From the Cold* with inexperienced actors and no money?[11]

11 Quoted in C. Tohill, 199.

So although we exalt filmmakers such as Walerian Borowczyk or Pier Paolo Pasolini or whoever – because they are 'serious' filmmakers, filmmakers who've made some 'serious' work which can be properly called 'art' – there are hundreds of other filmmakers and films of that period which contain just as much outrageous imagery. I mean filmmakers like José Bénazéraf, Jess Franco, Jean Rollin, José Larraz, Massimo Pupillo, etc. Or maybe it's because, somehow, filmmakers like Pasolini, Robbe-Grillet and Borowczyk have survived, while so many others have been forgotten.

WALERIAN BOROWCZYK'S INFLUENCE

One can easily discern the influence of Walerian Borowczyk on filmmakers such as David Lynch, Terry Gilliam and Jeunet and Caro (the latters' films *Delicatessen* and *The City of Lost Children* contain references to Borowczyk's *Goto: Island of Love*. Indeed, *The City of Lost Children* is a virtual remake of *Goto* in many respects, down to the humour, the surreal imagery, and the stylized, shabby wood and metal and stone *mise-en-scène*). Terry Gilliam said he and Terry Jones loved Borowczyk's *Goto: Island of Love* and *Blanche*. Of Borowczyk's short *Jeux des anges*, Gilliam said it was

> just extraordinary: the sense that you're on a train with the walls of the city going past, and then the sound of angels' wings – incredible... Terry Jones and I went crazy over Borowczyk because his films were so much about atmosphere and texture. (T. Gilliam, 39)

As well as Gilliam, the Quay Brothers and Neil Jordan have expressed their admiration for Walerian Borowczyk. (Jordan had a go at his own version of an erotic, Freudian update of a Grimm fairy tale in *Company of Wolves*, but although it's fêted in British film critical circles, *The Company of Wolves* ain't a patch on a Borowczyk movie).

Walerian Borowczyk has his fans among critics – such as Ado Kryou, David Thomson, Tom Milne, and Mark Kermode.

WALERIAN BOROWCZYK AND EROTICISM

Walerian Borowczyk's is a highly cultured cinema, a cinema of (for) connoisseurs – eclectic, subtle, stylish, mysterious and haunting. Many films were based on literary sources: Ovid (*Art of Love*), André Pieyre de Mandiargues (*The Streetwalker* and *Love Rites*), Robert Louis Stevenson (*Bloodbath of Dr Jeckyll*), Franz Wedekind (*Lulu*), and Stendhal (*Behind Convent Walls*). Borowczyk certainly delivered on one count: there was plenty of nudity, plenty of sex, but his films were also that rare thing, *erotic*.

André Pieyre de Mandiargues (1909-1991) is an important figure among Walerian Borowczyk's collaborators: he provided the stories for *La Marge, Love Rites,* part of *Immoral Tales,* and the narration, props and much of *Une collection particulière.* He also wrote the novel that was the basis for *Girl On a Motorcycle* (a.k.a. *Naked Under Leather,* Jack Cardiff, 1968). Aside from *Girl On a Motorcycle* and Borowczyk's films, no one else seems to have produced movies from de Mandiargues' fiction.[12]

⚜

Were there ever so many movies of one director so in love with women's torsos, bellies, hips, buttocks, thighs and vulvas? Walerian Borowczyk delights in the medium close-up of women's bodies, shot from the thighs to the belly. He has them turn this way and that, sometimes naked, sometimes draped with gauzy material, sometimes with the light shining from behind, sometimes in soft focus.

These shots go beyond softcore porn, or mere titillation, as

12 One of Borowczyk's short films, *Esgarot de Venus* (1975), was a document of the art of Mandiargues' wife, Bona Tibertelli De Pisis. It's a minor work in the Boro canon, partly because De Pisis's erotic art isn't very inspiring.

detractors call them; they become painterly appreciations of form, shape, tone, colour. They recall artists such as Eric Gill, Aristide Maillol and Auguste Rodin, sculptors who worshipped that part of the female form in bronze and marble. Walerian Borowczyk's endless images of women's bodies around the torso, buttocks and hips also recall 19th century nude paintings, by Gustave Moreau, Jean Auguste Dominique Ingres or Gustave Courbet, or the thousands of academy nudes.

Walerian Borowczyk certainly knows his history of religion and sex, the links between spirit and flesh, the Passion and pornography, extreme religious faith and erotic fervour, mysticism and masturbation. Among the 20th century artists who've addressed the fusion between sex and spirit are Georges Bataille, D.H. Lawrence, James Joyce, John Cowper Powys, Eric Gill, and directors such as Luis Buñuel, Ingmar Bergman and Pier Palo Pasolini.

Walerian Borowczyk is certainly very much in the same tradition of *avant garde* and modernist European literature that explores sexual and religious issues in extreme manifestations: Borowczyk is part of the tradition which includes Surrealists like Hans Bellmer with his dolls and fingers penetrating orifices; or Georges Bataille with his pornography of asses, eyes, eggs and mouths in *The Story of O*; or the dreamscapes of arch Surrealist prankster Salvador Dali; or the far superior Surrealism of Luis Buñuel; or the man behind it all in France: the Marquis de Sade. And those writers who were just as extreme, and still part of that 'no limits' modernist tradition: Henry Miller, Pauline Réage, Jean de Berg, Emmanuelle Arsan, William Burroughs, D.H. Lawrence, Anaïs Nin, etc.

Walerian Borowczyk maintained that he wasn't a maker of erotic films, and disliked that kind of categorization. It was too narrow, for a start, and was more to do with how people perceived him and his films, than who he really was, or what his movies really were. Besides, Borowczyk said, sex was no more unusual than eating or smoking cigarettes. When an interviewer called him a pervert, he replied 'who isn't a pervert?'

When you look closer, you can see that Walerian Borowczyk's films aren't particularly pervy – especially when compared to many strands of pornography. Even Borowczyk's most controversial production, *The Beast*, depicts heterosexual sex (apart from the curé and his choirboys, which's not really shown). And everything the beast does with Romilda is within the bounds of regular heterosexual sex. Indeed, there are sexual depictions in mainstream films which are much more 'perverse' than the sex in *The Beast*. And pictures such as *Ai No Corrida* are way more perverse and objectionable, if you want to see them like that, than the sex in *The Beast* (in *In the Realm of the Senses* the lovers literally fuck themselves to death!).

Walerian Borowczyk defended his films by saying: 'all I do is express everyone's dreams'. It was odd, wasn't it, he maintained, that critics always talked about him, rather than the thousands of viewers and consumers who watched his movies. Borowczyk resisted that biographical approach of most film criticism, which always relates films to the filmmakers, which always says that *Citizen Kane* is always ultimately about Orson Welles (even more than about about William Randolph Hearst).

SOME OF WALERIAN BOROWCZYK'S INFLUENCES

Walerian Borowczyk lived in Paris for much of his life; Paris seemed to be a favourite destination for Eastern European and Polish filmmakers – Roman Polanski and Krzysztof Kieslowski ended up there (some directors, like Andrej Wadja, remained in Poland). And many other filmmakers gravitated towards Paris and France: Luis Buñuel, Raul Ruiz and Pedro Almodóvar. Why Paris? One reason is that France has one of strongest film cultures in the world: France produces more films than any country in Europe, and people go to the cinema more times a year in France than anywhere else in Europe. In short, it's a very good place to make movies.[13]

13 And most of Boro's movies were made in French, his second language. And with mainly French crews.

Aspects of French art in particular have long been interested (even obsessed) with sexuality and (Catholic) religion: Gustave Moreau, Félicien Rops, J.-K. Huysmans, Gustave Flaubert, Odilon Redon, Jean Delville, and the whole *fin-de-siècle* Symbolist and Decadent æsthetic movements. (Consider Rops' riotous, blasphemous images of Satan, devils, phalluses and naked women).

Walerian Borowczyk's sensuous, intellectual art cinema is clearly informed by the history of 'high' European culture that goes back through the modernist *avant garde* and Surrealism, via Symbolism and *fin-de-siècle* Decadence, to the Romantics, to the Marquis de Sade and 18th century pornography, and further back, via Renaissance painting, to the flamboyance and debauchery of the Medicis, the Borgias and Catherine the Great. Thence to mediæval religion and art (monasteries and convents, and the highpoint of Catholic art), bypassing the Dark Ages, to ancient Greek and Roman times.

One could analyze Walerian Borowczyk's cinema in relation to any of those eras and cultural movements. The affinities between Borowczyk's films and the Symbolist and Decadent age are obvious. For instance, *fin-de-siècle* 'high' culture was marked by 'gory exoticism', as Mario Praz put it (289), by mysticism and black magic, occultism, Satanism, Catholic imagery, the macabre, the æstheticism of 'beauty', a love of costumes, dressing up, cross-dressing and dandyism, a love of Oriental and Byzantine culture, opulence and indulgence, where the key phrase is from Paul Verlaine: 'Je suis l'Empire à la fin de la décadence', Verlaine wrote in 1885 in 'Langueur' (1974, 180).

The age was summed up by works of literature such as Arthur Rimbaud's *Une Saison en Enfer*, Comte de Lautréamont's *Chansons de Maldoror*, Edgar Allen Poe's horror stories, Charles Baudelaire's *Flowers of Evil*, Gustave Flaubert's *Salambô* and *La Tentation de saint Antoine*, J.-K. Huysmans' *À Rebours* and *Là-bas*, Bram Stoker's *Dracula*, Joséphin Péladan's *Le Vice suprême*, and music such as Richard Wagner's *Parsifal*. (Some of the key artists of the Decadent and Symbolist epoch, apart from the writers and painters noted above, included Honoré de Balzac, Jean Moréas, Albert Aurier, Octave Mirabeau, Walter Pater, Jan Troop, Oscar Wilde, Pierre Louÿs, Arnold

Böcklin, Puvis de Chavannes and Stéphane Mallarmé.) Borowczyk is wholly at home in this cultural *milieu*, and draws on it.

Walerian Borowczyk is a follower of Surrealism, too – and Surrealism's preoccupation with sex and death, and with cruelty and absurdity, are an important element in his cinema. 'Beauty will be convulsive, or not all,' remarked the godfather of Surrealism, André Breton, and that's Borowczyk's maxim too.

Walerian Borowczyk also has the Surrealists' love of bizarre objects, and his cinema is full of them – from the fly-catching box in *Goto: Island of Love* to the metal finger extensions in *Love Rites*. (The fly-catching box, with its funnels ending in dog's hair, is a classic Surrealist device – it could be part of an exhibition by Max Ernst or Marcel Duchamp). And Borowczyk also employs Surrealism's use of juxtaposition: put two apparently innocuous objects together to form a third, strange being.[14]

Walerian Borowczyk's also fond of secret objects, objects that are hidden and have to be revealed – taken out of cabinets, or unfolded. In *La Bête* there's a family album with pages that are unfolded to reveal erotic drawings, and when a framed text is reversed it reveals a sketch of a horse coupling with a woman.

No need to mention the emphasis in Surrealism on dreams, on dream imagery, on the unconscious, or to cite Sigmund Freud or C.G. Jung *et al.* Walerian Borowczyk called *Immoral Tales* 'a sanctuary for liberty, an island of no restrictions': he has the 'no limits' philosophy of the Surrealists and the *avant garde* in Europe of the 20th century. 'All I do is express everyone's dreams', Borowczyk insisted: he was simply filming what everybody was dreaming about.

Carl Jung wrote:

> The cinema, like the detective story, makes it possible to experience without danger all the excitement, passion and desirousness which must be suppressed in a humanitarian ordering of society.

Linked to Surrealism is the Existentialism in Walerian Borowczyk's cinema: he is definitely a figure of the mid-to-late 20th century

14 Of painters, Borowczyk said he was impressed by Tomasso Capelli, a 14th century Italian painter, Henri Lecourbe, and his own father (J. Gerber, 171).

(or his artistic and political views seem to have been formed partly by the debates in Existentialism of the mid-century). There are also correspondences between Borowczyk's cinema and the Theatre of the Absurd of Samuel Beckett, Antonin Artaud and Eugène Ionesco. Part of that Existential belief is expressed in the cruelty and absurdity of modern life in Borowczyk's cinema. It's a view that encompasses pessimism, irony, and detachment. A view that sees the horrors of modern life and decides that not a lot can assuage them.

One of Walerian Borowczyk's notions was that Disney's films were more pornographic than his own (one imagines what the studio executives at the Walt Disney Company, viewing a DVD of *The Beast* or *Immoral Tales* beside their own *Aladdin* or *Bambi*, would make of that idea). Borowczyk said that *Snow White and the Seven Dwarfs* was much more erotic than any of his own films because of its 'stench of unsatisfied desire'.

Asked who'd he like to be in history if he had the choice, Walerian Borowczyk said: 'if I have to choose an epoch and an identity, it would be that of Leda's swan in antiquity (if she really was as beautiful as the artists represent her)' (J. Gerber, 172-3). The greatest representation of Leda is of course Leonardo da Vinci's lost painting - a copy gives some idea of the beauty of Leda.[15] There's also a lost version by Michelangelo Buonaroti, which's even more explicit: the giant swan lies between the woman's legs, its wing covering her vulva.[16] Both are known from copies.[17]

That is typical of Walerian Borowczyk's eccentricity - to be the swan that makes love to Leda. But the swan was of course a god - Jupiter - in disguise.

15 Leonardo's *Leda* was burned by Madame de Maintenon around 1700, or was destroyed by one of Louis XIII's henchmen.

16 There's a copy of *Leda and the Swan*, 16th century, in London's Royal Academy.

17 Anonymous, the 'ex-Spiridon version', *Leda and the Swan*, wood, 132 x 78cm, Rome; anonymous: *Leda and the Swan*, 112 x 86cm, Galleria Borghese, Rome.

WALERIAN BOROWCZYK'S VISUALS

Walerian Borowczyk has no superior when it comes to art direction in cinema. I reckon his art direction is the equal of celebrated examples, such as Cedric Gibbons and the MGM unit, or Walter Roehrig, Walter Reimann and Hermann Warm, who did the settings for *The Cabinet of Dr Caligari*. Is Borowczyk that good? Yes, I think he is.

Walerian Borowczyk has the credits of editor and production designer on many of his films. Many of the props and designs in Borowczyk's cinema have an appealing handmade feel to them, and I wonder if Borowczyk himself created some of them. You could mount an exhibition of the props in Borowczyk's films and it would be a great show (and more interesting than some other film exhibitions). A filmmaker such as Jan Svankmajer has a similar handmade, earthy feel to his props. In Borowczyk's cinema, it's the classic eroticization of the object – the (art) object as fetish.

One of Walerian Borowczyk's delights are boxes, cabinets, cupboards and display cases of all kinds – but preferrably nice old wooden ones. The cabinets and boxes often contain mysterious objects, like busts (Borowczyk is fond of statuary of all kinds). The sets of a Borowczyk film are *already* a museum display. They are like a Surrealist exhibition, or a 'secret museum' or 'private collection' of pornography and erotica of the 18th or 19th centuries. Or like a show of curios and antiques, arranged in old wooden display cases (recalling the Pitt Rivers Museum in Oxford, used so evocatively in Philip Pullman's *His Dark Materials* books).

Who knows where Walerian Borowczyk sourced all of the incredible objects in his films? Clearly some of them are manufactured just for the film, but many are existing pieces – partly because Borowczyk loves objects with a history, objects that have been used. Almost all of the objects in Borowczyk's films have been used; new, pristine objects are very rare in his films. So he must've scoured so many flea markets, antique stores, and art fairs.

The love of wooden boxes recalls all sorts of artists: the Surrealists loved boxes (like Max Ernst), as did the Minimal artists (like Donald

Judd, Carl Andre and Jackie Winsor. Judd, one of the two or three most important artists of the 1960-2000 period, made the box his fundamental form). But there's one artist to consider in relation to the boxes in Borowczyk's cinema, and that the reclusive American artist Joseph Cornell, not least because of the way that Cornell would use his boxes to frame and present an arcane array of objects: a bird, a star map, an egg, a photograph, a feather, a pebble. If you like Borowczyk's films, I'd highly recommend you look at Joseph Cornell's enigmatic art of boxes.

Aside from *Goto: Island of Love*, Walerian Borowczyk's feature films were made in colour. Some of Borowczyk's animations were in black-and-white. It makes sense that *Goto: Island of Love* should be in black-and-white, but Borowczyk was clearly happy in either medium. (All of the usual constraints of commercial cinema would have operated for Borowczyk – all film producers, distributors and studios would argue for colour films, for all the usual reasons – one of the chief ones being – what else? – money). But if you consider the range of techniques that Borowczyk employed in his animation and films, you can see that he was a versatile and adaptable filmmaker. If a producer or studio told him he could only make films in colour or only in b/w or only with three actors or only with one set, he could do it, and flourish.

WALERIAN BOROWCZYK'S CLOTHES

Clothes, clothes, clothes, it's all about the clothes in a Walerian Borowczyk film. Even when there is plenty of other stuff going on, Borowczyk's films make time to study clothes. Many historical movies are called 'costume dramas', usually referring to the lovely frocks that the stars wear. But Borowczyk's films offer a real feeling for clothes – how they move on the body, how they hang on the body, and what is underneath them. Few other filmmakers have filmed clothes like Borowczyk: there is a heightened, sensual apprehension of the materiality of clothes, of textures, colours, shapes, etc.

Walerian Borowczyk could easily have had an alternative career as a fashion designer, or a costume designer for movies. (And Hugo in *Love Rites* is a fashion designer).

And no other filmmaker has so enjoyed characters putting on or taking off clothes. In *Immoral Tales* alone there are scenes of characters taking off their clothes in every episode, and sometimes it's a slow process, such as when Lucrezia's father and brother undress her. At times Borowczyk's films look like a costume fitting. And when characters take off their clothes in a Borowczyk picture, it's usually down to nudity.

Walerian Borowczyk of course loves layers and things that are hidden then revealed, or partially revealed. No one could fail to notice that this filmmaker has a fetish for naked women clad in gauzy, filmy cloth (usually white). Nipples and pubic hair are visible underneath; it's a classic look in erotica. To emphasize it, sometimes Borowczyk has actors take off their clothes then put on something see-through.

WALERIAN BOROWCZYK AND RELIGION

Walerian Borowczyk's films are anti-clerical and anti-Catholic; there are many scenes, in movies such as *Behind Convent Walls, La Bête* and *Story of Sin*, of the hypocrisy and sexual repression of Catholicism. At the same time, though, Borowczyk clearly revels in some of the imagery and ritual of Catholicism (like many filmmakers), and many of his films seem to ambiguously celebrate as well as condemn organized religion (one sees the same ambiguity in the films of Pier Paolo Pasolini, Luis Buñuel and Federico Fellini).

Like Pier Paolo Pasolini, Luis Buñuel and Ken Russell, Walerian

Borowczyk delights in exploring the links between sex, death, religion, blasphemy and art. There is the same enjoyment in attacking institutions such as the church, Catholicism, morality and Christian tenets, using weapons such as Surrealism, sexuality, humorous irreverence, violence and blasphemy. Oh, and lots of nudity and sex.

Walerian Borowczyk was fascinated by institutions, and often portrayed them - the island of love in Goto, the convent in *Behind Convent Walls*, the Vatican in *Immoral Tales*, the brothel in *The Rites of Lurve*. And he's also intrigued by dictatorships - Erzsébet Báthory presiding over her house of women in *Immoral Tales*, the Mother Superior in the nunnery, Goto on the island. And Borowczyk was especially adept at depicting the daily life of institutions, and the numerous rituals and daily tasks - the lighting of candles, say, or the preparation of a bathroom for a mistress, or the decoration of a church. There's a strong impression of the real daily lives of the people who live in these institutions. It's one of the strengths of *Goto: Island of Love*, for instance: you really believe those people are living in that degrading, shabby place. Borowczyk grounds his fantastical narratives in realism.

PART TWO

THE FILMS

2

GOTO: ISLAND OF LOVE

Goto: Island of Love is one of the strangest feature débuts in the history of cinema (Walerian Borowczyk had already made many animated films before *Goto: Island of Love*). It's also one of the best débuts. That's an accolade bandied about by film critics so often it becomes meaningless: 'the best film début since *Kirsty and Bridget Go Nutzoid in Vegas',* critics bleat. But in the case of *Goto: Island of Love*, it really is true. *Goto: Island of Love* can take its place among the other films trotted out as great film débuts – *Breathless, Eraserhead, The 400 Blows, Badlands* – and the granddaddy of them all, *Citizen Kane.*

Boro co-wrote *Goto* with Dominique Duvergé, one of the key collaborators of the period; Guy Durban was DP; Charles Bretoneiche was editor; Serge Groffe and Renée Coulant did the make-up; Patrick Saglio was AD; sound was by Gérard de Lagarde and Norbert Gernolle; and Louis Duchesne and René Thévenet produced.

The world of *Goto: Island of Love* is dark, grim, fantastical, and very strange. It is shot in black-and-white, recalling sober Eastern European films, and with scenes and images flattened (as in Sergei Paradjanov's *The Colour of Pomegranates*). There are some colour inserts. It's in French.

Goto depicts a fantasy realm which recalls Mervyn Peake's *Gormenghast* trilogy, or Charles Dickens' London, or Franz Kafka's Prague (film critics related the world of *Goto* to Kafka's *The Prison Colony,* 1948).

The *mise-en-scène* is dirty, shabby, organic, a world of stripped walls, stone, wood, and Victorian furniture. Also on display are a collection of props and designs that form a unique vision. Totally brilliant.

It's also a film of walls: brick walls, stone walls, peeling plaster walls, tiled walls, and walls made from wooden planks. Walerian Borowczyk is in love with walls almost as much as women's bodies (actually, more so at times). He loves to place his actors in their extravagant costumes against really interestingly textured walls. Borowczyk will never use a simple, blank wall of plywood painted one colour (like a standard film set) if there's a old brick wall nearby which's got bits missing from it and holes in the cement. The only other director I can think of who enshrines walls with the same passion is Andrei Tarkovsky. It's part of their Eastern European/ Russian sensibility, maybe, to include so many peeling, cracked, decaying walls (you see it in the cinema of Jan Svankmajer).

It's all very stylized and abstract, but also wholly convincing. You can really believe that these characters live in this environment. It's to do with the texture, the light, the compositions, the unified vision. Plenty of films have delivered scenes of filthy, muddy, shabby environments (and not only in the mediæval films of Pier Paolo Pasolini or Ingmar Bergman), but few feel as striking and lived-in as this. While Hollywood films always give in and have glossy back-lighting and make-up smeared on its actors' faces (as in *The Lord of the Rings* or *Braveheart*), so that you don't *really* feel as if the characters really do live in those spaces, in *Goto: Island of Love* and other Borowczyk films it's all too believable. Hollywood constructs sets and brings in grass and mud; *Goto: Island of Love* has the real thing. And, no, it's not because Borowczyk and his team can't afford to build sets and have elaborate lighting or costumes; it's to do with *the way* those film elements are employed. With Borowczyk, you are in the hands of a master.

Goto: Island of Love seems to arrive on the film scene fully-formed, completely convincing and organic, and totally eccentric. Walerian Borowczyk wrote and directed *Goto: Island of Love* – the writing and conception being the really important contributions to the piece. It's the *conception* of this bizarre world that's so convincing, and the design and construction of it is equally impressive. This is filmmaking at its very highest pitch.[18]

The story of *Goto: Island of Love* concerns desire, loss, distance, and tragedy, as an underling, the fly catcher, dog keeper and boot-cleaner Grozo (Guy Saint-Jean),[19] works his way up in the bizarre kingdom of Goto, by cunning, persuasion and murder, to become king

18 Walerian Borowczyk is a total one-off in cinema, but there are affinities between Borowczyk and filmmakers such as Pier Paolo Pasolini, Luis Buñuel, Werner Herzog and Jan Svankmajer (Pasolini, for instance, also liked to use unknown actors, shoot on location, explore Catholicism and religion, draw on the history of art, and use the ancient world).

19 Grozo is given three tasks by the king Goto: flies, dogs and shoes. Each job has a ritual as well as an erotic component.

himself.

Grozo's passion for Glossia (Ligia Branice), the wife of the king Goto III (Pierre Brasseur),[20] lusting after her from afar through binoculars, and uncovering her infidelity with an officer, Lieutenant Gono (Jean-Pierre Andréani), ends in tragedy when, pursuing her up endless flights of stairs, Grozo fails to prevent Glossia from falling to her death (or she throws herself down to escape him). Everyone's name in *Goto: Island of Love* begins with a 'G': Goto, Glossia, Grozo, Gwino, Grymp, Gra, Gomor, Gonasta.

The radiant Polish actress Ligia Branice (b. 1932) was Walerian Borowczyk's wife at the time, and went on to star in *Blanche* and *Behind Convent Walls*. Apart from Borowczyk's films, Branice doesn't seem to have appeared in many other films or television. A pity: she's a fine actress (and kept in great shape – when *Behind Convent Walls* was shot, she was in her mid-forties). Later, Marina Pierro was the star of five of Borowczyk's features. Putting your wife in your films is a time-honoured practice in cinema. Borowczyk used his wife Branice, Godard used Anna Karina, Anne Wiazemsky and Anne-Marie Miéville; Woody Allen used Diane Keaton and Mia Farrow; and Orson Welles used Rita Hayworth.

Goto: Island of Love truly is a tragedy: Grozo kills three people in order to get Glossia, and reach the top: her father Gomor (whom he works for as a fly catcher), her lover, the handsome young lieutenant, Gono, and her husband, King Goto III. Grozo's a pretty ruthless character, really, resembling Macbeth or Iago.

Goto: Island of Love is also an allegory about a Communist state, echoing Walerian Borowczyk's own experience of growing up in Eastern Europe. It amused Borowczyk, for example, that *Goto: Island of Love* was banned in fascist Spain as well as Communist nations.

Not to be under-estimated is Walerian Borowczyk's grasp of social conventions and hierarchies: many of his cinematic worlds have clearly delineated social codes and relationships: everyone knows their place, everyone has their own situation and duties. Borowczyk is brilliant on social ritual and deference, on the manifestation of power

20 Pierre Brasseur (1905-72) was a veteran of over 130 films, including classics such as *Les Enfants du paradis* and *Les Yeux sans visage*.

relations within social groups. That he came from Eastern Europe only enhances his vision.

The isle of Goto is a military society, with soldiers, officers and a king. The populace have their own cells, and revere the king. And they have their own mythology and history, which's outlined in the early scene in the classroom, presided over by the eccentric professor (Fernand Berchet). (Let's not forget Borowczyk's great scriptwriting too: the classroom scene is a slick way of getting across plenty of exposition, but you don't notice it. That's skilful writing.)

Erotic desire is a key element in *Goto: Island of Love*, as in almost all of Walerian Borowczyk's feature films. Grozo desires Glossia: that simple but inescapable fact drives much of the narrative. Grozo is a condemned man at the beginning (for stealing some binoculars), and is forced to fight the giant criminal Gra (there's some slapstick comedy as Grozo is armed with a wooden plank while Gra is blindfolded with a hood).

Grozo manages to escape and beg for mercy, racing up some stairs and burying his head in Glossia's lap. That moment when he touched her dress and body haunts him – he remembers it at night, in bed, and later, when he's tupping a prostitute. The film makes memorable use of brief flashbacks. (It's also blackly funny when Gra is executed by guillotine, and Grozo emerges from a space some feet below him, as he lies face-down on a platform. You've never seen a guillotine scene like this, with the victim spitting on his enemy as the last thing he's able to do before dying, and Grozo insulting Gra's head when it lands in a basket below him).

Naked women are also a part of *Goto: Island of Love. Of course they are*, because it's a *Walerian Borowczyk film*! There's an enchanting *tableau* of a group of naked women bathing in tin baths (pipes, water, baths, nude women and set out on two levels). It's a bordello, and the women are picked off by the Madame to join men in cubicles. If this's the first Borowczyk film you've seen, it'll be the first time you'll see how Borowczyk photographs naked women: they don't *do* anything (usually), they are just *there* (often they're bathing, or dressing). And Borowczyk's camera doesn't only look at them from a distance, it also moves in much closer, to frame their torsos and, in particular, their buttocks and hips (never was a filmmaker so in love with women's asses – outside of hardcore pornography, that is. Or maybe including all of porn). Borowczyk's direction to the naked extras probably runs along the lines of: '*D'accord*, now stand up... *Bon*, now turn around, so we can see your ass. *Oui, ton cul*.. Ah, *magnifique*!'[21]

There is also a sex scene, a classic romp in the hay between Glossia and her soldier lover Gono in the stables. But Walerian Borowczyk's reference here, or the kind of sex romp he's thinking of, is not taken from cinema, but much further back: Borowczyk is a connoisseur of pornography and erotic literature – he is referencing erotic art of the 17th and 18th centuries, in written as well as painted or drawn form. The film knows that it's a cliché, well-worn like an old boot, to portray lovers tupping in the hay in the stables, but it's not a cliché from the history of *cinema*, but from the history of *literature*.[22]

In other words, when you're looking at a Walerian Borowczyk picture, you have to think in terms of literature and graphic art (painting, drawing, printmaking) going back centuries, not only to cinema as an artform with its roots in silent films from the early 1900s. Before erotic cinema there was erotic photography, for instance (there is some superb French photographic erotica, which Borowczyk has sometimes used in his films, dating from the 1900s-1910s. And before that erotic literature, and erotic prints, and so on and on.)

The eroticism in *Goto: Island of Love* is also voyeurism, one of Walerian Borowczyk's chief recurring themes (and also one of pornography's – and cinema's). Both Grozo and the king, Goto III, spy on Glossia and her assignations with Gono. They can't help themselves climbing up to that loft and using the binoculars to spy on the lovers (Grozo's crime, at the beginning, was to steal some binoculars, although we don't see Grozo ogling the lovers that early on).

Here we don't need to bring in philosophers such as Jacques Lacan and Elizabeth Grosz on voyeurism and the sexual lack, on voyeurism and castration, on scopophilia (the pleasure of looking), issues which

21 It's Jean-Luc Godard's 'civilization de cul', the 'civilization of the ass' that he satirized in 1960s movies such as *Contempt*.

22 And in numerous erotic prints – such as by Jean-Honoré Fragonard, Thomas Rowlandson, Johan Tobias Sergel, etc.

have been discussed to death in film criticism, cultural theory and contemporary philosophy.

Suffice to say here that Walerian Borowczyk's films certainly express the familiar concerns of voyeurism and desire, the links between scopophilia and the prohibition, the lack, and impotence – and, of course, death. *Goto: Island of Love* has both Grozo and Goto observing the lovers; there's a wonderful scene where Goto is watching them and Grozo is loitering around the loft (he says he's putting out his fly-catching boxes). Just before they both see the couple making love, there's a confrontation between the king and the worker. The object of contention? A pair of binoculars, the voyeur's modern weapon of choice.

Goto commands Grozo to take up the binoculars, and Grozo is very hesitant to do so, knowing that theft means extreme punishment on the Isle of Goto, possibly leading to death in the trial fight (the island has a curious custom of pitting a much smaller criminal against a giant, and that after they've both committed many crimes). After hesitating, and getting Goto's word that he won't come to harm, Grozo takes up the binoculars. Goto encourages him to look out of the window, as if he's encouraging Grozo to see the marital infidelity. In previous scenes, the characters sometimes look at the sea (with longing – Goto in surveying his kingdom, but Glossia in hope, looking at the boat that might take her and Gono away from the island, as Gono has promised. The boat is reprised in some of the mental flashbacks of characters like Glossia).

But this time the first thing Grozo lights upon with the binoculars is his beloved Glossia making love with Gono. The sight is as saddening to him as he knows it will be to Goto. Grozo moves away and Goto takes a look. The film cuts back and forth between Goto looking and the pair making love passionately. Surely no artform other than cinema can so perfectly depict the looker and the looked-at in voyeurism, and the reactions, altering over time.

The sight of the lovers means death, of course. The king gives Grozo his gun, and plainly means that Grozo should go out to the stables and kill Gono. But Grozo, remember, is consumed with desire for Glossia, and he shoots the king. It's positively Shakespearean, as well as distinctly Freudian (Sigmund Freud was the god of the Surrealists – or Freud as interpreted by André Breton). Grozo exits the scene as a murderer, carefully covering up his tracks before slipping on some boots downstairs (he spends much of the movie in his socks, as an early close-up revealed).

Glossia is the prize or trophy that's fought over by the three men in *Goto*, in the usual patriarchal manner that feminists have discussed *ad infinitum*. No need to quote the hundreds of feminists who have complained how women are traded between men (the marriage ceremony exemplifies that, when the bride is exchanged from the bride's father to the groom). Glossia is also of course an *idea* or *symbol* of a woman, of Woman, with her white costume like an *anima* figure (and her unusual hat – Borowczyk loves odd hats).

So concisely and neatly Walerian Borowczyk portrays all of the issues surrounding desire in these scenes – the intense desire, the prohibition (Grozo is forbidden to come near Glossia), the beloved object of desire (Glossia is radiant), the voyeuristic impulse (which neither Grozo nor Goto can resist), and the death that results from it.

But it all has to end badly; there's no other way for a tragedy to end. After the king's death, Grozo, like Macbeth or Iago, orchestrates things so that the leaders think that Goto committed suicide when he saw his wife and Gono tupping. Grozo's ambition knows no end now. He will have Glossia at any cost – he's already killed two people to get closer to her.

So the generals put Glossia under house arrest, but Grozo is able to win her trust (through the hatch window, her only contact with the rest of Goto – Walerian Borowczyk loves doorways of all kinds). When Grozo comes to Glossia's room, though, he makes a fatal error, by telling her that Gono has been executed, and was accused of killing Goto (Grozo wearing the king's uniform doesn't help, either). That sends Glossia into a madness; instead of eloping with Grozo, as he hopes, in his scheming but simple fashion, having won her trust (he thinks), she flees, in a lengthy chase, up stairs and along corridors, and all the way up the stairs near the loft. It's *Vertigo* or *The Hunchback of*

Notre Dame or *Frankenstein* territory now, pure Gothic horror, as the frenzy reaches its climax, and Glossia topples to her death.

She lands on the stage, scene of the first act, where Grozo was reprieved. The film might end there, with a fade to black, but Walerian Borowczyk adds a coda which enhances Grozo's misery: the man carries and drags Glossia back to his room (again, as it's a Borowczyk film, he doesn't simply carry her along corridors, but he's pushing her corpse through narrow hatches and up stairs).

The scene in his room is pitiful, because Grozo has turned it into a Glossia Shrine: he has collected her clothes throughout the film. The longest snatch of colour footage in *Goto: Island of Love* occurs here,[23] revealing the many dresses and objects that Grozo has collected of Glossia's (he's had access to her rooms because he cleans the king and queen's boots. *Goto: Island of Love* introduces audiences to Borowczyk's foot fetishism and shoe fetishism: there's a shot of Glossia which pans down to her shoes, for no apparent reason; and Grozo caresses Glossia's boots lovingly as he cleans them).

In the final shot of the 1968 film, after Grozo has put her on her bed, Glossia's eyes flutter open momentarily, she breathes a moment, before her eyes close (she is breathing, but the movie is clear that she opens her eyes only briefly, and then closes them – she is dead, she has to die). The film cuts from that image of the beloved woman dying to a close-up of Grozo in agony, weeping. Meanwhile the George Frideric Handel *Concerto* has been hammering throughout this sequence.

It's a moving close to the film: even if Grozo has been a nasty piece of work throughout, you can't help feeling sorry for him. All of his schemes have come to nothing. *Goto: Island of Love* powerfully demonstrates the gulf between Grozo's perception and erotic desires and reality – the voyeur and the object of desire. You see it all in his face, and the reverse angles of the dead woman on his bed (the place where they might have made love). He thinks he means more to Glossia, but for her he's just another of her husband's many subjects.

⚜

What an ending! And how amazing is this film! You can recognize

23 The other colour inserts include a bucket of blood (after Gra's guillotining), meat that's fed to the dogs, clothes in Glossia's room, and Glossia's boots.

all of the elements that Walerian Borowczyk and his production team have gathered together – the pieces from William Shakespeare, the designs from Expressionist theatre, the lighting and photography from German Expressionism, the objects and props from Surrealism, but the blending of them is wholly original.

Goto: Island of Love depicts the classic erotic melodrama, exploited by writers over thousands of years: Grozo and Goto love Glossia, but she loves Gono. The picture might not have the grandeur and tragedy of Sophocles, Eurypides or Shakespeare, but, in its own more modest way, it carves out a moving drama in a unique world. *Goto: Island of Love* also proves that Borowczyk is not only a great director and Surrealist animator who sank down to the level of a purveyor of soft porn films, as critics too often deride, but could construct a marvellous, humane, compelling and visionary drama.

⚜

It's not only the story that is so striking in *Goto: Island of Love*, though, but Walerian Borowczyk's extraordinary feeling for visuals, spaces, costumes, and designs (accompanied by a Handel organ concerto). *Goto: Island of Love* has a *mise-en-scène* like no other film, a combination of shabby rooms, railway tracks and flat cars, stables and horses, brick warehouses and factories, animals (cats, dogs, horses),[24] and a classroom scene (and a teacher) out of 19th century fiction. (There is no long shot establishing Goto's fortress or the fortress in its surroundings. Instead, there are views outwards from the stronghold, to the fields and trees, or to the distant shore. That helps to give the spaces of the film their particular quality: the fortress is like a maze, with endless rooms adjoining endless corridors.)

Goto: Island of Love is one of those movies that exist in their own space, which they have carved out for themselves. They are linked to other films assuredly, but manage to make such an impression, with their vivid *mise-en-scène* and idiosyncratic vision. The art direction in *Goto: Island of Love* is truly incredible, in *every* shot. *Every* shot is beautifully composed.

Goto: Island of Love takes its place among other films which have

24 *Goto: Island of Love* opens with shots of the stables, and horses exercising – horses would crop up notoriously in *The Beast*, of course.

created their own world so completely and convincingly, like *Blade Runner, The Wizard Of Oz* or anything by Hayao Miyazaki. Other movies you might cite in connection with *Goto: Island of Love* include *The Trial*, Orson Welles' incredible take on Franz Kafka, shot in Paris and Yugoslavia, which recreates a nightmarish realm of black-and-white and unreal spaces as compelling as *Goto*'s. And maybe Jean-Luc Godard's 1965 sci-fi film *Alphaville*, also made in Paris.

The cruelty in the dictatorial system is clearly significant in *Goto: Island of Love*: this is a regime presided over by a king whose every command is sacrosanct and who is worshipped by his subjects (in the early classroom, for instance, the portrait of Goto III that the teacher and children discuss is clearly meant to evoke political dictators of the 20th century).[25] And everyone wears military clothing, or the clothes of workers – shabby overalls. (Some of the labour on the island of Goto seems pointless – the soldiers dynamite a quarry but the fortress is old and nothing seems to have been built for centuries).

Music's again an important element in *Goto: Island of Love*: there's George Frideric Handel's *Concerto* no. 11, opus 7, the hymn the subjects of Goto sing (composed by Walerian Borowczyk), and the concert they attend (which features a solo on a saw and bow, and a man playing a home-made cello which has only one string).

Yet most of *Goto: Island of Love* is near-silent, with some distinctive spot sound effects, consisting of abstract sounds like scrapes, thuds, squeaks and rattles. So that, when the music comes, it really roars through the film: in two scenes Handel is employed to great effect; in the middle of the picture, when Glossia and Goto visit the beach and Goto nearly drowns in the broken boat, and in the climactic sequence.

25 And there are three rulers of Goto isle within that portrait – a classic Surrealist object from Borowczyk, but also a commentary on seeing things from a different angle perhaps, or maybe it's about each ruler being different but also the same (whoever you vote for, it's always the government that gets in). So all the Gotos that rule the island are the same.

3

IMMORAL TALES

Immoral Tales (1974) is a total masterpiece. Made in French, it was a collection of four erotic stories: *La Marée* (*The Tide*), based on a story by Walerian Borowczyk's friend André Pieyre de Mandiargues; *Thérèse Philosophe*, about a young woman locked up in a room who finds escape in masturbation; *Erzsébet Báthory*, about the original 'Countess Dracula'; and *Lucrezia Borgia*, about the decadent Italian Renaissance dynasty of the Borgias.

A short film, *Une Collection Particulière* (1973), a catalogue and documentary of Walerian Borowczyk's own collection of erotica, was going to be part of *Immoral Tales*, as well as *The Beast* (it was narrated by and starred de Mandiargues). *Une Collection Particulière* is an amusing and playful exploration of a host of erotica, including sex toys, dildoes, prints, photographs, and paintings. There are some early devices designed to titillate - wooden models and automata (such as a policeman getting an erection, a man fucking a donkey, and strip shows and silhouettes of people tupping). These quaint machines pre-date cinema, but simulate movement and life, being part of Borowczyk's fascination with animation, and animating the inanimate, which was such a large part of Borowczyk's early films.

Contes Immoraux continued Walerian Borowczyk's exploration of the erotic (for some it was a lapse into pornography, as Borowczyk's next film, *La Bête*, demonstrated for those nay-sayers). *Immoral Tales* starred Lise Danvers, Fabrice Luchini, Charlotte Alexandra, Pascale Christophe, Paloma Picasso (daughter of the painter, in her only leading role in a film), Florence Bellamy, Jacopo Berenzini and Lorenzo Berenzini.

Immoral Tales was produced by Anatole Dauman and Argos Films (Dauman, one of the key film producers of the period, had credits that included art house classics such as *Hiroshima Mon Amour, Masculin/Féminin* and *Mouchette*). *Immoral Tales* was apparently second at the box office in 1974 in France. (Is that true? Amazing, if it is. No: it must be by the week, that *Immoral Tales* was at no.2 for one or more weeks). Piet Bolscher was costume designer, Dominique Duvergé was first AD, Bernard Daillencourt, Guy Durban, Noël Véry and Michel Zolat were DPs, and Boro is credited with production design, editing, and direction.

One of the very striking aspects of *Immoral Tales* is how much of a silent film it is – or, rather, how little dialogue there is. Because it's not silent – there is plenty of music, and sound effects. Long stretches of the film are without dialogue. In the first movie, André is talking plenty about tides and such, but the sound of the sea and the seagulls is just as prominent. In the second film, most of the dialogue comes from God, no less, in voiceover. But most of the second film is still without dialogue. In the third movie, there's a little dialogue from the soldier, but virtually none from the two leads, Erzsébet Báthory and Istvan. The fourth episode, about the Borgias, has much more dialogue – a ranting monologue from Girolamo Savonarola, and and the conversations between the Borgias themselves. In this film, though, it's Lucrezia Borgia's laugh as much as the dialogue, that stays in the mind.

The music was by Maurice Le Roux, and also Guillaume de Machaut, Musique Espagnole Ancienne, Musique Hongroise Ancienne, and Walerian Borowczyk's favourite Domenico Scarlatti.[26] In many parts of *Immoral Tales*, the music is exquisite – particularly the recreations of Renaissance and 17th century music (presumably by Musique Espagnole Ancienne and Musique Hongroise Ancienne). The genre dubbed 'early music' in classical music circles is popular nowadays, and Borowczyk makes brilliant use of it. I will keep coming back to Borowczyk's use of music, and how it is overshadowed by the nudity and sex and visual eccentricities of his films.

Immoral Tales travelled back in time: the first story, *La Marée* (*The Tide*), was set in the present, the following stories moved back to the late 19th century, 1890, to 1610 for 'Countess Dracula', and finally to Renaissance times with the Borgias, to 1498. The first movie was set in France; judging by the chalky white cliffs in *The Tide*, it was somewhere in Northern France. The second film was also set in rural France. The third film, about 'Countess Dracula', moved to Eastern Europe, and the final movie to late fifteenth century Italy.

26 Domenico Scarlatti (1685-1757) was part of a musical family, and composed around 600 pieces for harpsichord.

LA MARÉE (THE TIDE)

A title card of a quote from Francois de La Rochefoucauld's (1613-80) *Maxims* appeared after the opening titles. The first story in *Immoral Tales* was about 25 minutes long,[27] and featured two cousins, a 20 year-old youth André (Fabrice Luchini) and a 16 year-old woman Julie (Lise Danvers) cycling to the beach, climbing along some rocks under the cliffs and making love. So far so familiar, but this is not a piece of softcore porn. There's never been a sex scene on the beach like this in cinema (or pornography); this is *very* far from the porn circuit of the San Fernando Valley.

There is a scene of the youths at a large, rural house, setting the scene in contemporary France: Julie waves at some parental figure who departs in a Citroen (with the parents out of the way, the children can play; Julie and André prepare to cycle off to the beach). The landscape they cycle through resembles Northern France – it might be Normandy, or Brittany. The imagery is of Summer, a day out, innocence (only the way that André is ordering Julie about and seems to be planning something hints at something else going on). There are hints, too, in the close-ups that the film selects – in particular, Julie's mouth, which becomes the central motif of this chapter of *Immoral Tales* (along with the sea). It's significant, perhaps, that Julie and André are cousins, or maybe it's just another of those standard tropes in erotic fiction of incest. It's certainly significant that André is 20 and Julie is 16 (and a virgin). He tells her that in Paris each Wednesday he visits prostitutes with his friends (yeah, right – doesn't every kid brag about that?).

Before any sex can occur, Walerian Borowczyk has the couple spending quite a while clambering over seaweed-strewn rocks and trudging along a stony beach, in and out of the surf. Throughout this, the film builds up images of the beach, the cliffs above, birds flying into their nests, and gulls flying above the waves. It's permanently overcast (well, it is in most of the shots).

André persuades his cousin Julie that they won't get cut off from

27 You get *The Tide* as part of *The Beast* on DVD.

the tide: he carries a newspaper clipping with the tide times on it, which he places on a rock, beside his watch. The girl seems to be complying mutely to what the youth wants (the youth is leading the narrative all the way; he talks about educating his cousin). Julie goes for a swim in the milky, grey sea, against his wishes.

The boy asks the girl to take off her black bikini and leave her see-through white cotton dress on. He then asks her to suck him while he explains to her about the tides. When the tide reaches its height, at 11.27, he explains, he will flood her mouth, and she will understand about the sun, the moon and the tide. It'll be a gift from the sea, he tells her.

The prelude to the sex act has Julie undressing, and the camera lingering on her breasts and vulva in a tight close-up, in the familiar voyeuristic gaze of mainstream and pornographic cinema (the woman's body is on display at many points, while André barely undresses – just pulls his jeans down a little but keeps his wellington boots on).

So far, so normal: well, kinda. Up to this point, though, the film has constructed painterly images, of the cliffs, the rocks, the waves, birds on the cliffs, gulls floating on the water, the stones, and the people dwarfed below the cliffs (in a slow zoom shot that tilts down from the cliffs to the beach).

Julie undressing and the camera lingering on her naked body is thus just one element among many elements, because Walerian Borowczyk's camera also dwells at length on the cliffs, the beach, the rocks and the sea. No porn director would waste precious 35mm film stock on such images. But Borowczyk seems just as interested in the setting, in the sound and sight of the surging waves, as in the couple making out.

André and Julie embrace; to presage the blowjob, there's an extreme, abstract close-up of the girl's mouth, with the boy's finger stroking her lips, circling round and round, then pressing inside it. It's a classic device to show what isn't allowed to be shown in softcore cinema (the 'meat shot' of cock sucking), but Borowczyk has the shot go on much, much longer than a conventional art film or softcore flick.

Borowczyk returns to the close-up of the girl's mouth a few times; after the sex act, the film again concentrates on Julie's mouth, her fingers abstractedly pressing her wet lips.

Immoral Tales features luscious close-ups of the girl's face staring up into the camera, as Julie looks at André and listens to him as he explains what they're going to do (Walerian Borowczyk has a magical ability to film women in close-up, staring into the camera – not every filmmaker can do it – the same radiant, soul-revealing shots appear in *Behind Convent Walls,* of Ligia Branice, for instance, and of Marina Pierro in *Love Rites*). It's another game, but a special game, he says, in which she'll learn something about the tides and the sea.

The couple move from the rocks to lie on the stones at the high tideline. André uncovers her breasts and plays with her nipple. When she's sucking him, he pulls up her white dress, to reveal her ass and cunt – and the camera lingers over such details, framing nothing but Julie's ass and cunt.

Walerian Borowczyk renders the everyday world, the surroundings (the stones, beach, rocks, cliffs, sky and sea) strange by cutting away from Julie with her head between André's legs to the waves, the seagulls flying above the waves or the nests in the cliffs. The roar and hiss of the ocean builds, until it is very loud, giving the scene a powerful rhythm (the scene plays without music, like many of Borowczyk's scenes). In Production Code 'classical' Hollywood films, cutting away to a shot of pounding waves was a clichéd trope for what couldn't be shown, people making whoopie; here, in *Contes Immoraux,* it's as if the boy and the girl conjure up the elemental powers of nature, of the sea and the sky, by their lovemaking. The roaring waves illustrate (embody) the couple's sexual energy, in the tried and tested metaphorical manner of poetry, but it also works back in the other direction: the raging sea seems to be infusing the lovers with a primæval erotic power. The *mise-en-scène* is primal, archaic, with only André's watch and the tide timetable as relics of the modern age (though set in the 1970s, the scene has a timeless, mythical quality).

Then, an extraordinary cut occurs, a long shot of the couple writhing on the beach taken from a boat 50 or so yards out to sea, approaching the shore. In a medium shot, taken from a reverse angle, above the couple on the stones, with the waves behind them, André comes, thrusting his hips upwards, his legs entangled with the girl's; the high tide washes over them from time to time, drenching them (the actors must've hated shooting it – cold water, hard stones, no wet suits – aside from that flimsy bit of cloth, poor Lise Danvers is naked – and you can bet that Monsieur Borowczyk asked for more than one take. Danvers was an unknown actor, and has appeared in only one other film, made around the same time).

It's like the famous scene in *From Here To Eternity* between Deborah Kerr and Burt Lancaster – well, actually, it's way beyond that scene. *Immoral Tales* has taken up the cliché of sex on the beach, which *From Here To Eternity* and other movies have drawn on, and given it a European, art film spin. The waves pounding the beach and drenching the couple don't need any gloss: Walerian Borowczyk has made manifest what other films hint at then draw back from showing.

It's a genuinely erotic sequence – and that's not entirely because of the sex act, or Lise Danvers' nude body. It's partly to do with the pictorial and aural elements that Walerian Borowczyk has orchestrated here. And it's also to do with the setting – being by the sea *is* erotic, and you don't need actors in films to reveal that to you (poets have been doing it for millennia).

The scene evokes notions of time, tides, rituals, bodies, skin, sexual fluids, as well as presenting an erotic act. What's memorable about the piece is not the sex, which has been seen a zillion times before, but the interconnection between the bodies and the landscape; the ritualistic aspect (these are not individuals or personalities having sex, but archetypes); and the way Borowczyk manages to turn the ordinary into the strange. It must rank as the weirdest blowjob scene in all cinema.

The elements of *The Tide* are deceptively simple: a boy, a girl, and a beach. It's the way Walerian Borowczyk orchestrates these apparently plain ingredients that marks him out as a master. And it's the way that he *balances* and *mixes* those elements. A Borowczyk movie is never *one thing alone*, never *just* arty, or *just* porny, or *just* comic, or *just* surreal. You could send a thousand film students to the coast armed with a camera, tripod, microphone, lights, a couple of actors, food and 1,000 feet of 35mm film stock, and none of them would come back with something a millionth as impressive as *La Marée*.

THÉRÈSE PHILOSOPHE

In the second film of *Contes Immoraux* (around 23 minutes long), *Thérèse Philosophe*, a world of Victorian repression and culture is evoked: a young woman, Thérèse (Charlotte Alexandra), is locked in a room for three days by a stern matriarch. Thérèse is young, attractive, pale, and clad in a virginal white dress. It's set in 1890. It was based on an 18th century novel (1748) by Jean-Baptiste de Boyer, Marquis d'Argens. Only part of the novel was filmed, and the episode only took up the idea of Thérèse being locked in a room for two weeks, surrounded by erotica, but trying to refrain from masturbation.

The sequence consists of the woman's masturbatory fantasies – at the beginning of the segment, Thérèse visits a church. Thérèse is filmed in a richly decorated Catholic church (apparently after Mass) suggestively caressing brass columns, eagles, statuary and church organ pipes (accompanied by Walerian Borowczyk's beloved classical organ music). Here, a deep male voice (identified as the voice of God) prompts her to reveal herself to Him sensually, to live for Him as she should. The church introduces Borowczyk's recurring themes of spirituality and sexuality, God and love (and how Thérèse interprets God's request for love erotically). The opening scene is steeped in Catholic imagery and religious repression – a young woman wandering around a church in an erotic daze and fondling statues and long metal organ pipes suggestively is fairly blatant and to the point. Borowczyk doesn't hold back: this young woman is horny, the film says.

One of Walerian Borowczyk's recurring scenes is a young person (usually a woman) learning about sex acts for the first time. She's curious, wants to know more, wants to do what she's heard about (or, more often, seen in erotic books). So films such as *Immoral Tales* and *La Bête* depict young people having sex for the first time (often it's masturbation).

Trapped in the room (because she was late coming home from church), Thérèse finds objects for her erotic fantasies: a book of 18th century pornography, called *Thérèse Philosophe* (Borowczyk's love of erotica, and cataloguing it, manifests itself in the sequence where the young woman leafs through the book at length, and the film cuts to close-ups of the 18th century black-and-white illustrations of people tupping in a variety of settings and positions).

As well as the book of erotica, *Thérèse Philosophe* also cuts to paintings in the room, and many other objects: Walerian Borowczyk has art directed the set with a host of antique items: a bust; a mirror; a chamber pot; old trunks; erotic photographs; a fairground wheel. It seems to be a lumber room, maybe a former nursery. A world of the past, with hidden mysteries, like the erotic photos Thérèse finds at the bottom of the trunk. Like other Borowczyk heroines, Thérèse embarks upon searching through the room for things to use, discovering the cache of French late 19th century erotica (probably from Borowczyk's own collection). Maybe they were her father's. Thérèse also has a *Station of the Cross* (*De la Croix*) which she hangs onto (she begs her mother/ guardian for it when she's locked in the room).

Thérèse's erotic desire knows no bounds. As in Walerian Borowczyk's other films, once women have become sexually aroused and intent on orgasm, nothing will stop them. By the end of the second episode of *Immoral Tales*, everything in the room has been appropriated by Thérèse for her masturbation session: a print of Edward VII (!),[28] a bath mat, a large wooden doll, the flowers on her hat, candlesticks and cucumbers. She takes up the battered wooden doll and kisses it on the mouth softly. Memories of childhood.

There's no music in *Thérèse Philosophe*, except in a couple of bursts: strident organ music is deployed when Thérèse discovers the

28 That's one of Borowczyk's themes – the all-consuming erotic power of women. Candles and cucumbers might be expected to be part of masturbation, but not a print of Edward VII or a bath mat!

book of erotica: it's as if she's discovering sex for the first time. Oh, so *that's* what adults get up to she maybe thinks. The film cuts back from the erotic prints to a C.U. of Thérèse reacting to them, disturbed and aroused. It's one of Borowczyk's main themes: a young person discovering sex.

God's voice talks to Thérèse. It's Joan of Arc time, voices of God in the head time – except God didn't tell Joan of Arc to masturbate with a cucumber. Thérèse undresses and offers herself to God, lying back on the bed, clad in a favourite Walerian Borowczyk costume, a white cotton dress. She starts to masturbate, first caressing her nipples, pulling off her dress, then squeezing her thighs together. The camera lingers over Thérèse's pale skin and pink nipples. Flashbacks occur – to the church, as if Thérèse is riffling through some erotic moments in her life, to find some moments she can use for her masturbatory fantasies.

Thérèse takes up a cucumber and traps it between her thighs. Finally, she sits up, her back to the camera, and pushes the cucumber inside herself, gradually working her arm faster until she is ramming it in, and gasping loudly, accompanied by the squelchy sounds of the cucumber in her cunt.

I guess some viewers would see this scene as pure soft porn. But Walerian Borowczyk is doing other things within the scene, such as cutting away to the objects that are included in the girl's masturbation trance: the paintings of aristocrats on the wall, the Edward VII lithograph, the doll. She kisses a portrait of a man (possibly someone she admires).

Much of the episode is shot in painterly close-ups of the woman's body, panning from her mouth to her breasts, or along her torso to her bottom, which abstract the sexual act into a series of beautiful images. Walerian Borowczyk's camera travels over the woman's writhing body in big close-ups, refusing to clarify exactly what's going on (pornography, by contrast, uses medium shots to include the whole body. And mainstream Hollywood cinema tends to use these same big close-ups as Borowczyk, but not for abstract, painterly reasons: rather, in order to avoid showing the whole nude body, for the opposite reasons of pornography).

As Thérèse reaches her orgasm, she sits on the bed with her back to the camera, thighs spread apart, and the shots consist of close-up expanses of white skin, accompanied by Thérèse's frantic moans. Only after she comes does the camera pull back to clarify the situation, and show Thérèse lying face-down on the bed.

The allusions to paintings do not stop there, though: Thérèse lying face-down on the bed recalls 17th and 18th century nudes (and in particular Francois Boucher's famous painting *Mademoiselle O'Murphy*, 1751. Even Hollywood movies have referenced the famous Boucher butt).

Walerian Borowczyk's penchant for frontal, flattened compositions is apparent throughout the scene: the bed is set against the wall, and the camera stays back, flattening out the elements within the frame. Where most directors might have blocked the action in flattering three-quarter views, covered in medium shots, Borowczyk favours a cinematic approach all his own. At the end of the scene, for example, Thérèse lies on the bed, but the composition is end-on, looking down from her head.

A coda ends the episode which takes *Thérèse Philosophe* into another area of historical erotica: the young woman pounced upon by a lecherous older man in a field. First, Thérèse escapes from the room into the sunny fields (including a very long shot as she disappears into the distance, a composition that recalls 18th century landscape painting. Right at the end of the scene, a stocky middle-aged guy appears, and poor Thérèse cries for help. A rape is suggested, but not shown, because the second episode ends abruptly, right there.

It seems as if Thérèse is going to be punished after all for her masturbation and erotic feelings. It seems that God didn't intend her to show Him her love by fucking herself with a cucumber.

ERZSÉBET BÁTHORY

The third episode in *Contes Immoraux*, *Erzsébet Báthory*, is set in 1610 in Eastern Europe, and opens with the Countess Báthory (Paloma Picasso) riding on a black horse accompanied by her aide Istvan (Pascale Christophe) and some soldiers.[29] There's a brief evocation of the Dracula myth, a little cinematic Gothic atmosphere: a roadside crucifix which the Countess glowers at, and birds cawing ominously in the sky. Most of *Erzsébet Báthory* plays without dialogue. The music is wonderful early music.

The real Erzsbét Báthory (1560-1614) was known as 'the Blood Countess' and 'the Bloody Lady of Cachtice'. She lived at Cachtice Castle and is one of the most notorious serial killers in history: she was accused of 80 deaths, but some witnesses said 600 or 650.

Countess Báthory was one of a number of historical figures in the early modern period who became infamous for their bizarre, blood-filled exploits: Vlad Dracul, the Wallachian prince in the late 15th century (ancestor of Dracula), and the alchemist Gilles de Rais (1400-40) who murdered 200-300 children in the pursuit of the philosopher's stone.

Countess Báthory is clad in an enormous black feather hat, and a lush black costume (it's a self-consciously over-the-top costume). Istvan, her cross-dressing aide (dressed as a page), wears white. The costumes are *fabulous*. Those hats! And boots! And cloaks! And corselets! Piet Bolscher, Borowczyk's regular costume designer (including the costumes in *Immoral Tales*), should be mentioned here (and the make-up and hair artists). *Immoral Tales* is truly a costume drama. It's a proper *costume* drama. It's all about the clothes.

Walerian Borowczyk's *Immoral Tales* isn't the only movie about Countess Báthory: there have been European flicks made in the 1970s, as well as films featuring female vampires (sometimes with lesbian elements). *Carmilla* (1872) by Sheridan Le Fanu was often an inspiration. The first Italian vampire movie, and the first proper Italian horror movie (C. Tohill, 20), *I Vampiri* (*The Devil's Command-*

29 This episode drew on *The Bloody Countess* by the Surrealist poet Valentine Penrose (1898-1978), wife of British Surrealist Roland Penrose. The book's still available.

ment, Riccardo Freda, 1956), was a version of the Countess Dracula legend.

Hammer, the British studio, produced *Countess Dracula* in 1970 (although it stars Ingrid Pitt, it's not a patch on Walerian Borowczyk's film. *Countess Dracula* is one of those flicks you think halfway through: *why am I bothering to watch this?*).[30]

The episode cuts to a village scene in rural Hungary (although it looks like it was probably shot in France); the calm of people going about their everyday business (old women gossiping, a woman treading grapes in a barrel, a young couple fucking in a barn watched by a little girl), is interrupted when the Countess's soldiers invade the pastoral scene and offer to take away the young women of the village. When some of the women resist, and try to escape, the guards turn violent.

The scene turns into an attack, with soldiers pursing the women all over the place (including a scene where the woman tupping in the barn is chased through a stream in a field, with her boyfriend leaping on the soldier to defend her). Walerian Borowczyk includes all manner of details in this sequence, including the classic images of an abandoned baby crying, an old man hiding, and people struggling to escape. It's clear that the soldiers are only after young women.

After rounding up suitable candidates, the Countess Erzsébet Báthory appears on horseback. The soldiers line up the women to be inspected. After examining the women (pulling up their clothes to reveal close-ups of breasts and crotches), they are taken to the Countess's home. The scene sexualizes the victims – it's quite different from the usual scene in movies where some lord inspects a potential slave's teeth, as in *Spartacus.* It's clear from the outset that the Countess is interested in the women sexually; she wants fresh women (not necessarily virgins, although virgins are part of this kind of myth).

At the Báthory mansion, the naked body count of *Contes Immoraux* increases dramatically (as opposed to Hollywood's dead body count), with endless shots of naked women in showers, washing each other, giggling, talking, walking down corridors covering their breasts,

30 There's also *Daughters of Darkness* (1971), and *Bathory* (2008).

kneeling and praying in front of a Christian shrine (a wooden crucifix), and, eventually, being ushered into a large red room by the aide, the Countess's inner sanctum (the 'bloody chamber' of fairy tales).

This set is a classic Borowczyk environment: it's the ultimate seduction setting: a large room with wooden panelling and deep red walls, dominated by an ancient carved wooden bed. (Unlike many of Borowczyk's sets, this seems to have been constructed in a studio – partly, probably, because so many naked extras were required, and logistically and economically a studio's a better idea).

Most of the first half of the sequence concentrates on showing the group of nude women in the showers and bathrooms, the camera lovingly panning over their naked bodies, again and again. The film concentrates time after time on women soaping their breasts, bottoms and vulvas. Some of the women wash each other. Walerian Borowczyk's camera lingers unashamedly over close-ups of pussies and nipples. It's a paradise of female nudity.

It all seems to be a grand build-up for some extraordinary erotic encounter. There are no men in this scene: apart from the group of some twenty naked women, and the aloof, aristocratic Countess herself, there is only her aide Istvan, another woman, dressed as a page. This 3rd part of *Immoral Tales, Erzsébet Báthory,* seems to be both an eroticist's fantasy of lesbianism and group sex, and some bizarre ritual which can't be reduced to mere titillation or porn.

Walerian Borowczyk has created the ultimate seraglio, a boudoir, a convent full of young naked women. Borowczyk is clearly in his element here: in one scene he has the women coming down the corridor, exploring it, then kneeling in front of Christ on the Cross, and praying.

Istvan and Báthory both spy on the women as they bathe, using tilted mirrors mounted above the showers (Walerian Borowczyk's art direction is inspired). The film plays with different gazes: the Countess is presumably lesbian, but Istvan is at first depicted as a young man, who appears to be enjoying the abundance of women. Only later, during a lesbian scene with the Countess, is Istvan revealed to be a woman. But after Báthory has been arrested, Istvan embraces and kisses the captain of the soldiers. So she starts off as a heterosexual boy, shifts to a female lesbian, then a heterosexual woman (one wonders how she got the job of Báthory's aide in the first place. It was probably a helluva interview).

Some of the women draw graffiti on the walls in charcoal - images of penises, of course (one woman draws an oval with lines sprouting out of it and says it's the sun, but it's the standard graffiti vulva). One of the bonuses of *Immoral Tales* is watching Pablo Picasso's daughter going around the showers and rubbing off the pictures of dicks - especially in view of Picasso's late erotic work, the series of mythological prints (which Borowczyk would have known).

From the group nude prayer scene (only in a Walerian Borowczyk film will you see a cluster of naked women praying to a statue of Jesus), the movie moves closer to the bloody chamber of fairy tales. First the victims gather around some windows, climbing on chairs in order to see the preparations on the other side. Again, with his cast of lovely young actors ranged on a table and chairs, with their backs to the camera, Borowczyk indulges in some more close-ups of their butts, thighs and legs.

The naked women are led into the chamber of horrors by Istvan. Throughout the episode, Walerian Borowczyk and assistant director Dominique Duivergé have asked the extras to be animated, natural, excited. In the bedroom, the excitement gets louder, as the women explore the room in clusters, touching the carved bed, and the furnishings.

The *Erzsébet Báthory* episode gets really interesting when the Countess herself enters. You know this is the climax of the sequence - partly because the film has reached the big set, partly because Báthory is in amongst the naked virgins, and partly because you know something extraordinary is going to happen. Maybe a mass orgy? Maybe the Countess is going to be serviced by the women one by one? But she is 'Countess Dracula', so we know she's going to dispatch the women. How is she going to do that?

But *Immoral Tales* does not show the mass murder. Instead, it goes off in a much more interesting direction. It's unexpected when the

Countess enters the scene that the women gather tightly around her as she moves among them, first admiring her clothes. But then the naked women converge on the carved bed, where Báthory has ended up, and start to rip the Countess's clothes apart, as if stealing the shreds as some token or religious relic.

The scene becomes a series of medium close-ups of writhing limbs, skin and hair as the women become more violent and hysterical. They steal the Countess's jewels, some of them eating them (there is a shot of a woman inserting a pearl between her labia, a typically Borowczyk-ian image). Báthory has her clothes ripped off her in tatters, and the women fight over the pieces. The tearing sounds are loud on the soundtrack, as well as the screams. The scene reaches a crescendo of violence as the naked women scratch each other, drawing blood.

It's a scene with a primal basis, going back to the mænads and bacchanalian or Dionysian rituals of ancient Greece. And it's an extraordinary addition by Walerian Borowczyk to what seemed to be the Dracula myth: a mass seduction which would run smoothly towards death for the women. Maybe there would be glimpses of some infernal machine out of Gothic mediæval horror through a doorway, and the women would be led through it, one by one. But to have the women turn on the Countess and vent their rage is an example of Borowczyk's genius for drama. There are psychological insights here, which go beyond language.

Maybe Walerian Borowczyk and his team are making a statement about how victims collude with their oppressors, a truly depressing thought. Maybe there are equivalents to be made here with Poland under Communist rule, or other countries with oppressive regimes. The *Erzsébet Báthory* episode is a mythical, dream-like sequence, and not meant to 'real' or 'literal', but if you look at the characters in it, there are only two people in that big red room and twenty women, who could easily overpower them. But instead, the women turn from shredding Báthory's clothes to attack each other. They revert to some primal, animal state, losing their humanity, and tearing at each other.

The chaos abruptly ends, the women disappear, and the Countess is alone once more with her page Istvan. A pool of red looms in close-up:

the Countess, naked, climbs into her bath and begins to wash herself with the blood of the dead women. Rather than the horror of the scene, Borowczyk concentrates on the painterly aspects of the red blood clinging in bubbles and swirls to the Countess's breasts, belly, buttocks and cunt. As in the previous episodes, the camera lingers in close-up on the woman's naked body.

It is a truly obscene sight – Countess Báthory bathing in the blood of twenty women. It's a literal bloodbath. The film calmly washes over the mechanics of extermination, and focusses on the pleasure the Countess gleans from her bloodbath.

Isn't it a marvellous idea of Walerian Borowczyk's to have Paloma Picasso play this mass murderer with a quiet, dignified charm? One can imagine many another filmmaker and actor being unable to resist an obscene leer or two, a lick of the lips, some evil-eyed stare, or some other Movie Villain Business. But there's nothing at all: Báthory just goes about her bath as if it's the most normal thing in the world. It's as if she's been doing it everyday. (A Hollywood film would no doubt add some narrative elements like Báthory doing all this because she is immortal, or long-lived, like Dracula. And Hollywood would no doubt design the Báthory mansion as a world of shadows and disturbing images, but Borowczyk resists all of that: it's all brightly lit).

But Walerian Borowczyk stages it with a quiet reserve, all nice manners and people going about their business. And instead of major theatrics, Borowczyk simply closes the scene in the bathroom with a close-up on the metal lid of the bath. No shots of the blood being flushed away down the drain. Having Báthory simply step out of the bath after the shower has washed off the blood and walk away is a deft way of depicting her complete insensitivity to what she has done. She is the calmest Bluebeard in cinema.

The *Erzsébet Báthory* episode is the longest episode in *Immoral Tales* (at around 35 minutes); so, instead of ending here, with Countess Dracula bathing in women's blood, *Contes Immoraux* continues: the Countess climbs out of the bath, aided by her page Istvan; they retire to the blood-red inner boudoir.

Some exquisite music opens the next scene in this incredible sequence. It is a lesbian scene of sex and marriage. It's played entirely without dialogue, and it's rapt stuff.

Istvan is revealed, when she undresses, to be a young woman, and Báthory's lover. Báthory takes off Istvan's clothes, revealing her slim form and small breasts, and lets down her hair. The Countess quietly and lovingly dresses Istvan in a bridal outfit, putting a veil over her head.

The women, clad in diaphanous material through which their genitals are discernible, climb onto the bed and begin to make love. It's all very tender and graceful and gentle. The film captures the love-making with big close-ups of their naked bodies.

The film then cuts to some time later, the blood-red chamber now darkened. A slow tilt, pan and zoom shows the lovers lying beside each other.

The ending is swift: Istvan slips away from the bed. In the next shot, an officer enters the dark boudoir; Báthory wakes, startled; the officer informs the Countess that she is under arrest. Two guards come in and wrap the Countess in a black blanket and carry her off (an odd notion, as if she's too evil to be led away, and shouldn't be given the dignity of walking, or as if she's an animal and must be treated like something that must be taken out and thrown down a well or to the dogs, with suggestions of contamination, like the end of *Night of the Living Dead*). In the final shot, Istvan is seen embracing the officer passionately; she loved him all along. Ah, bless! And the Countess gets her just deserts. Execution, presumably, after a rapid trial.

There are numerous historical precedents or analogies in *Erzsébet Báthory* – of inquisitions and pogroms and invasions. Walerian Borowczyk and his team have evoked a violent invasion in the village scene that wouldn't be out of place in many a historical epic movie. There are further layers to this episode in *Immoral Tales*, though – and that is the concentration camps. It didn't strike me the first couple of times I watched the film, but the images of women being rounded up and taken away and then prepared in showers in order to be killed for some tyrant evokes the ovens.

I don't think Walerian Borowczyk is making a statement about

World War 2, in terms of allegory or analogy. If he's thinking in those terms, it would be in the wider realm of invasion and imprisonment over the course of history. (Borowczyk's Polish contemporary, Roman Polanski, is often placed within a context of WW2 and the German invasion of Poland). But Borowczyk has created an episode where twenty or so young women are captured and killed. *Erzsébet Báthory* is about a mass murderer, after all, even though it seduces the viewer with beautiful imagery and plenty of nudity.

If you want, you can interpret *Erzsébet Báthory* as being partly about the seductiveness of evil, how the most vile people and situations can appear to be enchanting. And the episode also follows a movie tradition of portraying villains as sophisticated, attractive people. Certainly Báthory is presented as elegant, wealthy, well-dressed and beautiful. And, crucially, Báthory *doesn't* think of herself as evil. She is doing what she wants to do, with no thought of the consequences (she is an artist! a free spirit!), and no remorse.

In sum, *Erzsébet Báthory* is a masterpiece of modern cinema, brilliantly realized, very dramatic, and thematically very powerful.

LUCREZIA BORGIA

In the last episode of *Immoral Tales*, set in Italy in 1498, Lucrezia Borgia (Florence Bellamy) sleeps with her brother Cesare Borgia (G. Lorenzo Bernini), and their father, who's Pope Alexander VI (Jacopo Berinzini). The Borgia episode has Lucrezia and her relatives cavorting in a white Baroque interior; the section culminates with group sex, with Lucrezia's brother Cesare fucking her from behind while she sucks off her father. It's a clichéd scene from pornography, but in Borowczyk's hands it becomes about something else – richer, stranger, and with a level of detail that pornography never has the time to construct. Aside from being a group sex scene, it's also graphic incest: a father having sex with his children. And he's the Pope!

And, like the *Erzsébet Báthory* episode, the *Lucrezia Borgia* episode also has a historical basis. In taking on the Borgias, Walerian Borowczyk tackles one of the more notorious eras of Italian history. The Borgia sequence also combines sex and religion in a blasphemous whole.

The film takes place in the Vatican primarily, with the Savonarola scenes occurring in a church and a square. Historically, Girolamo Savonarola (1452-98), played by Philippe Desboeuf, was prior of San Marco in Florence, and was burned at the stake as a heretic in Piazza della Signoria, Firenze.

Lucrezia Borgia opens with a religious procession in the Vatican – the Pope, cardinals, a host of dignitaries, and the star of the piece, Lucrezia Borgia. It's a production value sequence, caught in a master shot which zooms in slowly, following the procession through a large doorway. The costumes are beautiful, and there's another lovely piece of Renaissance music.

Most of *Lucrezia Borgia* takes place within a single room in the Vatican, another classic example of Walerian Borowczykian art direction: white marble walls and deep red hangings. Statues. Religious ornaments. A white bench (which also resembles an altar).

There are four people in the room: the Borgias, and a man. Fairly soon the Borgias are up to no good: they pull out some drawings and paintings of horses, with cocks prominent. These amuse the Borgias, especially father and daughter, for some time. Lucrezia's laugh becomes one of the signature sounds of this episode in *Immoral Tales*. Everything is amusing to her. The man doesn't want to be part of this lewdness. And before long, he is arrested – the soldiers appear abruptly from a sliding wall behind a bust on a plinth (there are also bizarre insert shots, like a friar stealing one of the horse drawings).

Lucrezia is in her element, laughing with delight as she holds two drawings of a horse's prick against a wall, flicking between the two so the prick becomes erect. The film portrays an atmosphere of erotic pleasure which increases in stages. In one shot, Cesare, clad in scarlet cardinal robes, is masturbating under his robes, stroking a huge erection.

When the film cuts to Girolamo Savonarola in Firenze, he is declaiming in a church pulpit, castigating the congregation for the wicked, debauched ways of the country. The crowd is heard but not seen; occasionally they shout at Savonarola and he responds to their cries. The off-screen sounds of people suggest a tumultuous historical period.

Back in the Vatican, the orgy begins. Lucrezia is very much the centre of it, with the action staged around her and with her body usually centre frame. With her father the Pope and her brother Cesare on either side of her, she kisses them and they begin to undress her. The camera lingers over close-ups of fingers undoing buttons, tilting down to show the dress gradually slipping to Lucrezia's ankles, then back up to her naked breasts. The fetishistic delight in clothes is palpable (and it is a *fabulous* green dress).

Exquisite choral music plays throughout much of the *Lucrezia Borgia* episode. The Pope is often declaiming too (the film is in French and Italian), but Lucrezia's light laughter cuts through.

When Lucrezia is naked, she puts on a gown and stands on a chair, like a statue to be admired. Pope Alexander takes up a long peacock's feather and plays it over Lucrezia's body, with close-ups of the feather brushing over Lucrezia's pussy. These erotic games are unusual enough in a movie, but when you remember that it's the Pope and his daughter and son, it becomes outrageous.

Back in the church, Savonarola's diatribe against the debauchery and lasciviousness of Italy becomes more incensed. No need to remark upon the montage structure Walerian Borowczyk is deploying here, in cutting from an incestuous orgy at the top of the power structure in Renaissance Italy and the San Marco prior ranting in a church about declining morality. Borowczyk is being outrageous, and he knows it; and yet he can also say: well, it all really happened. And he can also say: there was much worse than this, which I haven't filmed, or wouldn't be allowed to film.

When the picture cuts back to the Vatican room, Lucrezia is being tupped from behind by her brother Cesare. She's bent over the bench, face-down, loving it. Dad gets in on the action by climbing onto the bench and encouraging Lucrezia to suck him.

When the Borgias change around, Lucrezia, nude, lies back on the bench with her arms outstretched: she is a naked crucifixion, a wholly secular – and sexual – mockery of Christian iconography. Her father climbs on top of her and fucks her.

When the film cuts again to Savonarola in the church, a couple of soldiers enter the scene, to drag him away for punishment. The prior is still urging the crowd to repent as he's dragged off.

One of the most outrageous cuts in Walerian Borowczyk's cinema (and therefore in much of contemporary cinema) occurs next. It's a truly, mightily wild juxtaposition: from Savonarola burning at the stake in a square, surrounded by flames and smoke, to a huge close-up of Lucrezia's hairy cunt.

If you wanted an example of Walerian Borowczyk at his blasphemous, outrageous best, it's right here. The images – of Savonarola burning as a heretic at the stake and Lucrezia Borgia's cunt – are extreme enough, but to put them together like that is incredible.

As the camera pans around the half-naked bodies of the Pope and Cesare, with the nude Lucrezia lying between them in the afterglow of orgasm, *Immoral Tales* has reached an extraordinary climax. But Walerian Borowczyk doesn't stop there. He wants to rub in the hypocrisy of Renaissance Italy even further, adding a *dénouement* of strangeness: the Pope, cardinals, bishops and dignitaries have gathered to perform and witness the baptism of a baby (presumably it's either the Pope's child, or it's Cesare's). The threesome of Pope, Cesare and Lucrezia is at the centre of this *tableau* of happy Borgias. The setting is the doorway of the procession (and as indicated by the baby, presumably some months later).

The film cuts to big close-ups of the baby, smiling into the camera. Do we need to state that this is a parody of the Nativity? (adding further layers of blasphemy). When the title card 'FIN' comes up, it's the end of one of the strangest films ever made.

Wow.

If you take everything together that's depicted in *Immoral Tales*, you have one of the most mind-boggling movies of recent times. There are scenes here which, once seen, are never forgotten. Who else could make a twenty minute film of a young woman discovering masturbation, encouraged by the voice of God? Or a film of the 'Countess Dracula' slaughtering twenty naked virgins, staged as a hypnotizing seduction of innocence by absolute evil? Or the tide timetables being used as an excuse for a blowjob in the surf? Or the Borgias, father, daughter and brother, having an orgy while Girolamo Savonarola burns at the stake?

4

AN EROTIC FAIRY TALE:

LA BÊTE (THE BEAST)

'Dear Beast, you shall not die,' said Beauty, 'you shall live and become my husband. Here and now I offer you my hand, and swear that I will marry none but you. Alas, I fancied I felt only friendship for you, but the sorrow I have experienced clearly proves to me that I cannot live without you.'

Charles Perrault, *Beauty and the Beast*[31]

Let me tell you what this business is about. It's cunt and horses!

Harry Cohn (head of Columbia Pictures)

31 C. Perrault, *Complete Fairy Tales*, Kestrel Books, London, 1962, 132.

The story of *La Bête* (a.k.a. *The Beast, The Beast in Heat* and *Death's Ecstasy*, 1975) involves an American heiress Lucy Broadhurst (Lisbeth Hummel) being brought to a French chateau with her aunt Virginia (Elisabeth Kaza) by the scheming owners (in particular the marquis, Pierre de l'Esperance [played by Guy Tréjan]), who need to marry her to the earthy, degenerate (and somewhat backward) son of the family Mathurin (Pierre Benedetti) in order to circumvent a will which'll keep the family home intact.

That's the framing story, about grasping aristocrats, decadent morality, degenerate priests and sexually repressed young women.[32] This part of the film's set in the 20th century, though it's not the conventional modern, urban world of most movies. *La Bête* takes place exclusively at the French chateau and its grounds (the film is in French, but there is English dialogue – Virginia, Lucy and their chauffeur speak English).

There are subplots woven into the main narrative of the imminent marriage of Lucy and Mathurin: the Cardinal de Balo, brother of the marquis's father, the disabled Duc de Balo (Marcel Dalio), who's supposed to come to the chateau to perform the wedding ceremony, but has fallen out with him, the telephone calls to the Vatican, trying to persuade him to visit, the marquis, Pierre de l'Esperance, who's orchestrating the marriage, the uncouth Mathurin, who's happiest outside with his horses and is terrified of being married off (he has a bandaged hand, which's part of his beast nature), the priest (Roland Armontel) with his pretty choirboys who follow him around meekly (one is called Modeste), the black man servant Ifany (Hassane Fall) who sneaks off to tup the marquis's daughter, Clarisse de l'Esperance (Pascale Rivault), and two children, friends of the marquis's daughter, who've come to witness the wedding.

The other main narrative in *The Beast* depicts Lucy's masturbatory fantasies of erotic encounters with a beast in a sunlit forest, set in the 18th century, imagining herself as Romilda de l'Esperance (played by Sirpa Lane, 1951-99), one of the ancestors of the marquis's family, meeting the legendary beast that has haunted the family for centuries

32 Borowczyk said he had written *La Bête* in two days, and had the initial idea in a café (of course – he was living in Paris, cafés being crucibles of many a creative venture).

(the legend is that a beast emerges every two hundreds years in the park).

Walerian Borowczyk called *The Beast* 'really more of a comedy than an erotic film'. Let that prepare you for this extraordinary movie. Because the central section, the fairy tale sequence of the beast pursuing and fucking a woman, is meant to be very silly, very over-the-top, very unbelievable. *The Beast is* a comedy, and it *is* erotic. And it's so completely mad you can't help but be swept along by it. Have a look at some of the comments on imdb.com and amazon.com for some funny takes on the movie.

It's not *Hill Street Blues, Friends* or *Avatar*, it's *European*, utterly non-American and un-American. Every question about *The Beast* can be answered by the statement: *it's a comedy.*

Walerian Borowczyk remarked that:

> *La Bête* is a fantasy film and especially an 'adult film'. But first of all it is a film about dream mechanisms. Dreams translate our deepest desires. Why then cover with a veil of silence the temptation of an intimate relationship with an animal? (J. Gerber, 169)

Walerian Borowczyk here outlines one of his central goals – which is to make manifest desires and fears that are hidden or suppressed (he's especially fond of exposing them within a religious/ Catholic context, partly because the desires, when they erupt, appear even more outrageous. Organized religion is a great environment against which to set explosions of desire).

Among the crew on *La Bête* were DPs Bernard Daillencourt and Marcel Grignon, Noël Véry, camera operator, Jacques D'Ovidio, production designer, set decorator Alain Guillé, wardrobe by Piet Bolscher, make-up by Odette Berroyer, production manager Dominique Duvergé and sound by Michel Laurent and Jean-Pierre Ruh (sound mixer was Alex Pront). No less than six assistant editors are credited (Alain Cayrade, Florence Dauman, Claude Delon, Jean-Pierre Platel, Monique Prim and Michel Valio), but it's Boro who has the main editing credit. Much credit should go to producer Anatole Dauman for backing this OTT movie. Many on the team were Borowczyk regulars.

It's unlikely that you will recognize any of the performers in *The Beast*: Sirpa Lane, Lisbeth Hummel, Elisabeth Kaza, Guy Tréjan, Pierre Benedetti, Roland Armontel, Pascale Rivault, Robert Capia, etc.

The 'controversy' surrounding *The Beast* from its release onwards pivoted on the fantasy scenes of Romilda de l'Esperance having sex with 'the beast'. There were the inevitable run-ins with censors and the media. *La Bête* retained its power to upset viewers, even shock, many years later. In the U.K., the British Board of Film Classification could not pass it; in 1978 it was granted an 'X' by the Greater London Council (and only after extensive cuts), and only allowed to be seen in London. It was not granted a certificate by the BBFC in Britain until 2001, due to the relaxation of censorship laws, turning up on video, DVD and the FilmFour channel.

⚜

The very first shot of *The Beast* is of Mathurin, the beast's incarnation in the present day; the second shot is a C.U. of a horse's cock. *La Bête* doesn't mess about: it begins with a copulation scene, complete with erection, vagina and penetration shots, of two horses in the courtyard outside some stables. The graphic scene's covered with a rapid montage of long lens images of the horses' bodies, which are always in motion, the male moving restlessly around the female. There are close-ups of the horses' genitals (the stallion's penis distended, the mare's vagina opening and closing, with squelchy sound effects), accompanied by loud snorts and the clatter of hooves (the echoey sounds of the horses are heard over the titles too).

The explicit imagery of copulating animals sets up the central erotic encounter of the film, between Lucy Broadhurst/ Romilda de l'Esperance and the beast, when Lucy and her aunt Virginia arrive at the stables in their limo. Immediately, Lucy gets out of the vehicle and starts taking Polaroids of the horses (a simple device to illustrate her sexual curiosity, which makes her *dopplegänger*, Romilda, venture out into the forest). In the car, Virginia had responded to Lucy's enthusiastic praise of 'beautiful France': 'beautiful France has always lived in lust'.

The Beast does take a while to get going after that extraordinary opening sequence (one of the strangest in cinema history. *Terms of Endearment* or *Great Expectations* this ain't). There's a bunch of characters to introduce, and their relationships. There's a lot of not very distinctive talk, but in the midst of it all (around ten or so minutes), Borowczyk is slipping in numerous details – such as a snail crawling on the duke's hand (snails crop up many times in *The Beast*). And the marquis and the duke have an ambiguous relationship (the marquis seems to keep his brother locked up – he is forever locking and unlocking doors like Bluebeard, as if he's always got something to hide).

As soon as the 1975 film cuts to Lucy and her aunt Virginia in the car, the film begins to gel: you know that something more interesting's going to happen with Lucy around – the marquis, the duke, Mathurin and the curé are rather unappealing characters. And all of that stuff about grooming Mathurin so he'll be presentable to meet Lucy is not particularly engaging. And notice how Walerian Borowczyk has Lucy play the character in her mid-teens here, rather than the 22 years old that actress Lisbeth Hummel actually is.[33] Lucy is excitedly talking about the world outside as they drive through it. And then, to emphasis the fairy tale nature of this movie, she jumps out of the car and disappears into the forest. The chateau is culture, sanctuary, safety, and the forest is danger, mystery, the unknown – and desire. By having Lucy stop here and run off into the forest, Borowczyk alludes to any number of fairy tales (yet this woodland is also full of sunlight and trilling birdsong).

He's also announcing: folks, this isn't going to be your usual film. One of the ways he does that is to have really strange things popping up. In the forest, in the lake, there appears to be a body under the water, the bubbles audible as they pop up. Truly weird, partly because it doesn't link up with much else in the picture (except the repeated images of Romilda's corset in the lake. Is it the beast? Is it Romilda's dead-alive corpse?).

La Bête incorporates characters and situations straight out of an 18th century comedy of manners, or French farce, or 19th century

33 Hummel was born in 1952, in Copenhagen; aside from *The Beast*, she hasn't appeared in many other films. She has done photos for softcore porn magazines.

erotica: the randy, aged curé with his two beautiful youths, the black man servant who fucks the marquis's daughter, the town girl who wanders into a forest and is raped by a man-beast (she hates it at first, then enjoys it).

People are constantly caught in mid-tup, mid-grope, mid-day-dream in *La Bête*. Clarisse de l'Esperance and the black servant Ifany are always disturbed when they get freaky, and Lucy's mastur-batory fantasies are interrupted.

La Bête was classic Walerian Borowczyk, with all of his favourite motifs and themes on display: an incredible sense of detail (a snail on a shoe); a painterly sense of colour,[34] light, and space; an elegant olde worlde setting (a French chateau); high art allusions (to, for instance, painting); and a pounding Domenico Scarlatti harpsichord soundtrack.

Oh, and there's lots of sex: erotic prints (one shows a winged horse entering a woman, which ties in with the bestiality theme – see below); close-ups of women's naked torsos through semi-transparent gowns; women masturbating; people fucking; and, most controversially, the beast fucking a woman.

One of the sources of *La Bête* was an 18th century French fable, *La veritable histoire de la bête de Gevaudin* (which Walerian Borowczyk had turned into an 18 minute short in 1973, entitled *La véritable histoire de la bête du Gévaudan*; it was shown as a work-in-progress at the London Film Festival, comprising the last of three self-contained films in *Immoral Tales*). Another was a movie that Borowczyk was hired to work on, Alain Fleischer's *Les rendezvous en forêt.* Producer Anatole Dauman wanted Borowczyk to spice up the ending, and Borowczyk constructed a beast suit.[35] However, Fleischer prevented Borowczyk from adding to *Les rendezvous en forêt* through legal action, and Borowczyk would later use his beast costume in *La Bête. La Bête* also, unlike too many of Borowczyk's other films, is not dubbed (or a large proportion of the movie has source sound). There's a much greater sense of performance and atmosphere.

Walerian Borowczyk sets up classic oppositions: the house and the

34 Red is the predominant symbolic colour in this contemporary erotic fairy tale – the red rose, blood, and the bright red walls in the chateau.

35 The beast has gorilla hands and a wolf head, and black hair all over. Borowczyk himself played the beast. Nah, just kidding.

forest; inside and outside; the dark rooms, with the windows always shuttered (even during the day), and the bright, sunlit woodland; repressed sexuality inside and unbridled lust outside; paganism vs. Catholicism. The interiors, richly furnished, hint at blood, virginal or animal, with deep red pre-dominating, and white and black also.

Clarisse de l'Esperance (who wears dreadlocks, boots and jeans and drives a 2CV when she's not naked, which's most of the time) tups the black man servant Ifany (he has a large cock, of course). Their couplings are always interrupted by the master of the house yelling for his butler. When Ifany leaves, Clarisse resignedly climbs onto the wooden end of the bed and rubs her clit to orgasm, the camera zooming in on her pubis. In one lengthy and striking sequence shot (it's striking how many lengthy sequence shots Walerian Borowczyk uses), Clarisse and Ifany are hard at it on his bed (Clarisse keeps her boots on, a nice fetishistic touch), when the marquis hollers for him. So the lovers break apart; the man climbs out of bed, his half-erect cock prominent, dresses, and leaves. Clarisse, frustrated, straddles the headboard to rub herself to orgasm. The camera zooms in slightly, reframing her body, concentrating on her cunt. But this isn't the end of an already lengthy take: Clarisse gives up and sits on the bed, then moves around the room, pulls on a dressing gown, then opens the wardrobe to let out the two young children brought for the wedding. And she's shut them up in a wardrobe so she can fuck Ifany! You won't see that in your average Hollywood movie.

The tupping of Clarisse and Ifany brings in a racial element again: kisses across the racial divide had been seen in earlier movies, but for 1975 it was fairly unusual outside of porno seeing two naked people, one pale white, the other black, fucking each other (thirty years and more on, it's still very unusual).

The ethnic angle is also noted by the black characters themselves – when Ifany goes out to the Rolls Royce and talks to the black chauffeur. Their dialogue includes allusions to slaves. Note also that the beast is black, and the women linked to the beast, Romilda and Lucy, are dressed in white. It's *Beauty and the Beast*, and it's *King Kong* too, with all the racial stereotyping of those stories.

Lucy's in an erotic limbo: she's been brought to the chateau to be married off to Mathurin, and exists in that vertiginous space in between singledom and marriage. Lucy spends much of her time mooning about on her own in her room, leaving the others, the aunt Virginia, the marquis Pierre de l'Esperance, his son Mathurin, the curé and the Duc de Balo, to scheme and plot.

When she's first seen alone, Lucy explores her room:[36] after looking at a painting of the Madonna and Child,[37] and some books, she soon uncovers an erotic book in a wooden cabinet (after discarding a duller book).[38] It contains black-and-white drawings illustrating some erotic texts, a spoof by Voltaire of Joan of Arc, called *La Pucelle D'Orléans* (1789). There's even a shot of the title page, just so's the audience knows exactly what piece of 18th century erotica it is (no doubt the book – a rarity – was from Boro's own collection).

It's another erotic moment for Lucy, and because it's erotic she is inevitably disturbed by the black chauffeur bringing in her things (erotic films always have to put off fulfilment – i.e., orgasm – towards the end of the movie, in the same way that the big action set-piece only occurs in a conventional movie at the climax. In *The Beast*, the climax is literal – actually, it's multiple, too: Clarisse comes, Lucy comes, Romilda comes, and the Beast comes many times).

Later, Lucy masturbates while perusing the Polaroids she's taken of the copulating horses spread on her pillow (the DPs frame the shot for the delectation of the viewer, with Lucy's legs and buttocks turned towards the camera on the bed, Lucy pulling down her stockings and panties and pushing her fingers inside herself from behind.) The shot concentrates exclusively on Lucy's ass and fingers, with her face out of shot (also, it's a lengthy take, and there are no cuts to Lucy's face). Only in a Borowczyk film does a character masturbate over photos of horses fucking! As before, she's interrupted in her erotic reverie by calls from outside her room.

36 Like Thérèse in *Immoral Tales*, Lucy looks round her room for something to entertain her; both women uncover erotica (which is never far from the surface of everyday life in Borowczyk Land).

37 As if admonishing Lucy: this is what women are supposed to be like – demure and motherly yet also virginal, like the Virgin Mary.

38 Lucy's inquisitiveness also uncovers a drawing of animals getting freaky on the back of a frame (once again, it looks as if Borowczyk has produced this sketch).

When the film cuts back to Lucy again, she's trying on a filmy white dress and veil, as if playing at being a bride. Walerian Borowczyk begins this sequence with a close-up of Lucy's cooch. In an erotic reverie, Lucy admires her naked body under the cloth in the mirror.

La Bête finally enters the famous sequence of the monster and the woman, Romilda: it's framed as Lucy's dream or memory: she is lying back on her bed, in her filmy white gown, holding the red rose. The past, two hundred years earlier, is a cultural world of Domenico Scarlatti music – Romilda is first seen playing it in the chateau on a sunny Summer's day (every time *The Beast* cuts back to the forest sequence, the Scarlatti music is pounding away. Why does the harpsichord sound so much heavier than the regular grand piano?).

Even this intro in *La Bête* is slightly skewed in Walerian Borowczyk's imagination: the establishing shot of Romilda in the chateau is a slow zoom from far off, revealing Romilda in a window. So far so good, but the camera zooms first onto a carving of the god Pan grinning lasciviously (or it could be Dionysius). In other words, primal, mythical desire (an ancient world, a Greek mystery). *Then* it tilts down to reveal Romilda (she's in her early twenties, pretty, white blonde (wearing a wig), refined, small, and alone).

There's more mythology evoked before Romilda encounters the beast: Romilda notices that a lamb has wandered away from its mother. No need to point out the symbolism of sacrificial lambs. So Romilda goes off in pursuit of the lamb, in a beautiful blue gown (you can see that actress Sirpa Lane has real trouble running through the overgrown fields and woods in that costume. She must've cursed Borowczyk. Bloody film directors! You come over here and run in this fucking costume!).

The first time that Romilda sees the beast is when she finds the bloody remains of the lamb on the ground, and the beast is nearby. The sight of the corpse and the blood trigger off this hysterical version of *Little Red Riding Hood* meets *Beauty and the Beast* meets arty Euro-erotica.

The sex with the beast takes many forms, as if Walerian Borowczyk and his team were riffling through the highlights of the

Kama Sutra. First, the beast, seen only partially for much of the first fantasies, pursues the woman through the forest. As he chases her, he pulls off pieces of her clothing, a classic sexual fantasy (cut to shots of the clothes flying through the air, catching on bushes, and the monster's point-of-view of Lucy running away from him up a path, the camera focussing on her jiggling cheeks).[39]

By now Romilda is down to a beautiful white corset and socks. The beast takes up the clothes and sniffs them, and drapes them over his penis (at the end of the first chase and rape, in one extraordinary close-up, the beast pulls off her blonde wig and rubs it over the end of his penis, the semen dripping from the hair.)

This's pretty wild stuff. It's so ridiculous, so over-the-top, yet utterly compelling, and it all takes place to the hammering of harpsichord music. Your average sex scene this certainly isn't. Oh, yeah, it is a guy in a very silly and unconvincing monster suit chasing a woman in a sunny forest. It's so dumb you can't believe it. It looks like a dumb-ass student movie. And the roars that Borowczyk and his team employ for the monster are taken from some Godzilla or dinosaur movie, and don't fit at all.

But all that is deliberate. It's meant to be dumb and unbelievable. As Walerian Borowczyk says, *The Beast* is more a comedy than an erotic film. Maybe. But wait. This isn't just a dumb-ass movie: no silly film would include in the midst of a sex scene sudden cuts to the trees, to a lake, to a snail crawling on a shoe (*no one* cuts away to shots of trees and leaves in the midst of a sex scene or a rape). Something else is going on here.

Romilda takes refuge from the priapic beast in, of all places, a tree. While the beast prowls below, brandishing his erection like a club,[40] Romilda falls from the tree, but manages to hold herself up on a branch. Their first sexual coupling is, typically for Walerian Borowczyk, eccentric, to say the least: while she's hanging from a branch, clad only in a white corset and socks, the beast grabs her, burying his muzzle between her legs, eating her pussy. Her feet, meanwhile, as

39 The rapidity of the cutting and the density of the images is like a chase in an action movie – a zillion details fly by the viewer.
40 Reminiscent of the ithyphallic Cerne Giant chalk hill figure in Dorset, U.K.

repeated close-ups reveal, touch his phallus. At first she seems to be kicking it or treading on it; then she loses a shoe, aided by the beast (another example of Borowczyk's amazing eye for detail), and masturbates his cock to yet another climax with her feet.

Romilda's screaming and yelling all the way through, and the beast occasionally roars – but Romilda seems to realize that it might be a good idea to get the beast off, and uses her feet to do so. It truly is out-there, off the chain, leftfield, outside the box, whatever: it's one of the weirder sex scenes in cinema: a monster eating a woman's cunt as she hangs from a tree masturbating his cock with her feet, and screaming all the time, while Domenico Scarlatti harpsichord music batters away at the eardrums.

Walerian Borowczyk has challenged the audience: *you want weird? I'll give you weird!*

Meanwhile, back inside the chateau, everyone is asleep – it's *Sleeping Beauty* time, with the people under a spell. Maybe they are all dreaming of Romilda in the forest. A group dream. As if the brutality of the encounter with the beast isn't enough, the violence erupts in the modern-day chateau scenes, as the marquis wakes, and secretly murders his disabled brother (covered with anxious point-of-view shots, into the camera).

Lucy writhes on the bed in her erotic dream, scissoring her legs, pulling her gauzy nightgown back and forth between her thighs. Once again, Walerian Borowczyk & co. hold on this scene far, far longer than dramatically necessary (and also shoots it frontally, from the end of the bed). Twice Lucy visits Marthurin in his little room nearby, but he remains resolutely asleep (the first time, she goes in and takes off his shoes, presumably to help him sleep better – he tosses about from time to time, as if in fitful dreams. The second time she visits him, she crouches down and puts her hand over his crotch. Like Sleeping Beauty, Mathurin still doesn't wake). There are shots of Lucy's naked body underneath the semi-transparent gown, creeping along the corridors at night, one of Borowczyk's signature images. Borowczyk cuts between Lucy masturbating and fantasizing on her bed and her erotic, 18th century dreams.

This is one horny girl: getting no joy out of Mathurin, she returns to her bedroom and starts to caress the bed knob like it's a dick. Then she takes up the rose (which the marquis gave her with his faked letter from Mathurin), and lies on her bed.

One of the longest masturbation scenes in Walerian Borowczyk's cinema ensues (he is certainly one of the kings of the cinema of self-pleasuring – I can't think of another major filmmaker who loves masturbation scenes so much), as Lucy lies back, opens her legs and starts touching herself. An incredible, big close-up: Lucy's cunt, her thighs undulating on either side, her hands covering her sex and she rubs the red rose petals into her labia and clitoris. The shot goes on and on, the red and green of the flower enveloping the woman's vulva, and shielding it from the viewer, her fingers wet, her hands moving back and forth. The shot ends with Lucy's hands moving out of shot, revealing a close-up of her lips and clit. Wow! *The Beast* then cuts to the final scenes of the woman and the beast.

The last of the sex scenes between Romilda de l'Esperance and la bête in the woodland occur straight after the remarkable extreme close-up of Lucy masturbating with a red rose. The beast grapples the woman onto a tree trunk and begins to fuck her from behind. Close-ups of his penis, his balls, her buttocks, her face. She seems to swoon away from the pain of the experience. Then she comes back to consciousness (expressed with a close-up of her hand, resting on top of her white dress, which begins to move with the rhythm of the beast's movements), and she starts to enjoy what's happening (her gasps are loud, and she licks her lips lasciviously).

The tempo of the cutting increases, as the lovemaking reaches a climax, which occurs with a money shot, a close-up of the beast coming over the woman's ass. The film then ascends to a plateau of orgasmic pleasures, as the woman and the beast are seen enjoying a variety of sexual acts: Romilda squeezing her breasts and nipples to tantalize the beast... the beast fucking her tits... copious amounts of sperm dripping over her body, down to her vulva... Romilda putting her fingers inside herself from behind... Romilda licking the beast's cock as she straddles him... Romilda jacking him with her feet, and so on.

Down on the ground, Romilda masturbates la bête, and licks him again, and he dies (there's blood around his muzzle). It's an ecstasy (the 'death's ecstasy' of one of the film's many alternative titles). And that, of course, is one of the recurring fantasies of Western literature, And it's very Surrealist and Sadeian, too: dying at orgasm.

During the sex scenes with the beast, Walerian Borowczyk doesn't just concentrate on genitals contacting each other, as in conventional pornography, he cuts away, many times, to images of the trees and bushes, to a white cloth with blood on it, and to the progress of a snail crawling over Romilda's shoe (the snail, one of many creatures in *La Bête*, is obviously a symbol of phallic fecundity: the snail and shoe features prominently when the beast is fucking Romilda from behind – she stares at it. A phallic snail, a vaginal shoe. The snail and shoe fall to the ground symbolically, just before the beast dies in a series of rapid cuts). *The Beast* also employs subjective shots of Romilda's views of the forest as she's being schtupped: the forest floor, the trees above, with the camera swinging back and forth to simulate the rhythms of sex (Ken Russell used the same technique in *Women In Love* and *Valentino*).

Is it rape? As far as Romilda is concerned, and as far as Lucy fantasizing about the past is concerned, it is rape. But it's a rape they're fantasizing about. Pro-pornography and anti-censorship critics and feminists might say that *The Beast* is extreme, but it does articulate fantasies that some people have (it's not only women who sometimes fantasize about sex with animals). Anti-pornography and pro-censorship critics and feminists might get outraged at that suggestion, and campaign for banning *The Beast* and all of Walerian Borowczyk's films. For them *The Beast* would be a rape fantasy perpetrated by a lecherous film director and pornographer.

For the beast, though, it plainly isn't rape: he just wants to have sex with the woman. Walerian Borowczyk is clear about that: the opening scene shows animals having sex. It's one of the things they do; get used to it. Issues like neurosis, sexual repression, religion, taboo and the like are human constructs, having *nothing* to do with the animal world. So the beast is like the horse (even his penis looks the same as the horse's). And Borowczyk has explained in interviews that *La Bête* is about the fantasy of having sex with an animal. The *fantasy.* As Borowczyk put it, he is revealing what people dream about. (I'd say that other rape scenes are far more disturbing than the one in *The Beast*: *The Accused, Deliverance, Straw Dogs,* etc).

✤

Walerian Borowczyk deploys archetypal tropes in *La Bête*: a lamb, a forest, blood, a man-beast, a woman alone. The motifs and narratives derive from mythology and fairy tales. What is *La Bête* really, but a European art movie version of *Beauty and the Beast?* It's *Beauty and the Beast* (with a little of *Bluebeard* and *Little Red Riding Hood*) with 1970s eroticism prominent. 'Beauty' and the 'beast' don't dally with each other in restrained conversation, as in Jean Cocteau's 1946 version of the fairy tale: they get down to some serious fucking.[41]

La Belle et la Bête is a famous story in French literary history, of course. The most famous fairy tale version was by Charles Perrault[42] – with the Grimm brothers and Hans Christian Andersen, Perrault is one of the founding fathers of fairy tale literature. Walerian Borowczyk's film of course draws on Perrault's story. The beast/ bridegroom story goes back a long way – to Apuleius and the myth of Cupid and Psyche, for instance. The story of a woman and an enchanted or supernatural animal is found in many, many places.[43] Although *The Beast* is a crazee Euro-art movie, it also displays a deep and subtle understanding of folklore and fairy tales.

The most famous film version is the 1946 black-and-white fantasy movie by Jean Cocteau, starring Jean Marais. *La Belle et la Bête* has been influential in cinema, not least in the realm of the European art movie, and Walerian Borowczyk also draws on it. More recently, the Walt Disney Company produced a Broadway musical-style interpretation (1991), which drew on Cocteau as well as Perrault's original

41 *The Beast* also draws on vampire stories, such as *Carmilla* by Sheridan Le Fanu.

42 But Charles Perrault's version was preceded by other 18th century interpretations, such as by Madame Le Prince de Beaumont (1756) and Madame Gabrielle de Villeneuve (1740).

43 In folklore studies, *Beauty and the Beast* is a type ATU 425 tale, known as 'The Search For the Lost Husband'. This folk tale type includes 'The Vanished Husband', 'The Animal as Bridegroom', 'The Son of the Witch', 'Beauty and the Beast', 'The Enchanted Husband Sings a Lullaby', 'The Snake as Bridegroom' and 'The Insulted Bridegroom Disenchanted'.

tale, and added plenty of Disney touches (such as the animated side-kicks and secondary characters – teapots, candlesticks, clocks). There are many other versions of *Beauty and the Beast* in cinema: Jack Zipes notes 8 silent movies, from 1899-1924, and 29 sound movies, from 1934-2007, in his fantastic book on fairy tale films, *The Enchanted Screen*.

In Walerian Borowczyk's and Anatole Dauman's film, though, there is no magical transformation of the beast into the prince. Nope. Instead, Romilda kills the beast, and Lucy appears to kill Mathurin, the modern-day beast (or he dies). No happy ending, then. The ending of *La Bête* is fairly ambiguous: Lucy exits in hysteria and remorse, devastated to think she might have killed her bridegroom (whom she liked). And Romilda rushes off along a forest path, now nude (her corset was flung into the lake), and looking distraught.

None of the well-known versions of *Beauty and the Beast* come anywhere near the outrage and wildness of Walerian Borowczyk's 1975 film. There have been other modern interpretations in literature – feminists have tackled fairy tales, writing their own (sometimes eroticized) versions. (For the best introduction to fairy tales, go to the writings of Jack Zipes).[44]

The Beast also draws on aspects of *Little Red Riding Hood*: the young woman in the forest and the wolf (some modern fairy tales have eroticized the encounter between the young woman and the wolf). You don't have to know anything about Sigmund Freud or Bruno Bettelheim or Jack Zipes to see what's going on in *Little Red Riding Hood*. In a way, *The Beast* is *Little Red Riding Hood* in the forest (and in the past), and *Beauty and the Beast* inside the chateau (and the present day).

There is also a little of *Bluebeard* – Walerian Borowczyk loves the trope of the forbidden room or the tabooed cabinet, and uses it in other films. In *Immoral Tales*, the ultimate *Bluebeard* story is enacted by the

44 All of Jack Zipes's books are truly wonderful, but some of the best are *Don't Bet on the Prince: Contemporary Feminist Fairy Tales in North America and England*, Methuen, New York, NY, 1983, *The Oxford Companion To Fairy Tales*, Oxford University Press, 2000, *Breaking the Spell: Radical Theories of Folk and Fairy Tales*, University of Kentucky Press, Lexington, 2002, and *Sticks and Stones: The Troublesome Success of Children's Literature From Slovenly Peter to Harry Potter*, Routledge, London, 2002.

Countess Bathóry who has virgins slaughtered for their blood.

The red rose in *The Beast*, one of the talismanic objects of the film (including Walt Disney's version), also comes straight out of fairy tales, including *Beauty and the Beast*. But fairy tale heroines like Belle or Snow White would never dream of using a rose to rub over their clitorises.

In *The Beast*, a young woman enters a forest: the forest is typically the place in fairy tales where characters enter in order to encounter obstacles and mystery. The forest is the place of initiation and trial. It lies on the edge of the familiar, everyday world of the fairy tale. It is where the protagonist gets lost, meets strange creatures, undergoes transformations and spells. It is, typically, one of the first places the protagonist enters on the journey outwards from the home, in *Snow White, Little Red Riding Hood* or *Hansel and Gretel*, for example.

In *The Brothers Grimm*, Jack Zipes writes of the forest in fairy tales:

> Inevitably, they find their way into the forest. It is there that they lose and find themselves. It is there that they gain a sense of what is to be done. The forest is always large, immense, great, and mysterious. No one ever gains power of the forest, but the trees possess the power to change lives and alter destinies. (43)

The forest is a zone of otherness, strangeness, enchantment and the unknown. In (Jungian) psychological terms, it is the unconscious, or confusion, a realm of instability, a *regressus ad uterum*, a place of re-creation and re-birth, where the ego/ soul/ hero/ine is tested and initiated. The enchanted or dark forest is a place of wild things, such as dragons in caves, or witches in their gloomy houses; it is also a place of death (and dragons, witches, caves and darkness are linked with death or the 'dark side' of life). *The Beast* evokes many of those aspects, with love and death foremost.

Walerian Borowczyk takes up mythic material – a woman and a monster – which's the basic stuff of countless horror films. And it's filmed like a horror movie, too – with blurry, handheld shots, the camera operator (Gérard Wurtz) running behind or in front of the actors, with the woman's screams prominent. Like horror pictures, the viewer sees glimpses of parts of the bodies, and only fragments of the beast. And yet, no horror film I've seen would think of putting (or dare to put) Domenico Scarlatti harpsichord music over a monster chasing a woman. The music is simply *unbelievable*. I bet that Scarlatti has *never* been used over a monster chase in a movie.[45]

In horror films, one of the things the monster threatens to do is to fuck the heroine. Well, Walerian Borowczyk simply makes good that threat, and the monster really does fuck the heroine. In horror cinema, the question is, will he catch her?, and what will he do to her if he does? In American horror movies, the monster's going to kill her, or torture her, but Borowczyk's *La Bête* makes it all very clear: no, he doesn't want to cut her up like your typical slasher villain, he wants to fuck her. In this respect, again, *La Bête* is not pornographic: rather, it's all those stalk 'n' slash and serial killer movies that are really pornographic, with their truly twisted emphasis on violence and endless suffering.

One of the central motifs of *La Bête* is the beast's phallus – the spectator sees much more of this than the whole of the beast himself. Indeed, one of the first sightings of the beast is of his massive penis. It's permanently erect, dribbles healthy doses of sperm (over the woman's breasts, buttocks, vulva, mouth, feet), and is the target of much licking, stroking and tupping.

The Beast is a movie of many cocks, actually: there's the horse cock at the beginning, in the second shot of the whole movie, and Ifany's large joystick, and drawings of penises that Lucy finds on two occasions. And the beast's schlong of course is shaped like a horse's penis.

The ithyphallic beast is the incarnation of wild, unbridled sexuality, restlessly, endlessly priapic, a totally stereotypical embodiment of male sexual lust, with an unstoppable carnal drive. He is the epitome of lusty satyrs and Pans out of Greek mythology, the wolves, bears and ogres of fairy tales, the monsters of legend and horror films. Walerian Borowczyk gives the beast (and the design of its phallus) a clear origin in the horses that Lucy stumbles upon copulating in the

45 And you can bet that Scarlatti would never have dreamt his music would be used in *this* manner!

stables at the beginning of the film. (The beast itself resembles, apart from a man in a hairy suit, a wolf and a bear).

The revelation, in the final scenes, that Mathurin is really the beast, is a hackneyed but effective way of connecting the fantasy and 'real life' narratives, the past and the present. Mathurin is found dead beside his bed by Lucy, on one of her visits to her future husband; she becomes hysterical, and Walerian Borowczyk has Hummel play the subsequent scenes at the height of hysteria. The madness comes from Lucy thinking she has killed Mathurin, just as Romilda killed the beast in her fantasy and in the past. Lucy thinks she has killed him in her erotic fantasies: in her dreams, as Romilda literally fucks the beast to death, using all her charms until the beast lies down and dies (both beasts die at the same time).

It's as if women, once sexually aroused, have too much desire, too much orgasmic pleasure, for the men or beasts to sustain. It's as if female erotic desire overwhelms the men, in the end, and kills them. Although the beast has multiple orgasms and is the embodiment of pure sexual lust, in the end it's Romilda's sexual desire that kills him. And notice how Lucy arrives at the chateau in a state of erotic excitement: she's leaping out of the car and photographing the forest; she's searching around her room and finding erotic illustrations; and she's masturbating a number of times. Once aroused, her erotic desire becomes unstoppable (though not necessarily insatiable – she just wants a man to love, and is eager to get on with her marriage. Note that in the dinner scene, Virginia is repulsed by Mathurin suddenly talking about tobacco and chewing it, but Lucy is more forgiving. And it's Virginia who undresses Mathurin at the end to reveal him as the beast).

It's noteworthy, too, that it's *Lucy* who pursues *Mathurin*, not the other way around. Mathurin is actually scared, he tells his father, and would prefer not to be presented for marriage. In the forest/ past sequence, it's the beast who pursues Romilda (although Romilda does go into the forest willingly, to catch the lamb). In the chateau/ present-day sequence, it's the woman pursing the man.

Notice, too, that Lucy never stops wanting and loving Mathurin:

despite his appearance, despite countless signals, and her aunt's misgivings,[46] Lucy holds fast to her love for this uncouth, unappealing guy (one of the aspects of *The Beast* that stretches credibility is that Lucy and Mathurian have been corresponding b4 meeting. No way would Mathurin be able to string to two words together; once again, it has to be the scheming marquis).

In the scenes which close *The Beast*, Walerian Borowczyk employs negative space: characters move out of frame for some moments, although they can be heard talking. Mathurin is picked up by the others, woken by a hysterical Lucy banging on the doors; he's put into a chair in the hall, then taken into the living room, where's he's laid on a table.

It's Virginia who undresses Mathurin, revealing a very hairy body and a tail. It's a grotesque image of a man-beast (actually quite creepy, and more effective than the beast costume). At that point, the reaction of Virginia is to get out of there as quickly as possible, taking Lucy with her (Lucy eventually calms down when she's in the Roller).

What the discovery of Mathurin as the beast does is to unleash a vitriolic denunciation of bestiality by the Cardinal, who has finally arrived. The Cardinal's detestation of bestial sex is absurdly graphic (he talks about women who use dogs and cats to lick their vulvas).

There's plenty of religious subtext to *The Beast*, too, as in all of Walerian Borowczyk's work. At the top layer, the marquis brother, Duc De Balo, is constantly telephoning the Vatican to speak to the Cardinal whom they hope will come and marry Mathurin to Lucy. The marriage, like the baptism, will they hope nix the curse of the beast.

Deeper layers of religiosity in *The Beast* include the familiar oppositions of paganism vs. religion, nature vs. civilization (the forest vs. the chateau), 'normal sex' (Clarisse and Ifany) and bestial sex (Romilda and the beast). The Cardinal condemns bestiality, yet this wilfully over-the-top movie has Romilda being raped by an animal but then enjoying it, and going further than the beast himself in sex, and fucking him to death.

46 Notice too that there are no scenes of Lucy and Mathurin alone together: the only time is when Mathurin is asleep and Lucy creeps into his room. Apart from that, they are always in social situations, surrounded by people.

The blasphemy of the 1975 movie is to reveal a morality that Christianity and civilized society would prefer to repress or ignore: that humans have lusts and appetites that can be as unbridled as that of animals. Animals fuck – it's one of the things they do (the horses are seen coupling at the beginning of *The Beast*), and some humans love to fuck, too (if they didn't, we wouldn't be here). The film depicts lustful characters: Lucy, Clarisse, Ifany, the beast, Romilda – even the curé has his pretty boys.

The Beast is thus an attack on the hypocrisies of organized religion (and Catholicism in particular). It makes it clear that the people who run religion are themselves degenerate (*viz.*, the priest with his underage boys).

⚜

I see I've written quite a bit about *The Beast* – there is a lot to it, once you get beyond the sheer silliness of it all. On a script and narrative level, *The Beast* is actually cleverly worked out (including how the fantasy two hundred years ago impacts on the present day story). And while the monster suit and the chase is pure pantomime or vaudeville, there are some impressive technical effects in *The Beast*, but many of them are invisible: the editing, for a start (courtesy of the maestro and an army of editorial assistants). Nearly always the last thing viewers and critics comment upon in Walerian Borowczyk's cinema (hell, there's all that naked flesh to contemplate first), the editing in Borowczyk's films is virtuosic. It's as impressive as any of Borowczyk's contemporary European art filmmakers. Really? Yes. Oh sure, Jean-Luc Godard or Ingmar Bergman are taken so seriously in other areas of filmmaking (politically, psychologically, socially), but at the level of editing and organizing material, Borowczyk is a magician. Just look at the way he's bringing together all of the characters in *The Beast.*

One of the curious aspects of Walerian Borowczyk's montage style of editing is that he leaves in parts of shots most other editors would automatically throw to the cutting room floor: wobbly camerawork, parts of shots where the camera operator is lining up a shot, or the sudden slew of a camera up and down as they finish a tilting move.

Borowczyk seems to like those parts of shots before he called 'action!' and after he'd called 'cut!'

The other invisible technical element in *The Beast* is the music. Oh sure, Vincente Minnelli or Martin Scorsese are regularly trotted out as amazing film directors when it comes to music (and they are), but just for the use of the Domenico Scarlatti score alone in *The Beast*, Walerian Borowczyk is the equal of his contemporaries.

And for simply taking the viewer to a place all of its own, a dream-like forest of the unconscious, where desires run rampant, *The Beast* is extraordinary.

5

THE STORY OF SIN

The Story of Sin (a.k.a. *Dzieje Grzechu* or *The Story of a Sin*, 1975), which charted the changing fortunes of Eva (Grazyna Dlugolecka) in early 20th century Poland, was a big movie and countered the common view of Walerian Borowczyk as a purveyor of small-scale European art movies which tend towards softcore porn. *The Story of Sin* was a historical melodrama involving many costly production values (such as extras, horses and carriages, extensive location shooting, period sets, props, costumes and a large cast).[47] Zygmunt Samosiuk was cameraman, Lida Pacewicz was editor, Teresa Barska was art director, Jerzy Szeski designed the costumes, Zbigniew Dobracki did the make-up, Marek Iwaszkiewicz was set decorator, Jan Czerwinski did the sound, Helena Nowicka was production manager, Anna Izykowska-Mironowicz was music consultant, and Eva Smal was first AD (there were a large proportion of women on the crew, as there often was on Borowczyk movie).

Of course, there *was* nudity in *The Story of Sin* (mainly featuring Grazyna Dlugolecka), and some sex scenes. But, considering the other films Borowczyk was making in the mid-Seventies – *Three Immoral Tales, Behind Convent Walls* and *The Beast* – *The Story of Sin* was fairly restrained. Take away the few sex scenes, and *The Story of Sin* might be mistaken for the more sedate kind of European historical dramas of the time. Except of course that this was a Walerian Borowczyk movie, and couldn't have been made by anyone else. The painterly compositions, the plentiful references to the history of art (with numerous cutaways to paintings on walls), the rapid insert shots of secret gestures, the very unusual props (old wax cylinders, telecommunications equipment, fans, phials, mirrors, etc), the bursts of classical music (including Borowczyk's beloved organ music), and the flower petals (strewn on a nude woman, of course), were among the many touches particular to Borowczyk's cinema.

As a historical drama, *The Story of Sin* was a beautifully made

47 Borowczyk recalled that the producers 'gave me complete freedom over subject and script', with only a scene depicting the Czarist army marching in a town in Poland being cut.

piece.[48] It didn't have the slickness (and showiness) of European co-productions and 'heritage' films – it was filmed, according to the DP, Zygmunt Samosiuk, 80% handheld, for a start, giving the movie a loose, spontaneous feel for a period drama (and Samosiuk, operating the camera himself much of the time, allowed a far looser kind of handheld movement than usual. I do think the handheld quality of *The Story of Sin* does get tiresome at times).

In some respects, *The Story of Sin* recalled *Katy Tippel* (1975), Paul Verhoeven's Dutch historical drama which followed a woman growing up in 19th century Amsterdam (Verhoeven's film contained far more sex than Walerian Borowczyk's film, incidentally, and dirt, squalor, greed, and poverty). Like *Katy Tippel, The Story of Sin* was also a story about a woman starting out with good intentions who falls into prostitution and other bad ways. Many European *auteurs* were fascinated by prostitution (typically exploring – and condemning – the social values and the societies that pushed women towards it). As well as Borowczyk and Verhoeven, Jean-Luc Godard, Ken Russell, Ingmar Bergman, Federico Fellini and Rainer Maria Fassbinder also directed films about whores.

According to Grazyna Dlugolecka, she was cast when she met Walerian Borowczyk in a corridor, not at an audition. Dlugolecka recalled that shooting *The Story of Sin* hadn't been so wonderful (although she regarded Borowczyk as a master director). She wouldn't want to go through it again (Borowczyk had been angered by Dlugolecka complaining about the film in the Polish press). But she had a friend on set in cameraman Zygmunt Samosiuk, she added.

But what a killer role for a young actress: you get to do everything in this story. And the acting, across the board, is superb (except for Zbigniew Zapasiewicz, who plays the priest and, in the confessional scene, is continually reading his lines right in front of him. And it's a long, long shot which editor Lidia Pacewicz doesn't cut away from).

⚜

48 Michael Richardson put *Story of Sin* next to *L'Age d'Or* as a film of *amour fou*, 'one of the great explorations of the disruptive impact of love on social relations' (114). *Story of Sin* also has affinities with *That Obscure Object of Desire* and *Letters From an Unknown Woman.*

The Story of Sin doesn't appear like your usual costume drama: there are no establishing shots, for instance. Occasionally there's a railway station sign, but no big wide shots of Monte Carlo or Rome, that you'd find in a typical historical drama. And no sweeping camera moves, either: the action is kept close to Eva all the time. So it can be a little confusing, because *The Story of Sin* is a globetrotting movie, shifting around Warsaw, Berlin, Rome, Shuttenbach, etc (my Polish isn't great and the subtitles don't translate everything. Are we in Berlin here, at the boating lake? And does it matter?).

No, it's not the subtitles, or lack of establishing shots, it's the film itself, and Walerian Borowczyk's style of making films. One can imagine a film producer viewing a screening of the second or third cut of the movie and saying, 'Boro, can we just put in an establishing shot or two or some captions, so the audience knows what's going on and where we are?' And Borowczyk would probably retort with a flat no.

Walerian Borowczyk's movies simply dispense with cinematic devices that act as lead-ins or set-ups that conventional movies employ. In a word: exposition. He simply expects the audience to work a little and keep up. That's quite common in the European art film, though.

In Walerian Borowczyk's cinema, everything in the picture has a function – in particular his art direction, which's second to none: the objects, the furniture, the animals, the lighting, the scenery, the people, and those fabulous costumes.

The *mise-en-scène* in *The Story of Sin* is Walerian Borowczyk at his best. He is in his element art directing numerous interiors of the post-*fin-de-siècle* period. Teresa Barska and Marek Iwaszkiewicz were art director and set designer, and Jerzy Szeski and Roswita Stern did the costumes (but you can bet that Borowczyk was overseeing every detail). The art direction of *The Story of Sin* is teeming with references from the history of art: there are more references to painting than you'll find in many biopics of painters. Virtually every single interior set is art directed with paintings and prints. Cyprian Bodzanta (Mieczyslaw Voit) sends his paintings out into the world so they'll be seen (they're loaded onto a cart and covered with straw). And of course

Borowczyk finds many occasions where his collection of popular erotica of the period can be displayed too.

There are too many paintings for the film to contain, and one long scene is staged in an art exhibition, as if to collect the rest of the paintings that couldn't be squeezed in elsewhere. And a large, voluptuous reclining nude forms the background to much of the scene, where Eva meets Count Szczerbic (the Count romancing Eva is too good to be true).

The Story of Sin is a film of mirrors. Voyeurism is let loose everywhere. Characters spy on people through keyholes, via mirrors, and through windows. In one memorable scene, Pochron (Roman Wilhelmi) spies on Eva's liaison with Count Szczerbic by arranging a set of three folding oval mirrors. And the camera covers the scene looking through those mirrors. Spellbinding.

Among the classic Borowczykian images in *The Story of Sin* are Eva alone in bed, semi-nude, her body strewn with red rose petals, given to her by her lover, Lukash. And the incredible scene where Eva makes love with Count Szczerbic then kills him.

More and more as I look at Walerian Borowczyk's cinema, I get the impression that it's not only the visuals, the props, the art direction and the costumes that are sacrosanct: it's the *editing.*

Music is another striking element of *The Story of Sin:* Borowczyk has selected some favourites from the world of classical music (including his beloved organ music), and used them sparingly but very effectively. Some scenes (such as the love scenes) play silently, with music.

The Story of Sin uses many devices of the costume drama, though – such as voiceover reading from letters, and close-ups of letters (plus a classic Borowczykian addition of C.U.s of postcards – from Vienna, Florence, Rome). Even the voice of God is heard (when Eva reads a religious book). And Eva is seen reading Charles Baudelaire's *Flowers of Evil* (what else could it be? – *À Rebours* by J.-K. Huysmans, perhaps, or Comte de Lautréamont's *Chansons de Maldoror*).

You get sucked into the story of poor Eva in *The Story of Sin,* and her search for love and being. But it is a brutal movie, and Eva is doomed from the beginning. Whatever she does, she can't win. She is, she says, Eve, the 'first sinner'. She is often sad and lonely, and has no true companion. *The Story of Sin* describes a decline and fall. From what? From innocence, from youth, from hope. It's a story of corruption, and exploitation: everybody wants something from Eva.

Sexual desire begins her journey, and at first it seems as if Eva's found if not true love, then some kind of love. One can't help feeling that her beloved, Lukash Niepolomski (Jerzy Zelnik) is a bit of a drip. I mean, really not worth Eva's film-long desire for him, her continuous search for him. In every scene she's asking someone about Lukash, where is he? when can she see him? Oh well, I guess he's just a cipher, then, just a goal that she wants to reach but never can. In which case, his bland persona only makes her tragedy even stronger.

Eva is surrounded by men who desire her: Lukash, Horst, the factory man who once boarded with Eva's parents, Pochron, and Count Szczerbic. Her treatment at the hands of Pochron and his partner in crime Plaza-Splawski (Marek Walczewski) is abysmal.

The idyll in the snow, as Lukash recovers from his wound following the duel with Szczerbic, is Eva's happiest time in the 1975 film. It's followed by a love scene which again is tinged with quirky Borowczykian eroticism: Lukash, like squintilliions of other people, is a connoisseur of erotic images. He has a book of erotic photographs beside him (which he hid from Eva earlier). As they make love passionately on the bed, Lukash finds a favourite photo (a nude woman lying face-down) and encourages Eva to do the same on the bed. She copies the photograph and he fucks her from behind. And all the while a feisty violin concerto plays.

In the central section of *The Story of Sin,* following Lukash's disappearance, an erotic network is set up, but it's all unconsummated, it's all love from afar: Eva pursues Lukash; the Count pursues Eva (and Horst offers himself too); and Pochron is spying on them, following Eva across Europe.

The story rattles along, taking in location after location, and doesn't let up. *The Story of Sin* is a film you want to watch all the way through (unlike many other flicks one could mention). In one scene,

Eva is leaping out of a moving train at night, to escape Pochron; not long after that, he's caught up with her and is raping her in a hotel. The film doesn't halt for a second, and next it's mounting a big scene in a restaurant, including a dance and a vaudeville show (with a tightrope walker).

Manual labour is another element of *The Story of Sin:* Eva is no Jane Austen heroine who pines away in enormous country manors, ringing the bell when she wants another cup of tea. Eva works – in an office, in a clothes factory, at a sewing machine, in the greenhouses of Ciprian's utopia, and ultimately as a prostitute. In *The Story of Sin,* prostitution is labour at its most pure, in a modern, capitalist system.

The Story of Sin is a sexy movie too – it's entirely driven by Eva's longing (primarily for Lukash). Many scenes are played with Eva naked or half-naked. When she turns to prostitution, she's clad in the fetish favourite of black corset and stockings.

✤

The murder of Count Szczerbic is a *tour-de-force* of eroticism and death. It's a truly despicable murder, and a textbook piece of film-making. This scene alone should be enough to convince many critics of Walerian Borowczyk's greatness.

It begins erotically enough, with Eva and the Count making love. The room's been arranged in the style of a boudoir out an old libertine's fantasy: a couch, lit from the side, is positioned centre stage, with a small circular mirror above it, and a chest of drawers behind it. Hidden in the darkness in the next room are Pochron and Plaza-Splawski (but only Pochron is revealed at first). When Eva persuades Szczerbic to part with some money, she hands it through the drawers to Pochron. And he, in turn, slips her the poison in the syringe, which she puts on the floor.

The orchestration of Gothic details and the montage style of editing is gobsmackingly good here. There's the brilliant use of a scratchy, ancient wax cylinder playing. And when the death comes, and Eva really does stick the guy with the poison, it's shocking. And only then do the lights come up and Pochron and Plaza-Splawski are seen behind it all. Eva has truly fallen, led to this sleazy murder for money.

You might've seen all of these elements in movies a million times before – lovemaking turning into murder, the woman who becomes a murderess. Alfred Hitchcock was particularly fond of staging scenes which slid from sex into death, often with black comedy touches. And this scene in *The Story of Sin* is easily the equal of Hitchcock.

⚜

The Story of Sin is one of those films where you're not sure where the movie will go next. One of the oddest sequences occurs towards the end, when Eva finds herself at Cyprian Bodzanta's utopian country estate. Cyprian meets Eva when she goes out onto her balcony in her hooker's outfit of corset and stockings and calls up to him (after seeing off a portly, clingy client). Cyprian takes Eva to a socialist utopia, where the inhabitants can work or rest, or do whatever they like. Borowczyk stages some intriguing scenes in a series of greenhouses, where women dressed all in white are gardening.

In this idyllic setting the film moves into a fantastical realm – a lake, swans, a Classical temple, sunshine, gardens. It's heaven. One of those movie places that you know can't last forever, or are doomed to fail (and that happens, though offscreen, described in dialogue). Yet, when Plaza-Splawski turns up (with his customary monocle and bald pate, a caricature of a German noble), Eva leaves straight away. Cyprian is disappointed, naturally, but it was inevitably the promise of seeing Lukash again that made Eva leave this paradise.

Eva's quest for fulfilment and beingness seems doomed to fail – especially if she relies on a guy like Lukash to give her heaven. *The Story of Sin* is a compelling portrayal of one person's struggle to make their way in the world. And it completely overturns the view that Walerian Borowczyk is a pedlar in softcore porn, or that his powers tapered off after *Blanche.*

6

BEHIND CONVENT WALLS

Behind Convent Walls (1977, a.k.a. *Interieur d'un Convent, Sex Life in a Convent* or *Within a Cloister*) was shot in Italy, and again starred Walerian Borowczyk's wife, Ligia Branice (as Sister Clara) and the future star of his later films, Marina Pierro (as Sister Veronica), who was only seventeen at the time. *Behind Convent Walls* was produced by Giuseppe Vezzani, shot by Luciano Tovoli, cut by Boro and Roberto Olivieri, designed by Francesco Chianese, Luciano Spadoni and Filippo Bufo, scripted by Boro, with costumes by Maria Laura Zampacavall, makeup by Franco Ruffini, sound by Carlo Palmieri and Alberto Tinebra, and music by Sergio Montori.

Behind Convent Walls was based on Stendhal's *Roman Walks* (I haven't read *Roman Walks*, but somehow I bet Stendhal wouldn't have thought it would be adapted someday into a story with nuns masturbating with dildoes. However, men sneaking into the convent to tup the nuns sounds like Stendhal – he did write a fabulous treatise on love, after all: *De l'Amour*, 1822). Stendhal does give *Behind Convent Walls* powerful literary associations, though.

Films featuring nuns are a sub-genre of cinema. Some famous examples include *The Bells of St Mary's, Black Narcissus, The Miracle, The Song of Bernadette, The Sound of Music, Sister Act* and *Nuns On the Run*. *Behind Convent Walls* is very much in the tradition of the convent or nun film which concentrates on the hothouse atmosphere of an institution, as in Ken Russell's wonderful film *The Devils* (1971) and *Black Narcissus* (1946). *Behind Convent Walls* must be among the most sexually explicit, as well as the strangest, movies about nuns and convents in cinema.

Behind Convent Walls was familiar Walerian Borowczyk territory: a historical time period (early 19th century), a labyrinthine interior of corridors, doors, windows and intimate rooms, a social hierarchy, repressed sexuality, Catholic imagery (tons of it), anti-clerical themes, painterly visuals, slow pace, and an atmosphere of mystery. Oh, and *plenty* of nudity.

No one else makes movies quite like this. The story was fairly straightforward: a group of lusty nuns in a convent are presided over by a strict Mother Superior, Abbess Flavia Orsini (Gabriella Giacobbe) who tries to stamp out their sinful desires. Indeed, the narrative boiled down, on one level, to a stern authority figure, like a surrogate parent, trying to stop her charges from masturbating and fucking.

Behind Convent Walls is a film of masturbation, of young women trying to find secret spaces where they can get off, or meet their lovers.

The Mother Superior is ruthless in her desire to find and persecute sexual activity, to search for erotic material: in many scenes she sneaks into the nuns' rooms when they're at prayer and goes through their drawers, cupboards and beds (she brandishes a long metal spike which she unsheathes like a sword and she pokes through mattresses to find concealed letters or sex aids; she finds erotic watercolours and douses them in a hand basin; she confronts the nuns with her findings).

The Mother Superior is an alarming embodiment of sexual repression and religious fervour taken to psychotic extremes. *Behind Convent Walls* is as effective as any film at exploring the hypocrisy, the lies, and the dangers of religious belief and practices, and specifically the suffocating sin and guilt of Catholicism.

The marketing for *Behind Convent Walls* would inevitably emphasize the sexuality and nudity, and there is quite a bit in *Behind Convent Walls*: the nuns dancing in the chapel, lesbian sex in a confessional, nuns stretching and exercising half naked, a semi-clad nun carving a dildo, another one painting watercolours of a man with a large phallus, and the local butcher rutting on top of, underneath and behind various nuns behind closed doors.

But this's a Walerian Borowczyk film, and although it has not a few erotic moments, and images of Borowczyk's beloved actresses Branice and Pierro nude, Borowczyk is just as interested in the social hierarchy of the convent, the relationships of the nuns to each other, the arcane use of props, furniture and interiors, and the endless to-ings and fro-ings of the actors down corridors, past windows, and through rooms. In terms of screen time, there are far more dialogue scenes, or near-silent scenes of the nuns travelling about the convent, than there are of sex. And Borowczyk is great on the social and religious rituals of the institution. There are a striking number of scenes of people praying, for instance (one of the nuns, Veronica, prays in the nude, assuming a kind of yoga position on her knees, on the floor in front of a painting of Christ on the Cross). Sister Clara is often depicted in the chapel, praying and reading her tiny prayer book.

⚜

In the first few minutes of *Behind Convent Walls*, Walerian Borowczyk introduces the world of the convent, the atmosphere of quiet labour and religious piety, which's instantly disrupted by the arrival of the local butcher (Howard Ross) with an enormous side of meat. As he enters the convent, he has to put on eye shades, a wonderful touch of the stupidity of suppressing sexuality in Christianity (there are many locks on the main door of the convent, and the nuns are never allowed to pass through the door).

Within moments, the butcher's in the kitchen with the nuns, distracting them from their chores with his arrogant bragging about the size of his muscles, and pounding away at the meat with a cleaver (unsubtle tropes of sex, hammering the meat like a woman). The kitchen sequence also includes numerous details of food and the nuns preparing it, lyrical evocations of the daily life of the nunnery.

Cut to a scene of the nuns in the gardens outside, pruning roses (bathed in the hot light of Italy and full-blown Summer). Sister Clara (Ligia Branice) appears for the first time; back in the chapel, Sister Veronica (Marina Pierro) pricks her finger on a rose thorn and sucks her finger in extreme close-up (Roberto Olivieri then cuts back to a close-up of the meat).

With a deft economy, then, Walerian Borowczyk and his mainly Italian team evoke scenes of sexual repression and intense erotic desire, and clusters of images around roses, blood, thorns, meat, flesh, the colour red, and tropes of penetration (thorns, meat cleavers, fingers). The fusion of eroticism and religion continues in the next scene, set in the chapel.

Covered in all manner of detailed shots, the nuns are shown cleaning the interior, dusting down statues of Jesus, his wounds leaking blood, accompanied by two nuns playing a violin and the church organ (the altarpiece is Simone Martini's beautiful *Annunci-*

ation).

The scene descends into a bit of a festivity: the nuns begin playing jaunty music (by Sergio Montori), some of the nuns start dancing, Sister Clara lies on her back with her legs in the air, doing exercises with her bare legs,[49] two nuns creep into the confessional, undressing and embracing. Borowczyk and Luciano Tovoli shoot the party with rapid, loose, handheld shots. Inevitably, it's at this point that the Abbess storms into the chapel and castigates her charges for their un-Christian activities. (Visually, one aspect of *Behind Convent Walls* does become irritating, for me, and that's the prevalence of handheld shots. Indeed, it appears as if most of *Behind Convent Walls* was shot handheld. It doesn't matter, really, but there are scenes where the camera's meant to be locked, but it wobbles too much.)

In the subsequent scenes, Sister Clara, the heroine, is shown as a God-fearing, pious nun, keen to do well in the convent. Significantly, she begins the film not as one of the nuns who go against the grain and defy the authority figures. Clara is a virginal innocent, someone pure and good, and the film is partly the story of her gradual initiation into sex (like Lucy in *The Beast*). Clara asks the Mother Superior if she can pray in the chapel sometimes at night, because then she'll be nearer to God. She visits a nun, Lucrezia, in the library who's working on a tapestry. No sooner is Clara out of the room, though, than Lucrezia is rutting her lover, Paolo Visconti, behind the tapestry (while being watched by another, older nun, who hides behind a chair – the voyeurism aspect is maintained throughout the film). Yet again, the Abbess storms in to disrupt the sex.

Later, after Clara has read aloud from the good book during supper, the nuns repair to their rooms to engage in... what else?, but lascivious thoughts or acts. One nun plays the violin in the nude. Veronica prays to the Lord while doing yoga-like exercises, crossing her legs and rising on her knees, or lying on her back with her legs pawing the air. She mutters litanies to a large *Crucifixion* painting on the wall above her. She embodies the nun as the 'bride of Christ' in a literal form, undressing before a painting of him like a bride in her

49 Borowczyk loved to have Marina Pierro do this, the gesture crops up again in *The Art of Love*.

bedroom. (Later, she visits the father confessor (Mario Maranzan) in the confessional, and tells him about her experiences at night of Jesus visiting her bed and making love with him, their legs entwining. The priest's titillated but tries to deflate her erotic desire. Veronica's accounts recall mediæval female mystics, such as St Catherine of Genoa or St Teresa of Avila, who spoke of the spiritual union of the soul with God in explicitly erotic terms. For example, St Catherine wrote: 'Love, I want You, the whole of You').

A man visits the convent by climbing a knotted rope, and tups one of the nuns. Another nun (a portly figure who's the resident painter in the nunnery) paints watercolours of men with enormous phalloi (in exchange for food the nuns bring). A nun visits her and commissions the artist to paint her an erotic picture. Later, the nun masturbates with the dildo she's carved out of wood; it's not wholly a simple masturbation scene, though: Borowczyk adds his artistic details: the image of the dildo digging back and forth is shot in a hand mirror, and there's a watercolour of a bearded man glued to the end (masturbating with a dildo would probably be enough for some filmmakers, but adding the image of the nun's beloved on the end enhances the scene, and, to go even further, to add a mirror so the nun can watch the image of her man fucking her).

Inevitably, the Abbess disturbs the masturbating nun, finds the mirror, then the dildo, then demands the nun show her what she was doing. Bizarrely, the nun complies, sits on her bed, legs open, and mimes what she was doing with the dildo. Naturally, the Mother Superior orders her to the chapel, and confiscates the offending artefacts.

Walerian Borowczyk's ingenuity for the oddball is mesmerizing. For example, in one sequence, the convent's butcher and handyman Rodrigo is cutting wood with an axe in the convent courtyard; shards of wood fly up and strike the convent's windows a number of times until one smashes a pane and lands on the floor. A nun passes by: she picks up the piece of wood and one or two shards of glass, and crosses herself (a great touch – the building material for a dildo seems to have dropped out of the sky, from heaven). Later, she sits carving the wood into a dildo, half-naked, breasts spilling out of her clothes, legs astride a white bowl.

At times it seems as if Walerian Borowczyk were the reincarnation of some mediæval French monk, or an eighteenth century dandy, or an aristocratic acquaintance of the Marquis de Sade, or some highly intellectual æsthete like J.-K. Huysmans' Des Esseintes, a nobleman with a penchant for European painting and high-class pornography. Certainly, in *Behind Convent Walls* he deploys every cliché about nuns and convents.

There are many high art allusions in *Behind Convent Walls*, aside from the images of masturbation and the internecine warfare among the nuns: Francesco Chianese and Filippo Bufo have art-directed the convent like a museum: behind the opening credits is a Renaissance *Pièta* painting (it looks like a Titian or Tintoretto); there are other Renaissance and Catholic images and paintings; statues of Jesus on the Cross; statues of the Madonna; images of the Madonna and Child are seen behind actors.

The underside of these public images of Catholic faith are the secret images of the nuns, created behind closed doors: the dildoes the nuns carve with pictures of their beloved men drawn on the end; images of their beloveds hidden in prayer books; erotic drawings or letters hidden under beds. To give an idea of the very different concerns of Borowczyk from the run-of-the-mill softcore erotic film: Borowczyk cuts from images of nude women masturbating to images from Renaissance paintings. Only in art cinema does one find that kind of juxtaposition. In some *auteurs* it might be pretentious, but Borowczyk is clearly serious as well as playful.

In the middle of *Behind Convent Walls*, Sister Veronica punishes herself for her carnal thoughts by pressing her hands over the roses she's placed over the statue of Mary and Jesus. She interprets the bleeding wounds on her palms from the thorns as stigmata, and rushes about, showing off her holy hurts.

Walerian Borowczyk trots out the familiar stereotypes about convents and nuns, the clichéd situations and characters of porn (the dildoes, masturbation, sexual repression and desires, lesbianism, strict authority figures, secret lovers, punishment, and self-flagellation). But there's also an awareness of mediæval mysticism and Catholic spirituality, of religious ritual and daily duties, and of female saints such as St Catherine of Genoa, St Teresa of Avila, Hildegarde of Bingen and Julian of Norwich, who wrote astonishingly passionate accounts of their religious experiences of God, using erotically charged terms such as 'beloved', 'union', 'spiritual marriage', 'consummation', 'surrender', 'submission', 'penetration', 'love' and 'ecstasy'. This kind of Catholic mysticism is full of erotic imagery, from sensations of burning and bleeding hearts, to notions of masochism, self-torture, submission and orgasmic ecstasy. Borowczyk knows his mediæval mysticism well, alongside the sadomasochism and barely repressed eroticism behind Catholic mysticism and faith.

Towards the end of *Behind Convent Walls* there is an unusual sequence in Walerian Borowczyk's cinema – a rapid montage of images (unusual because Borowczyk favours long takes and a stately pace). It's as if someone thought the film was flagging, and needed a boost (it does appear that the picture sort of meanders and there's not much of a story developing).

The rapidfire montage of the images (all to music) are thoroughly Borowczykian: nuns masturbating; the large nun, nude, painting and later eating grapes; a naked nun playing the violin; Veronica dreaming of Jesus, lying on her back with her legs open (cut to the *Crucifixion* painting in her room); Clara dancing and singing alone, but with her breasts exposed; the butcher fucking his nun lover from behind; two nuns in bed, holding hands; a nude nun carrying washing; another nun carving a dildo; a nun masturbating by dragging her undergarments between her legs; a nun in bed on her side, squeezing her legs together, her buttocks presented to the camera in a low angle shot; the musician nun now masturbating with the violin clutched between her thighs on the back; a nun urinating; a pregnant nun sleeping; a lesbian threesome (in which they stroke their eyebrows); and Clara pressing her breasts up against the iron bars in the chapel (the iron bars are where men are allowed to be in the chapel – they are segregated from the nuns; this was the last place she saw her admirer, Rodrigo).

It's an amazing sequence, this night of passion, in which everyone seems to be having sex in some form or another (Roberto Olivieri and Walerian Borowczyk also cut back to religious paintings, and a relief the Madonna and Child, emphasizing the religious, ritual nature of the sex acts, and their transgressive nature).

The sequence climaxes with Clara breaking the rules, and leaving the convent to go to her lover, Rodrigo Landriani, at night, banging on his door. It's another case in Borowczyk's cinema of female sexuality suddenly exploding and becoming uncontrollable and infinite. Clara won't be stopped, but rushes upon Rodrigo hysterically. But then she is overcome and faints away.

Of course, they wind up getting freaky, but first Rodrigo carries her to the convent, and through to the rose garden of the convent grounds (where she was first seen at the beginning of the film). Rodrigo puts Clara on her back on a stone bench. Clara's undressed, in a swoon, and swiftly brought to orgasm by her lover's mouth and tongue. A lengthy close-up on Clara's face and she mutters prayers which turn into imprecations to her lover, accompanied by loud organ music. This's the highpoint of the film's fusion of religious and sexual ecstasy. (It's typical of Borowczyk's fetishism that Clara keeps her white wimple on, and her boots.)

Then the lovers tup energetically, with Walerian Borowczyk's camera panning up and down his wife's body, paying particular attention to her breasts and crotch. Many handheld close-ups of Rodrigo's thrusting buttocks, his mouth and hands on her breasts. Borowczyk makes it explicit that Clara's orgasmic experience is also a religious, spiritual experience; when she comes, he cuts to brief shots of paintings of Jesus.

Behind Convent Walls ends with a series of deaths from poison, including the Mother Superior, Clara and another nun (one of the nuns persuades another to give the Abbess some opium, and, in the bathroom, the nun pours in the whole bottle). The poison that was intended for the Mother Superior appears to have taken the lives of the nuns too. So the movie is a tragedy, like some of Borowczyk's other films.

After the Mother Superior dies, the convent is in an uproar. The father confessor rushes around trying to find out what happened, and to quieten down the hysterical nuns. A bishop (Rodolfo Dal Pra) and some other religious officials arrive to find the convent in an apocalyptic state. The father confessor calls the place a charnel house.

In a subsequent scene, Clara, semi-naked, haughty, consumed with passion, informs the father confessor that she's madly in love, and renounces the Catholic faith. As in *The Beast*, Borowczyk and his team stage scenes where half-naked or completely naked characters (usually women), in states of desire or madness or dislocation, face people (usually authority figures) who are fully dressed. And the authority figures don't know what to do with these naked women. The father confessor has no idea how to react to Clara – she has gone far beyond what he can comprehend. In a way, it's the key scene in the film, in terms of what Clara is saying, about the importance of love over religion, of love between two people over religious worship (her views seem to be close to Borowczyk's).

The scenes of sex followed by the (far longer) ones of death take *Behind Convent Walls* far away from the 1970s porn movie. *Behind Convent Walls* ends not with joyous images of love or sex, but with the death of love, youth and beauty, making the film a condemnation of sexual repression, and social and religious oppression. And Clara, the central character (and top-billed actor) is dead, just as she has become sexually fulfilled. Just as Clara has seen the light and will no doubt move out of the convent into the wide world, she dies. The movie condemns the repressive, authoritarian regime of the convent, which uses religion to justify (or excuse) its oppressive make-up. No doubt one could read into the dictatorial Abbess a comment on political dictators of the 20th century, and the repressive regime at the convent like that of Communism in Eastern Europe, which critics have done with some of Borowczyk's other movies (such as *Goto: Island of Love*). Communism or Catholicism, they're both oppressive, cruel systems in Borowczyk's cinema.

And the Abbess's investigation of the nuns' rooms, sneaking in there and prodding around with that long metal spike, evoke the mediæval Inquisition, as well as witchfinders (witches in the Middle Ages would be pricked with spikes as one way of testing if they were witches). It's as if the nuns are turning into witches, turning towards the Devil, with their lust for dancing, music, food, and fucking. Indeed, Walerian Borowczyk stages the party in the chapel like a witches' sabbath. The film is clear that the religious system in the convent condemns all the enjoyable aspects of life – eating, drinking, dancing, making music, making art, and sex. (For an artist like Borowczyk, it's abhorrent that the Catholic oppression in the convent forbids music or painting, and proves that this kind of organized religion is psychotic with its endless rules and taboos). The human spirit, the movie offers, will always desire to break through boundaries and taboos. And even repressive social systems can't hold it back.

It's interesting, too, that towards the end of *Behind Convent Walls* male authority figures enter the narrative and take over: the bishop, the father confessor, and soldiers. To them it seems as if the nuns have gone crazy: in one scene, Veronica hysterically throws herself at the bishop, rubbing her bloody hands on his face. The themes orchestrated here include hysteria, uncontrollable energies (of sex, of spirituality), of the religious and social repression of the convent system (i.e., organized religion, and Catholicism in particular). The system breaks down, the rules and taboos are broken, patriarchy can't contain this explosion of erotic desire here (the sexual sublimated into the spiritual backfires). Life's pleasures shouldn't be sublimated into other things, like religions, which end up suppressing them.

7

THREE IMMORAL WOMEN

Three Immoral Women (a.k.a. *Les Héroïnes du mal, Heroines of Evil, Heroines of Pain* and *Immoral Women,* 1979) is classic Walerian Borowczyk: it's truly outrageous: this is a film where a young woman masturbates with her pet rabbit.

Three Immoral Women has everything, all of the classic Walerian Borowczyk touches and obsessions: women in lead roles; tons of art on display; plenty of sex scenes and acres of nudity; floaty white see-through dresses; historical settings; period music; women bathing; still-lifes; animals; organ music; fabulous costumes and hats; and it's been art directed to perfection.

Three Immoral Women was produced by Pierre Braunberger, a veteran producer, whose credits included Jean Renoir movies of the 1920s-1930s. He produced some of Jean-Luc Godard's early movies, prior to *Breathless,* as well as *Vivre Sa Vie.* Jean-Paul De Vidas, Michel de Vidas executive produced; Gisèle Braunberger was associate producer; Bernard Daillencourt was cinematographer; Jacques D'Ovidio designed the show; Philippe d'Aram and Olivier Dassault provided the music; Khadicha Bariha was editor; Boro co-wrote André Pieyre de Mandiargues.

MARGHERITA

The first story of this three-part film, entitled 'Margherita' (*Three Immoral Women* a kind of sequel to *Immoral Tales* in narrative structure), concerns Margherita, played by Marina Pierro (who has never been more radiant); she was 19 at the time of production. Born in 1960, Pierro has appeared mainly in Borowczyk's films, as far as I can tell.[50] Pierro did star in *The Living Dead Girl* (a.k.a. *La Morte Vivante,* Jean Rollin, 1982).[51]

50 At least, according to the Internet Movie Database.

51 *The Living Dead Girl*'s not a great movie, and has many of the attributes of the low budget European mondo sex-'n'-horror production. But it does contain some mystery and power – the theme of vampires goes a long way.

'Margherita' is set in Renaissance Italy – in Rome, in fact, with most of the action taking place in the Vatican (a favourite Borowczyk location).[52] It's a world of Catholic religion, of institutionalized religion, of rich patrons of the arts, of painters and models.

Three Immoral Women evokes important historical figures: Michelangelo Buonaroti (1475-1564), Raphael (1483-1520) and Pope Julius II (1443-1513). In the middle of it all is Margherita Lutti, the baker's daughter who becomes an artist's model (Lutti, known as 'La Fornarina',[53] a famous woman in Renaissance art, was a real person; some said she was Raphael's wife, some his mistress, and some his model. It's a familiar scenario: the artist and his mysterious model/ mistress/ muse. Raphael's famous painting, *Portrait of a Young Woman* (1518-19, in the Barberini Palace in Rome), is said to be a portrait of Lutti. The film shows Lutti sitting for this painting).

Walerian Borowczyk and co. are here exploring familiar themes: the relation between patrons and artists, between money and art, between love and art, between sex and art, and between artists and models. The role of the artist in society is a key theme, too – how they are exploited by the rich patrons and cardinals, and how art fits in with religion.

Three Immoral Women opens with evocations of ancient Roman ruins – pillars, colonnades, arches, pools, walls. It's ancient, sun-drenched Italy,[54] with period music to help set the scene. Within a minute of *Three Immoral Women*, Margherita is being fucked from behind on a stone pillar by her rough-and-ready peasant lover Tomaso (Gérard Falconetti). Already the movie has evoked the ancient world, beauty, plenty of art, and sex. It's love among the ruins, it's love in Italy (with from the back being the preferred position in this film).

And the scene of Margherita and Tomaso doing the dirty on the column is not only classic Walerian Borowczyk, it's classical pornography. So when the film now cuts to images of ancient Roman

52 If you're going to attack Catholic religion, where better than the Vatican?

53 Pablo Picasso took up the same subject, of Raphael and his muse, in *Raphael and La Fornarina* (1968), in which a painter makes love to his model while Picasso draws himself as the Tiresias-like old man observing the Freudian primal scene. J.M.W. Turner and others also painted Raphael and La Fornarina.

54 The light is particularly beautiful – one reason why so many painters have visited Italy.

porn (the kind seen in murals, and at Pompeii),[55] it's as if the film-makers are saying, you know, people have been fucking for millennia, well, since forever – and they've been making art out of fucking, too, for a long, long time. *Three Immoral Women* is thus Borowczyk's version of ancient Roman erotica, the European art movie as ancient erotic art.

The painter Raphael Sanzio (François Guétary) is surrounded by arty images when he's introduced in his natty red costume: he's drawing out of doors, but it's as if he's carted his whole studio outside (Raphael's *Three Graces* (1504, Chantilly)[56] is a key image in *Three Immoral Women* – the Pope is seen examining it closely with a magnifying glass in classic voyeur/ art connoisseur style, until he's embarrassingly interrupted by one his lackeys).[57] And as soon as Raphael is introduced, the recurring theme of voyeurism in Borowczyk's cinema comes up: Raphael spies on the lovers through a telescope (maybe, as Borowczyk has suggested elsewhere, all artists are voyeurs, or maybe it's that voyeurism is inextricably a part of art).

But *Three Immoral Women* is as happy to depict scenes of Margherita alone, wandering around the classical ruins of Rome, as it is of sex or painting. Margherita sports a semi-transparent white dress throughout much of *Three Immoral Women,* and she looks as attractive as possible. So of course she's washing herself, too – no Walerian Borowczyk film is complete without a scene of women bathing. The film's sound's classic Borowczyk, too: bells chiming, organ music, and period Renaissance music. But much of the first few scenes are near-silent, with atmospheric sound like birdsong.

When *Three Immoral Women* cuts from the classical ruins in sunlight to Raphael's studio, the art direction heats up three thousand degrees: this is Walerian Borowczyk in his element: creating an artist's studio in Renaissance times, with the artist and his model in the studio. He could make two or three films just about this scenario on its own.

55 The film puts some of the well-known images of Pompeiian erotica onto the walls of the ruins surrounding Raphael, as well as erotic Renaissance art.

56 As well *The Three Graces*, other famous Raphael paintings quoted in *Three Immoral Women* include *The Liberation of St Peter.*

57 Michelangelo is shown creating his own, homoerotic version of *The Three Graces*, when he has three youths (nude, of course) posing holding apples.

Certainly Walerian Borowczyk and his team (Bernard Daillencourt, Borowczyk's regular collaborator, was the DP; and Jacques D'Ovidio was production designer), have gone to town on the art direction and design of this particular studio. It's jammed with artefacts (still-lifes of musical instruments), rolls of paper, hanging tapestries, busts, statuary. Every image is a carefully composed still-life. And it's in the Italian Renaissance, an era Borowczyk and his team know backwards. *Three Immoral Women* is riot of eclectic props: boxes and bejewelled caskets; fruit; paintings; cloth; curtains; mandolins; hats.

And Margherita is being fucked from the back again – this time by the painter Raphael (and she's lying on his work table, right on top of his sketches, of course, which she screws up – art and sex and life – you can see the art historians in the audience squirming in their seats – either with pleasure at the fusion of sex and art, or with horror as priceless works of art and ruined).[58] Sure it's a cliché upon a cliché, but somehow Borowczyk can make this kind of scene work.

The film now shifts to the Vatican, with scenes evoking the power of Catholic Rome – cardinals in red, and the Pope (Jean Martinelli), who visit the studio of Michelangelo Buonaroti (Roger Lefrere). The gay imagery – of Michelangelo horsing around with naked youths – is a little predictable, but also demonstrates how Borowczyk is not shy of putting in quite a bit of male nudity as well as female nudity (it would be good to see more of the Michelangelo story – there's a whole other film there, which Borowczyk is better qualified than almost anyone to make).

The scenes of the Pope and cardinals discussing art and commissions with a near-naked Michelangelo[59] are certainly a departure from your average Hollywood version (Chuck Heston and Rex Harrison in Hollywood's *The Agony and the Ecstasy*, for instance).

With the scenes in Raphael's studio, Walerian Borowczyk and his production team have recreated one of the recurring scenes of art cinema: the artist and his model. What makes *Three Immoral Women* a little more intriguing than your average arty flick is that Borowczyk

58 Raphael's homosexuality isn't part of this film – that given over to Michelangelo.
59 Michelangelo's costume is a comic expression of masculinity.

and co. have delivered heightened versions of the cliché: Margherita is modelling for angels, Madonnas and Eve, for instance (and the staging, the props, the art direction and the rest is also quirky, as one expects from Walerian Borowczyk).

And Walerian Borowczyk and his team thankfully avoid many of the clichés of artist and model scenes, too. This is opulent filmmaking, by a filmmaker who is clearly really enjoying himself. Borowczyk is completely at home in this environment: an artist's studio in Renaissance Italy.

Of course, the artist and model scene turns into something erotic – this is a Walerian Borowczyk film: and there's the addition of a voyeur, of course (this time, it's the shaven-headed, vain, pompous and horny art patron and banker Bernardo Bini, played with gusto by Jean-Claude Dreyfus). Peeping through the keyhole, he watches while Raphael pulls up Margherita's dress and strokes her round ass (and gets stabbed in the eye with a paintbrush for his trouble – there's always a cost to voyeurism). The camera lingers over a big close-up of Margherita's pretty bottom, and Raphael squeezing it and kissing it.

In the second half of the first episode of 1979's *Three Immoral Women,* the narrative shifts to the Vatican rooms which Raphael, Michelangelo and other artists are decorating[60] (the frescoes Raphael's working on include *The Liberation of St Peter* (1512-14) in the Stanza dell'Eliodoro, used for private audiences; the theme of St Peter was linked to Pope Julius II). The film's designers have created an extraordinary set of new pine wood structures – scaffolding, ladders, platforms and corridors, with special doors and entrances for people visiting the artists at work. The idea being, Raphael explains to the Pope, to keep visitors out.

There is a remarkable scene of Bernardo Bini visiting Raphael at work on the frescoes (hoping to meet Margherita). The space becomes an erotic labyrinth of corridors, windows, ladders, doors, rotating boxes and traps operated by levers.[61] There's also an elaborate system of mirrors and periscopes which enable Raphael and Margherita to spy

60 There's a mad painter, played by Pierre Benedetti, who chucks black paint at some canvas, recalling action painters such as Jackson Pollock.

61 Reminiscent of the crazy house scene in *The Lady From Shanghai* (1948), or an art installation by Alice Aycock or Mary Miss.

on their victim down below in the wooden labyrinth (Raphael is acting like a film director here, feeding La Fornarina the lines she calls down to Bini).

This is truly bizarre filmmaking – it's way beyond conventional drama or the usual art film. It's Walerian Borowczyk's own brand of surrealism and the poetry of cinema. And the violence underneath the scene (the link between violence/ death and sex is never far from the surface in Borowczyk's cinema) is very apparent: Bini is tripped and spun, and is thrust out of the wood maze into a wooden box of flour (white here symbolizing the fool, and death), ruining that gorgeous red costume and hat.[62]

When Margherita and Raphael get freaky again, it's depicted in Walerian Borowczyk's idiosyncratic style: only Borowczyk could – or would – depicted a sex scene (of two people fucking from the back) in a *single shot* focussing on the lovers' *bare feet* kicking around a *Roman helmet*, ending with an orgasm. No cutaways, no establishing shots, no close-ups of bodies or faces, just bare feet and a helmet.

Margherita, though, plays the courtesan in the Vatican – sleeping with Raphael, and also with Bernardo Bini, the patron (plus she has her lover Tomaso back in the Roman *campagna*). Margherita is leading the narrative, she is in control. As played by the wonderful Marina Pierro, Margherita is a woman millions of heterosexual guys couldn't help falling for.

She visits Bini in his rooms, pretending to Raphael that she's going to see her parents: before making love, they contemplate a selection of images from a famous series of Italian pornographic drawings (similar to the *I Modi* (*The Ways*) by Agostino Carracci). As Bini shows Margherita each image,[63] she decides whether she wants to try a particular sexual position. There is a narrative purpose to this, though: Margherita (eventually) chooses a position which has her lying on her back, Bini lifting her buttocks, with her leg in the air. Thus, when Bini is fucking her she uses her toes to pull out a wooden draw in a high

62 Later, Margherita is haunted by a dream of her father being covered in white, a dream of death.

63 The mechanics of the presentation of the erotic prints evokes early cinema, with Bini pulling on cords which change the slides which're projected on a screen. Technology has of course always been vital in the dissemination of pornography – and of cinema itself.

wooden chest which contains poisoned cherries on top of cakes[64] (the element of poisoning is completely in tune with Borowczyk's evocations of an arcane institution – in this case, the Vatican in Rome).

Margherita is like the clever, resourceful girls in fairy tales – skilfully manipulating the monster and distracting him so she can orchestrate his demise. Except in the hands of a filmmaker like Walerian Borowczyk, the distraction occurs right in the middle of sex.

Meanwhile, Raphael is painting Adam, Eve and the serpent – with Margherita, a.k.a. La Fornarina, as Eve, corrupting the men in her life (the scenes are intercut – Raphael is a painter who paints non-stop, including through the night, lying on his back on the wooden scaffolding to paint the serpent).[65] Margherita gets the better of both Raphael and Bini – Raphael is poisoned, too.

✤

There's a wonderful musical montage at this point, when Margherita and Raphael are re-united (before she poisons him): to Renaissance trumpets and drums,[66] the film assembles brief images of fruit, of food, of eating, of Margherita in close-up, of many paintings (including Adam and Eve) – oh, and sex, of course.

The first episode of *Three Immoral Women* closes with Margherita re-united with her lover in the Classical Roman ruins, having played powerful men at their own game and won. The final images are of Margherita and Tomaso caressing each other among the ruins, with Tomaso pouring the jewels and coins that Margherita obtained from Bini over her body in repeated close-ups. And it's typical of Borowczyk that the final shot is a giant close-up right between Margherita's thighs.

---

64 To set this up *Three Immoral Women* depicts Bini visiting an apothecary.
65 That the movie puts the artist on his back may be a deliberate echo of Margherita lying on her back when she makes love.
66 Music was credited to Philippe d'Aram and Olivier Dassault.

MARCELINE

The second episode of *Three Immoral Women,* 'Marceline', focusses on Gaëlle Legrand as a young woman in 19th century France, the daughter of bourgeois parents. The episode was based on a story by Walerian Borowczyk's regular collaborator André Pieyre de Mandiargues. Again, this episode is a slice of prime Walerian Borowczyk: only Borowczyk would depict an extended scene of a young woman masturbating on a lawn with her pet rabbit.

In the second part of *Three Immoral Women*, Walerian Borowczyk and his team depict a world of ferocious animosity between children and parents. The mother, Madame Cain (France Rumilly) and father, Mr Cain (Yves Gourvil), and the family maid Floka (Lisbeth Arno) are truly grotesque: the film exaggerates their sadism with manic laughter and venal behaviour worthy of the Borgias. These are very nasty people, ugly additions to Borowczyk's gallery of loony, out-size characters. Borowczyk doesn't hold back when it comes to depicting how truly revolting people can be to each other.

Yet again, Walerian Borowczyk depicts an oppressive system and how an individual manages to survive in it. It's Communist Poland all over again, but this time set in 19th century middle-class France, with healthy doses of Surrealism. It's the individual versus authority, the lone voice in the repressive regime, and it's youth versus age, children versus parents.

Gaëlle Legrand[67] plays the young, virginal but sexually curious daughter of the family, an innocent in a world of corruption and violence. Marceline is victimized by everyone around her – her parents, the maid, and the butcher. Marceline's only crime seems to be her youth or her innocence. Her very existence, as a young, sexual woman, seems to threaten the bourgeois regime of the period. Or maybe it's the fact that she's a little too attached to her pet bunny rabbit, and uses it in her masturbation fantasies.

Certainly the scene where Marceline masturbates with the rabbit

67 It was Gaëlle Legrand's first movie – a helluva debut! A demanding role in many respects. Unlike quite a few actors in a Borowczyk movie, Legrand went on to appear in many other productions.

between her legs on the lawn in the Summer sun, early on in the episode, is one of the more outrageous chapters in the Walerian Borowczyk cinematic *Book of Erotica*.[68] Framing is everything here, as the film includes a parasol prop which partially obscures Marceline's naked body and the rabbit nibbling at her vulva. The film also selects very low angles throughout the scene, a kind of rabbit's-eye-view of female masturbation, the camera squints along Marceline's nude form from between her legs, to her breasts and face. Borowczyk knows better than anyone that *selective* images of the body or a sex act are classic elements in erotica (but he's not averse to having plenty of wholly nude people in his films too). The movie lingers over Marceline caressing her breasts in close-up at length, erecting her nipples.

The rabbit masturbation scene is truly Out There, and it's made even more peculiar because of Walerian Borowczyk's touches – the clever framing and camera angles, the performance of the actress, the near-silence (just Marceline's gasps and whispered encouragements to her pet rabbit). And as it's masturbation, of course it has to be interrupted – by the maid calling Marceline to dinner. A huge number of Borowczyk's sex scenes are interrupted – just as they are in erotic art throughout history.

But this second episode of *Three Immoral Women* is the most violent of the three episodes in a way, because of the way that Marceline takes revenge on her oppressors. She kills her mother, her father, and her rapist, the butcher, Petrus (Hassane Fall, who was the butler Ifany in *The Beast*), hangs himself. It's as if her unbridled expression of female sexuality and *jouissance*, masturbating with the rabbit, disturbs the bourgeois household to its foundations, and the punishment is severe. Women can't have fun – and especially not on their own.

There are two punishments eked out: the first comes when poor Marceline unknowingly eats her pet rabbit which the family has cooked for her. In the second, Marceline enacts her vengeance in a spectacular fashion. Marceline is depicted as a virginal innocent: she wears a

68 The 'Marceline' episode opens with the girl dancing on the lawn with the rabbit. One can imagine the auditions for this film: 'what do I have to do, Monsieur Borowczyk?' 'Oh, you have to strip off in a garden in the sun and masturbate with a rabbit.' 'Oh.' 'Yes.' 'OK, *d'accord*, I'll do it!'

white lacy blouse, a white skirt, and white socks. And when she's raped later, the filmmakers spread plenty of blood around her crotch (blood on white cloth is a favourite with filmmakers everywhere, from low budget horror filmmakers to the latest Hollywood blockbuster).

Three Immoral Women is careful to show that Marceline hasn't done anything wrong. Masturbating with her pet rabbit is depicted as a pastoral, innocent pastime – it's not meant to be sleazy or repressed or even weird. So the punishment of killing and cooking her pet rabbit and feeding it to her unknowingly is a viciously cruel act by her parents. All of the adults in that dinner scene – Madame Cain, Mr Cain, and Floka the maid – are shown as truly malignant and vindictive. And they're kind of pointlessly vindictive (they don't offer much of a reason for killing and cooking Marceline's rabbit). The adults have the senseless adherence to violence of characters in *Alice's Adventures In Wonderland* (a favourite with the Surrealists). Mr Cain says something about Marceline having to grow up and lose her childish ways, but it's vague and unconvincing.

The 'Marceline' episode of *Three Immoral Women* has enough extreme elements on its own for a whole film – masturbation, murder, rape, and a kind of cannibalism. The setting – dreamy, sun-filled, rural and bourgeois – enhances the violence and extremity of emotion. The visual imagery is pastoral, glowing, in a word, *pretty* – as if Borowczyk and his team were shooting an adaption of Jane Austen or a shampoo commercial. Very genteel it all is – lovely costumes, a big old house, maids and dinners. And shot at the height of Summer, with the lawn and flowers and trees looking their best.

The film's sympathies are wholly with Marceline: the second episode is wholly seen from her point-of-view. Through her eyes the world of adults is depicted as a realm of hideous individuals – selfish, lascivious, law-bound, and above all, repressed. Repression is of course one of Walerian Borowczyk's targets, and here he attacks it aggressively. Sexual repression is part of the malaise at the heart of the bourgeois West, with its ridiculous bourgeois families with their claustrophobic rituals, meaningless manners and oppressive attitudes. Borowczyk is fairly Freudian here: if a society is wrong in its sex (its sexuality), as Lawrence Durrell or D.H. Lawrence might put it, it will be wrong everywhere.

One of the goals of the second episode of *Three Immoral Women* is to demonstrate how damaging it is to suppress or punish expressions of sexual feeling. Walerian Borowczyk is clear which side he is on: there are two sex scenes: one is a dreamy, pastoral masturbation fantasy which is, crucially, gentle as well as pleasurable, when Marceline masturbates with her pet rabbit.

The other is where Marceline is raped by the black butcher Petrus. Marceline's sexual curiosity and pleasure is punished twice (there is the race element, too, of course, which also cropped up in films such as *The Beast*, with its negative stereotyping of black men).

The rape scene takes place in that mythical Borowczykian realm – a perpetual twilight, not day, not night. And it's very much amongst the animals: Marceline wanders into the abattoir with its hanging meat, and Petrus corners her there (when Marceline leaves the house, it's half-naked, of course, and half-naked European style – from the waist down). He attacks her in a sheep pen, having her from behind right on top of some sheep (I bet the actors loved that – shooting for hours and hours fully naked in amongst twenty frisky sheep and prickly hay. No, these aren't animatronic sheep, either. One imagines that Legrand and Fall were cursing Borowczyk by the end of the day's shooting. You come down here and dick around in the hay naked!).

One of the prominent motifs in the 'Marceline' episode of *Three Immoral Women* is a cluster of linked elements: meat, food, cooking, eating, killing, sacrifice and animals. *Three Immoral Women* explores the familiar tropes of lambs to the slaughter, virgins and animals being sacrificed, and the links between eating and killing. There a scene of animals on hooks being cut open at the slaughter house. Depicting the bourgeoisie as a bunch of cannibals, or having cannibals eat the bourgeoisie, occurs in other movies of the time – in Jean-Luc Godard's *Weekend* (1967), for instance, or Pier Paolo Pasolini's *Pigsty* (1969).

So when Marceline enacts her revenge on her oppressors, it reverses the sacrifice and violence: Petrus, thinking Marceline is dead, hangs himself above the sheep, but he isn't quite dead when Marceline climbs down from the loft. He calls for Marceline to get his knife, on the ground, to cut him down, but Marceline instead takes it up, and sneaks away, leaving Petrus to die.

And then it's *Bluebeard* time, a fairy tale vengeance, every teenager's dream come true: Marceline goes up to her parents' room and cuts the throats of her parents. The imagery here is iconic and brutal: Marceline is naked, holding a knife, with blood spattered on her; blood spurts from her parents onto photographs of their ancestors (Marceline throwing Petrus's cap and knife onto the corpses implicates the butcher as the murderer). Marceline becomes the butcher, the priest of the sacrifice.

And it all becomes one extraordinary tale when, in the final scene, Marceline, now in a boarding school run by nuns, tells the tale of her bunny rabbit to her friends who gather around her after bedtime. It becomes a gruesome tale shared amongst friends. Extraordinary.

MARIE

The third episode of *Three Immoral Women* ('Marie'), is set in the present day, in contemporary Paris. The third of the three 'immoral women' is a young wife of a successful businessman, played by Pascale Christophe (Christophe was memorable as Istvan the page in *Immoral Tales*). It's the story of a kidnapping, and involves a woman, her husband, and her kidnapper – oh, and her dog. Like the rabbit in the second episode in *Three Immoral Women,* Marie's dog Caesar is her faithful friend and helper.

Much of the film consists of scenes set on Parisian streets and in the kidnapper's van, as Marie is snatched on the street near a shop, while her husband waits in his car. There are endless shots of Caesar the dog running through the streets of Paris. Much of the 'Marie' episode is shot with very long lenses, and looks as if the film crew didn't have permission to shoot on the locations, so situated themselves far away from the actors. (There's an electronic score to the third episode, by Philippe d'Aram and Olivier Dassault., which suits the contemporary setting, but isn't particularly distinctive; it also crops up in the the second part, where Marceline searches for her rabbit by the waterfall).

The first scenes evoke Marie and her husband (Henri Piégay) as a bourgeois couple – nice clothes, nice car, nice house, nice life. The husband is an art dealer (older, well-dressed, wearing spectacles), and there are more images of paintings. The husband drops Marie off at a bookstore so she can collect a book, but Antoine (Gérard Ismaël), a scruffy no-good in his 30s, kidnaps her by pulling her into a pile of cardboard boxes he's constructed on the sidewalk (very silly – especially when they edge towards his van).

It's a story of power games, with the kidnapper demanding money from the husband; and it's two men fighting over a woman. So there are scenes of Marie telephoning her husband, while Antoine trains a rifle on her, and listens to her conversation on a radio, scenes of Marie meeting her husband by a fish stall, and scenes of Marie buying the kidnapper newspapers at a newsstand.

As with the previous two episodes, the viewpoint – and the film-maker's sympathy – is strictly with Marie. And the revenge that Marie enacts on her oppressors is violent, although she doesn't do it herself – her faithful hound does! The climax is certainly unusual (and, it has to be said, filmed not particularly convincingly):[69] it's Marie's dog who rescues her, after she's been driven to a warehouse by the kidnapper. The dog attacks Antoine – in the crotch, of course, so the guy bleeds to death, rolling over and over and crying in agony – rolling and staggering so far he ends up tumbling into the River Seine.

So far so good; the movie has left any kind of realism far behind (from the moment the dog magically follows Marie's scent all the way across Paris to the warehouse). But then Walerian Borowczyk and his

69 Like Jean-Luc Godard, Borowczyk doesn't seem bothered by shooting action scenes, or spending too much time on an action-fuelled climax to his films. In contrast to Hollywood, which spends a lot of time and money on climactic scenes, stretching them out endlessly.

team add another death: the dog attacks Marie's husband. He too is bitten in the crotch, and writhes in pain all the way to the river, and topples in. It doesn't matter if anything's unbelievable at this point in this particular movie, because it's been full of larger-than-life events and images anyway. (For instance, how does the husband know where Antoine has taken his wife? Oh, who cares?).

Marie's reaction to her husband's death seems at first to be fear and anxiety, but changes to relief and even celebration. It's as if Marie wants to punish her husband as well as the kidnapper: maybe he's not the husband she thought he was, maybe he let her go too easily, maybe he should have protected her properly. Whatever: the third episode ends with a naked girl and her dog, embracing in the back of the van. (It's certainly odd that when her husband drives up in his Jaguar and yells for Marie, she doesn't say anything, but remains in the back of the van. She seems to be willing the dog to attack her husband).

There are two sex scenes in the third episode of *Three Immoral Women* – the first is when the kidnapper orders Marie to strip and rapes her; the second is where Marie, still naked, cavorts with her dog in the back of the van (Borowczyk is one of the few major filmmakers who really enjoys depicting sex between women and animals). The rape scene is intercut with garbage being collected by a night crew: the montage here, between rape and images of refuse being squashed in a garbage truck, is blunt and to the point.

The third episode of *Three Immoral Women* – 'Marie' – is easily the weakest, and the first episode is easily the most successful (and enjoyable), not least because it features the wonderful Marina Pierro (and most of the budget seems to have been spent on the first part, so that the last part, set in contemporary Paris, looks decidedly low budget). That's reflected in the length of each episode: 'Margherita' is around 50 minutes; 'Marceline' is about 40 minutes; and 'Marie' is around 24 minutes.

The third episode is still very much a film by Walerian Borowczyk, but it's as if the contemporary setting is just too pedestrian, too everyday to stimulate the filmmakers' talents (*Love Rites*, though, is also set in present-day Paris, but Borowczyk and his team turn Paris into a fantastical place, a place of myth and dream).[70] But there's more the sense in the third part that Borowczyk and his team are simply going through the motions of making a film, and the Borowczyk flourishes are thin on the ground.

But, as with other multi-part movies, it doesn't matter too much, because the previous two episodes in *Three Immoral Women* are so strong. Maybe if the third episode had been sandwiched between the other two it might've strengthened the film overall.

On the other hand, even if the second and third episodes sucked, the first was so striking and original, it wouldn't damage the film too much. You can allow a filmmaker moments where they're coasting if they deliver some extraordinary moments the rest of the time.

70 Michael Richardson remarked that 'in all of his films, Borowczyk creates a world that is simultaneously apart from this one but inseparable from it' (108).

8

THE ART OF LOVE

1983's *Ars Amandi* (*The Art of Love*) was produced by Walerian Borowczyk and company in Italy, loosely based on Ovid's famous love poems, and set in ancient Rome (in 8 A.D.). Borowczyk had visited similar territory with the first episode in *Three Immoral Women. The Art of Love* was co-written with Wilhelm Buchheim and Enzo Ungari.[71] *Ars Amandi* starred Borowczyk regular Marina Pierro (billed above the title) as the bored wife Claudia of a Roman soldier Macarius (Michele Placido) who has an affair with Cornelius (Philippe Taccini), one of the young men Ovid (Massimo Girotti) is instructing in the art of love in Rome. Marcel Albertini, Jacques Nahum, Mario Lupi, Camillio Teti and Ugo Tucci were the producers; Noël Véry and Borowczyk were DPs; Luis Enriquez Bacalov provided the music; Luciana Marinucci did the wardrobe; Gianni Ricci was AD; and Boro is also credited as editor.

This is Marina Pierro's film: she looks stunning (what a body!), and sports a fabulous array of costumes (and she was only 23 when *The Art of Love* was made). And she fulfils the potential of a terrific role. It's a movie of a love affair between a director and his leading lady, or between a director, his costume designer (Luciana Marinucci),[72] the make-up and hair assistants, and his leading actress, or between a director and *clothes* (courtesy of Luciana Marinucci). Pierro wears a fabulous collection of dresses – many of them consist of layers of gauzes in white or black. These are not so much dresses as layers of transparent cloth. (And a superb collection of headdresses, another Borowczykian specialty, including a giant grey feather hat). *The Art of Lerv* gets to the point straight away: it opens with a lengthy shot of Claudia bathing naked in an elaborate and unusual bath which includes a fish tank. (the scene introduces the star, the eroticism, the ancient Roman setting, the luxury, the narcissism, and the eccentricity – not so many movies open with the star bathing naked).

The Art of Love moves from scenes of Ovid lecturing to an assembly of youths in central Rome to various erotic entanglements and sexual dreams. (It's not all guys, either: the female students pile into the lecture hall later on, with Claudia of course arriving stylishly

71 Enzo Ungari worked on Bernardo Bertolucci's *1900* and *The Last Emperor*.
72 Luciana Marinucci deserves a lot of the credit for making *The Art of Love* look so good.

late). Ovid (43 B.C. - 17 A.D.) was one of the three celebrated ancient Roman poets, alongside Virgil and Horace. His *Ars Amatoria* exists in three books, published in 1 B.C. (there were other editions and books). Ovid's most famous work is *Metaphoroses.* Ovid's a big influence on the historical periods that Walerian Borowczyk loves to explore – the Middle Ages and the Renaissance (he is cited many times in courtly love poetry, for instance, or the writings of Dante Alighieri and Francesco Petrarch).

The structure of the whole film is based around Ovid's lectures on love: many times the picture is illustrating Ovid's teaching, which continues in lengthy sequences of voiceover over Borowczyk's montage editing. *The Art of Love* probably has more voiceover than any other Borowczyk film (Cornelius also has plenty of voiceover, as he further outlines Ovid's teachings, and Claudia does too).

Ovid lectures his students on how to love, how to treat women, how to seduce and entrance, and how to talk to their beloveds. Much of the film consists of Walerian Borowczyk's signature montage style of editing which illustrates Ovid's lectures: as Ovid talks of love, the film cuts to couples in beds, for example, or lovers preparing themselves, or bathing, or sending flowers. After the feast, for instance, there's one of Borowczyk's special nighttime sequences: a rapid montage of multiple story-lines, following a variety of couples having sex, or creeping along dark corridors to assignations.

The Art of Love is also Walerian Borowczyk's chance to mount some ancient world epic spectacle: he's doing his bit of *Quo Vadis?*, *Ben-Hur, Spartacus,* and *The Fall of the Roman Empire.* So there are evocations of Roman centurions, a procession, soldiers on campaign in snowy hills, Roman feasts, a Roman mythological ritual, and even an apocalyptic climax where Rome burns, masonry and pillars topple, and poor Claudia rushes around in panic.

The Art of Love is low budget by Hollywood standards, but it does contain tons of props, furniture, costumes, extras, animals, fire, snow and smoke effects. It uses existing architecture, but also sets beautifully decorated with frescoes and walls in reds and oranges.

There's a link between *The Art of Love* and the films of Pier Paolo

Pasolini: a veteran of Italian cinema, Massimo Girotti, who plays Ovid in *The Art of Love*, was King Creon in *Medea* (1969), and the father in *Theorem* (1968). *Theorem* also starred Laura Betti as the maid (Betti, who played Clio, the mother of Macarius in *Ars Amandi*, is a well-known figure in Italian movies, and was a fervent supporter of Pasolini).

The Art of Love is violent too: General Laurentius (Philippe Lemaire) strangles his wife when she's caught fucking a youth (and he beat her earlier); Macarius slays Cornelius when he returns to find him with his wife Claudia; and in a drunken stupor Rufus slashes at a bust of fruit with a sword.

The Art of Love is art directed by the maestro and assistants to perfection: it's a film of vases of flowers, mirrors, statues, bowls of fruit, boxes, brass vessels, paintings and pillars. The lighting is typical of the early Eighties: heaps of backlight, and glowing highlights. It might be a Kate Bush or Prince music video.

There are many erotic moments and sex scenes in *The Art of Love*, as one would expect from Walerian Borowczyk: Roman orgies, of course, Claudia bathing in a bath surrounded by a fish tank, her black servant Sepora (Mireille Pame) kissing and fellating the phallus on a statue of Priapus (plus one of the nobles, General Laurentius), Macarius's mother Clio (Laura Betti) sucking a guy, and various couples writhing on beds.

Perhaps the oddest sex scene in *Ars Amandi* is Claudia's dream of copulating with a bull in a misty, smoky forest, as she imagines herself as Pasiphæ, Queen of Crete; in this bizarre ritual, surrounded by Roman guards and heralds with trumpets, Claudia climbs (naked, of course) into a wooden replica of a cow, and presents her buttocks through a circular hole at the rear to a man dressed in a giant wooden bull's head and wielding a huge bull's pizzle.[73]

Yes, but it's not that simple: the movie cuts from Claudia on her bed fantasizing, to Claudia as Pasiphæ inside the bull, to the man

73 There's a wonderful depiction of the Bull Court at Knossos in the ancient world novel *The King Must Die* about the Theseus myth by Mary Renault. *The King Must Die* also contains a reference to a woman hiding inside the wooden bull used for training so her lover could fuck her.

fucking her,[74] to Ovid narrating the scene in the lecture hall, and finally to a real bull and cow going at it in a field (in a different setting). Wow – Borowczyk's editing here is extraordinary. Sometimes the montages in Boro's films are so rapid and so deft, you're not quite sure what you've seen. It's so many layers of narration, of dreams within stories.

In the museum Sepora fondles the genitals of a horse, and in Claudia's imagination a woman caresses a real horse's cock, shot from the same low angle (the museum seems to feature plaster reproductions of statues, a common way of displaying sculptures). It's not all sex in *The Art of Love*, though: the film illustrates Ovid's teaching on dealing with illness in a lengthy sequence (on how to look after your beloved when she's sick in bed), and on topics such as old age, preparing one's body for love, and adultery.

The Art of Love has Walerian Borowczyk's customary high art allusions (a visit to a gallery filled with statuary, references to ancient Roman, Renaissance and French Neo-Classical paintings),[75] and his acute painterly sensibility. He also squeezes in references to Leda and the swan (a favourite Boro topic) – and even features a live swan flapping about (plus children – as Leda's offspring Castor and Pollux).[76] And he recreates the famous paintings of Giuseppe Arcimboldo of a man's face constructed from fruit (but in three dimensions, as a bust).[77]

Prayers and ancient Roman ritual are another aspect of *The Art of Love*: Claudia has her own shrines and altars (including secret ones in cupboards), while Claudia's maid Sepora prays to a statue of Priapus which includes a golden phallus which she kisses. It's classic Borowczyk when Claudia makes Sepora swear an oath by putting her finger on a small painting of an erection (it's the famous painting of Priapus from Pompeii, which also appeared in *Three Immoral Women*).

The Art of Love is filled with details on daily life in ancient Rome,

74 There are of course close-ups of the red pizzle entering Claudia.
75 For instance, Jacques-Louis David's famous *The Oath of Horatii* (1784, Louvre, Paris).
76 This goes by in a flash, but it's beautiful.
77 Giuseppe Arcimboldo (1527-93) was a painter from Milan taken up by Salvador Dali and the Surrealists. Arcimboldo's influence also appears in Jan Svankmajer's films.

too: it's not only rounds of coupling; there are many domestic details, and the film offers a fresh look at everyday life in the ancient city. Some of it has a documentary feel, and it's very different from big Hollywood epics about the period, like *Cleopatra* or *Spartacus*, where there's far less of how people really might have lived. In the Hollywood epic movie, people stand about talking in those gigantic sets, while Borowczyk's settings do appear lived in.[78]

However, *The Art of Love* seems a little sloppier than some of Walerian Borowczyk's best work. The acting, apart from Marina Pierro and Massimo Girotti's Ovid, is ropey, and some of the action is staged with a haughty or clumsy indifference (maybe that's again partly because so much of the film is shot with a handheld camera, and the dubbing, in the English dub, is poor). Apparently, the Italian producers (credited as Marcel Albertini, Jacques Nahum and Ugo Tucci) added some hardcore sex to the picture (including faking letters from Borowczyk), which didn't help.[79] Adding sex scenes to existing pictures is quite common in exploitation, mondo and underground cinema.

The Art of Love does look at times like an excuse for some softcore porn (it recalls the infamous Bob Guccione/ Penthouse *Caligula* in this respect, which came out a few years earlier. *Caligula* was also filmed in Italy (an American-Italian production), also set in ancient Rome, and also had extra sex scenes added to it).[80] But *The Art of Love* is about love, and desire, not sex.

So *The Art of Love* isn't quite the movie Walerian Borowczyk intended – apart from re-editing and additions by the producers, there were also blurs and cuts imposed by censors. (Borowczyk does seem fated to be one of those filmmakers, like Orson Welles, to have their films interferred with after they'd completed them. Actually, almost all filmmakers of commercial and theatrically-released movies *do not* have

78 For Cathal Tohill and Pete Tombs, *The Art of Love* 'is kept expertly on the boil with an endless series of fascinating images showing private life in ancient Rome in all its minutiæ. You can't keep your eyes away from the screen for a second, it's so rich in colour and incident' (226-7).

79 It's ironic that someone would want to add *more* sex to a Walerian Borowczyk film! Usually most people want to take it out.

It's easy to spot the added footage: it looks different (lighting, set-ups, costumes, etc), and features people, in the orgy, for example, who don't appear anywhere else in *The Art of Love*.

80 Walerian Borowczyk is on a whole other level from a filmmaker such as Tinto Brass, the hapless 'director' of *Caligula*, though.

final cut – even the ones you'd think would, being gifted veterans. Movies are 99.99% of the time owned by the people who paid for them. Which means that even geniuses like Borowczyk or Welles could have movies taken away from them and re-cut. It's heart-breaking).

The Art of Love is given a false action climax out of keeping with the rest of the movie: Ovid is arrested by Roman soldiers in a panic-ridden scene which includes a woman giving birth (!) like some silly Hollywood disaster movie. Then it's fire, smoke, columns toppling, and poor Claudia rushing about or standing frozen in fear. Why all this craziness? As *The Art of Love* presents it, Macarius is so pissed with Claudia tupping the youth Cornelius, he takes it out on Ovid, who's encouraged Cornelius in the art of love (and he's already slain the hapless, naked Cornelius).

Doesn't work, does it? No need for it, is there?

The coda of *Ars Amandi*, set in the present day, doesn't help, either: it's a cliché-ridden and lame attempt at linking the ancient world with the present, as characters from the past crop up in modern day guises (Macarius, for instance, turns up as a Catholic priest).

In the coda, Claudia wakes from a nightmare in her Land Rover, as she's travelling from an archaeological dig in Pompeii back to Paris (maybe echoing the filmmakers' own journey after they'd wrapped the movie – 'let's get back to Paris!'). The hints of murder mystery and archæology just don't add anything to the movie. It all has the look of something imposed by film producers.

Most of the coda takes place at a busy roadside, and later a village: Claudia gives a priest (played by Michele Placido, who was Claudia's husband Macarius) a ride to his church. A newspaper that the priest reads at the church door reveals that Cornelius has murdered the chief archaeologist, played by Massimo Girotti, who was Ovid. As Claudia drives off into the sunset (accompanied by some bland Euro-pop), the movie ends.

⚜

The Art of Love isn't one of Boro's great works – it doesn't all fit together like *The Beast* or *Goto: Island of Love*, or have their dramatic or emotional power, but it does have a lot going for it: the sublime Marina Pierro, for a start, a seductive presence who's in most scenes. Pierro alone is worth the price of admission. And there are plenty of Borowczykian touches, plenty of eccentric moments, and some dazzling technical aspects, like the luscious art direction and the rapid montages. Yeah, and *The Art of Love* also has *lots* of sex.

9

EMMANUELLE 5

I was prepared for the worst when I ordered the DVD of *Emmanuelle 5* from Amazon – I'd read the reviews of this particular *bête noire* in the Borowczyk *œuvre*. The film didn't disappoint. It has every fault you can think of, and some others you didn't think possible. Certainly I will never watch the movie again – and once was too much.

If your first impression of *Emmanuelle 5* is of a truly dreadful film, you're not far wrong. It is hard to believe that the creator of masterpieces like *Blanche* and *Goto: Island of Love* had anything to do with *Emmanuelle 5*. I guess Walerian Borowczyk needed the money.

Walerian Borowczyk was hired to direct *Emmanuelle 5* by the producer Alain Siritsky,[81] working for A.S.P and Sofima. There are problems with including *Emmanuelle 5* in Borowczyk's canon. One is that there are clearly parts of the film not directed (or written) by Borowczyk (some of the soft porn sex, for instance, has the bland gloss of a bad made-for-TV movie). The Internet Movie Database credits Steve Barnett as a director. The credits for the movie, though, within the print itself, have Borowczyk as director and, crucially, as writer.[82] And the title card also comes up: 'un film de Walerian Borowczyk'. Now that *is* embarrassing.[83] The assistant director, Thierry Bazin, apparently directed many of the action scenes. Yet another problem is censorship – the version released in the United Kingdom had twelve minutes sliced out of it.

In *Emmanuelle 5*, Walerian Borowczyk was sending up his own films, and the porn industry. There are references to his earlier pictures, to Walt Disney, and the erotic objects from *Une collection particulière*. *Emmanuelle 5* globe-trots from Cannes to Paris to Las Vegas and the Seychelles. There's a film-with-a-film in *Emmanuelle 5*, called *Love Express*, which's shown at the Cannes Film Festival. *Emmanuelle 5* was later re-cut to form a pilot for the *Emmanuelle* TV series.

Emmanuelle 5 plays right into the hands of those film critics who really don't like Walerian Borowczyk's cinema, and think he was

81 Alain Siritsky is best-known as the producer of a number of television franchises focussing on sex and eroticism, including the *Justine* series, the *Passion and Romance* series, the *Sex Files* series, the *Scandal* series, and of course the *Emmanuelle* movies.
82 Howard Cohen and Alex Cunningham are also credited, and Emmanuelle Arsan's book *Emmanuelle: The Joys of a Woman*.
83 Maybe Borowczyk could've taken his name off the film, but maybe he'd lose his fee.

always a dirty old man anyway. *Emmanuelle 5* becomes the endpoint for those critics who saw a steady decline from the around 1975, the time of *The Story of Sin* and *The Beast*, onwards.

But always drawing attention to an artist's worst work is a negative way of looking at anything. It's like saying, oh, Steven Spielberg directed the flop *1941*. Er, yeah, but he also directed some extraordinary films (*Jaws, Close Encounters of the Third, E.T., Empire of the Sun, Schindler's List, Saving Private Ryan*, etc). So, to counter the critics who point to *Emmanuelle 5* and snort, we can say, yeah, but Borowczyk also made *Goto: Island of Love, Blanche, The Story of Sin* and *Immoral Tales*. And the 'continuous decline' is rubbish, too: *Love Rites,* which followed *Emmanuelle 5,* is a terrific movie, the equal of *The Story of Sin* for me.

Emmanuelle 5 is heartbreakingly bad, though – considering that Walerian Borowczyk is a genius with mind-boggling talents. Yes, Borowczyk may be sending up the porn industry with the film-with-a-film *Love Express*, and his own films, and answering some of his critics... but, somehow, that doesn't make up for such a bad movie.

Even the first two *Emmanuelle* films were far better than this.

✤

THE *EMMANUELLE* FILMS.

The *Emmanuelle* movies are instantly recognizable as classic examples of 1970s softcore porn – or the art film as porn, or the arty porn film. They were marked by exotic locations (like Bangkok or Tibet), glowing soft focus, backlit cinematography, partial or full nudity, and starred Dutch actress Sylvia Kristel (b. 1952). The first film was directed by Just Jaecklin. And the *Emmanuelle* pictures were enormously popular, playing to packed cinemas – there were a number of sequels (1975, 1977, 1984, 1986, 1988, 1992, 1994, 2000, 2001, 2003, 2004, etc), plus a TV series (*Emmanuelle In Space*, 1994), and many imitators and spoofs (some cash-in films took to using the name 'Emmanuelle' with one 'M', and there was a *Carry On Emmanuelle*). The first *Emmanuelle* drew more cinema-goers than any other French film of the Seventies, with nearly 9 million admissions.[84]

84 According to R. Prédal, *Le Cinéma Français Dupuis 1945,* Nathan, Paris, 1991. But it must have been more than that.

Emmanuelle Arsan's books launched the *Emmanuelle* movies (*Emmanuelle 5* is credited as being inspired by Arsan's book *Emmanuelle*, and includes a quotation from Arsan at the beginning). The *Emmanuelle* books were bestsellers, too. This is from *The Further Experiences of Emmanuelle*:

> Then he makes her bend her knees, to move towards him: when the moist cunt touches his prick, he inserts it, using his fingers, then takes hold of her buttocks and makes her envelop it completely.
>
> He says:
>
> 'Now ask me to make you come.'[85]

You get the idea. The *Emmanuelle* books were fairly standard European erotica – and very French, like the movies (and Walerian Borowczyk's *Emmanuelle* film, bad as it is, is very French).

The basic narrative of the first *Emmanuelle* film was a young female innocent being inducted into the wild and wonderful world of adult sexuality. It's the basic story of cult favourite *The Story of O*, and many examples of pornography, and one which Borowczyk used too.

Sylvia Kristel went from *Emmanuelle* and *La Marge* to become a star on the European art/ porn circuit, appearing in films by Alain Robbe-Grillet, Just Jaecklin's version of *The Story of O, Lady Chatterley's Lover*, and further *Emmanuelle* pictures.

✤

It was the relaxing of censorship/ film classification laws that enabled the *Emmanuelle* films – and Walerian Borowczyk's films – to receive wide releases. It was a particular historical period, around 1974, which legitimized the porn movie. It was the golden age of the X-rated movie, with 167 porn flicks being released in France in 1978. At this time, porn films accounted for more than a quarter of all film production in la France. The French government passed a law in 1976 aimed at limiting the production and release of porn films. The government wanted sex movies to go back to their marginal situation, as the Minister of Culture, Michel Gay, explained, of 10% of the market.

The films of Walerian Borowczyk, then, have to be understood in this historical and cultural context, when X-rated movies, or films with

85 E. Arsan, *The Further Experiences of Emmanuelle*, Mayflower, London, 1976, 63.

sex and nudity, took up a large amount of the market, and a large proportion of film production. Had Borowczyk begun making his feature movies ten years later or ten years earlier, they probably wouldn't contain so much sex and nudity (though no doubt some). But because he started making features around 1968, and continued through the height of the porn movie in France – the early-to-mid Seventies – helps to explain why there's plenty of flesh and fucking in *La Bête, Immoral Tales, La Marge* and *Behind Convent Walls.*

Emmanuelle Forever (Francis Leroi, 1994) is typical of the later *Emmanuelle* films. In *Emmanuelle Forever* James Bond appeared (well, George Lazenby), as well as Sylvia Kristel, though the sexploits and beautiful body were supplied by Marcella Walerstein, literally a younger incarnation of Emmanuelle (via some Tibetan magic). The story was hackneyed, the sex uninspired, the performances dire, but *Emmanuelle Forever* contained some very impressive second unit footage of Tibet that wouldn't have looked out of place in a Discovery Channel special.

✤

Back to *Emmanuelle 5.*

Apart from two scenes where Walerian Borowczyk appeared to be directing – the *Love Express* train journey and Rajid's harem – *Emmanuelle 5* looks like a film in which:

(1) Every other shot has been left out.

(2) Or maybe the editors dumped the film stock fresh from the lab into a trash can and pulled out shots at a random and slammed them onto the Moviola.

(3) Or maybe the movie was assembled using some arcane system of ancient Chaldean numerology: shot 1 here, if it's a Tuesday, then shot 98, if the Moon's in Virgo, then shot 24, if your mother was born in Lyons, then ten feet of shot 348, if you've always wanted to work in movies.

Who cares? *It stinks.*

IT IS SO BAD.

The Cannes sequence of *Emmanuelle 5* contains some of the shoddiest camerawork you'll ever see (if it's deliberate, it's a convincing illusion of the totally inept). Maybe it's meant to be like that... The montage editing is dazzling. But great editing can't save a sequence with such appalling initial footage. At the end of the sequence, Emmanuelle is dashing through the city streets near-naked, clutching her boobs, to escape a horde of (male) admirers. Even a bad *Carry On* film is more amusing than this.

In short, if the Cannes Film Festival episode is meant to be a send-up, it doesn't work on that level either. No one sets out to make a bad film, they say – that would be just dumb. But it does appear at times that Borowczyk was deliberately producing something inept (what about those stock footage shots of American aircraft carriers and helicopters?!). Maybe he had some score to settle. If so, what a waste of time.

Emmanuelle 5 is not 'so bad it's good'. It's not camp 'n' bad but really quite fun. It's not a dumb-silly-stoopid but secretly a work of genius.

No: it's a crock of shit.

Emmanuelle 5 is further wrecked by the music, dreadful bland 1980s pop (by Pierre Bachelet and Bernard LeVitte). Maybe some ætheric Bach or pounding Scarlatti would help. And the star, Monique Gabrielle, is a truly appalling actor (it didn't help that Walerian Borowczyk didn't get on with her). Oh, if only Marina Pierro was there.

The problem with Monique Gabrielle is that you *can't bear* to spend any time at all with her. Her character and acting are so dreary and obnoxious. By comparison, Sylvia Kristel in the first *Emmanuelle* films oozes mystique and charisma. (The inserts of pornography magazines in *Emmanuelle 5* are taken from *Penthouse* – Gabrielle seems to have been a *Penthouse* model. As if to emphasize the sleaziness of the *Penthouse* spreads, crumpled and tatty pages are included in the montages).

On the plus side, there are some Borowczykian flourishes in *Emmanuelle 5:* the best occur in the film-within-a-film, *Love Express* – basically, it's the Orient Express train journey, Borowczyk-style. The lighting, the props, the extreme close-ups, the fetish costumes, the nighttime setting, and naked bodies are instantly recognizable as being conjured by Borowczyk – even more so because they are orchestrated by very rapid cutting.

No one, in the middle of a sex scene, will keep cutting back to a box, or a glass of champagne, or an egg, or a purse, but Walerian Borowczyk does, all the way through the *Love Express* sequences. Only Borowczyk stages a sex scene but never once shows the action from a few paces away, in a wide shot, so the audience can see what's going on and who's doing what to whom.

Instead, Walerian Borowczyk conjures up a series of close-ups which never linger, and the montage editing presents a world of fetishized components, fleetingly glimpsed. Musically, Borowczyk employs visual repetitions (the close-ups of a waiter delivering drinks to train compartments, for instance). It's as if ten or so different sex acts are going on in a series of compartments on the train simultaneously. A Hitchcock train journey was never this wild.

Borowczyk indulges his penchant for the Little Bit Out There. A woman pisses into a jug, which an old man drinks. And it's covered with the camera on the floor, in a close-up of the woman's ass as she crouches down. That's a classic Borowczyk camera angle. (It's the 'ass angle'; it's the 'civilization du cul' of Jean-Luc Godard).

The scenes from *Love Express* are inserted into *Emmanuelle 5* and are far and away the most impressive aspects of the piece. Even so, not all of them seem to be directed by Walerian Borowczyk. The shaky helicopter shot, travelling towards Monique Gabrielle making love with a guy on a cliff overlooking the sea, that can't be Borowczyk, surely (the lovemaking's way too tame, for a start – they are standing and caressing each other's backs and shoulders). And the moment where her lover departs and she's looks bereft was repeated in the film with the thudding subtly of a hammer. Talk about padding!

Why didn't the key grip push Gabrielle off the cliff?

Cathal Tohill and Pete Tombs described the better sections of *Emmanuelle 5* as being 'like extracts from a nineteenth century novel taken straight out from the Private Collection of some wizened old libertine' (227), which's a description that could apply to many of Borowczyk's films.

The harem scene was full of Walerian Borowczyk's eye for detail, though. You can tell it's Borowczyk filming it immediately: the camera's far back, it's zoomed right in, there are floating curtains and plants between the women and the camera, which obscure the women, the women are partially naked (they wear white dresses and head-dresses), and the camera frames parts of bodies (concentrating, as one would expect in a Borowczyk film, on breasts and vulvas). It's mutual masturbation time – images of hands rubbing between thighs and lips (and, for once, that bloody abysmal music isn't grinding away). It's reminiscent of *Behind Convent Walls.*

And there are numerous cutaways to paintings (not antique ones this time, but contemporary Indian paintings, mainly of religious figures). Again, that is a Borowczykian speciality – to cut away from lovemaking to paintings.

One of the intriguing aspects of the harem sequence is the voiceover. Forget the character Rajid and the actor playing him (which you have to do to survive this movie), but listen to the narration of the prince relating how he built up his harem. Walerian Borowczyk or maybe someone else clearly wrote the voice-over and other dubbed roles after the film had been shot, in response to the footage.

Yep folks, someone slaved away in the editing room,[86] probably with the producer holding a revolver to their skull, and worked out where the film needed patching up with ADR. Then some poor schmuck had to write the blasted lines, and organize a recording session or two, and then some bozo had to contract actors to dub in those lines, and then someone mixed them into the film. *Emmanuelle 5* is full of ADR shots – shots where lines have been inserted to make sense of this meandering and hopeless story.

Hard to think of a tougher job in movies than editing the garbage of this movie.

And what about that dance number, in the middle of the film, in the rehearsal room? It's very Eighties, with the leotards and 1980s hair-dos, and might have come out of *Fame* or *Flashdance* (and, once again, the music is beyond awful). In the midst of it, in the U.K. version of the film, there are brief glimpses of sex – a black guy banging a woman

86 Nina Gilberti and Kevin Tent were the editors.

from behind and being sucked – which don't fit at all into the film. The twelve minutes lost from the British release print maybe played a part here, but *Emmanuelle 5* is one movie where restored footage wouldn't help any.

You could re-edit *Emmanuelle 5* into quite a good movie, following these steps:

(1) Delete all scenes featuring Monique Gabrielle.

(2) Drop many of the dopey scenes, like the Cannes Film Festival, and the boat journey. Alternatively, you could compress the sequence, lose the voiceover, and anything with Gabrielle in it (but actors Westburg, Shane, Dana, Khan, Miklas and all the rest aren't much better).

(3) Lose the music.

(4) Re-dub the movie (if you're going to have actors loop lines, at least do it properly).

The re-cut film would be about 15 minutes long, though.

But the *Love Express* sequences – those on the train specifically – are fine Borowczykian moments: you could just take those out of the film and you'd have an intriguing 10 minute erotic picture.

Alternatively, I guess you could watch *Emmanuelle 5* with the sound off and the music of Domenico Scarlatti or Johann Sebastian Bach playing. Or you could pretend that Walerian Borowczyk never made it, that he went from *The Art of Love* to *Love Rites*.

If you thought the Cannes Film Festival episode took some beating as Deep Shit, the last couple of reels of *Emmanuelle 5* are even worse: Emmanuelle goes East (as usual in the *Emmanuelle* films), this time visiting the fictional island ruled by Rajid (Yaseen Khan), who sports one of the worst hairstyles ever perpetrated on celluloid (a revolting mass of wavy grey hair). He's an Indian prince with bare-chested henchmen out of *Arabian Nights* carrying machine guns, and a harem of 50 women. Emmanuelle's American billionaire lover and saviour Charles Foster (Burns Westburg) pops up from time to time (he's basically Howard Hughes with big Eighties specs).

Emmanuelle becomes part of Rajid's harem, but wisely escapes, aided by another Yank. (They escape with the help of the United States Navy (!) who winch them to safety inside a wooden hut!). And in the final scene, Foster gets to fly his Howard Hughes *Spruce Goose* plane from the desert near Las Vegas, but when it gets into difficulty – as Foster and Emmanuelle are about to fuck in the cockpit – Foster crashes and Emmanuelle bails out, achieved with some more library footage and some ropey model shots.

Well, that's the essence of the story, but this part of the movie is so appalling, it has to be seen to be believed. My kids, when they were 16, made better movies than this in the local woods with a digital video camera. The chase, involving hills, a river, trees, a helicopter, a hut, and machine guns, is some of the most inept filmmaking you'll ever see (I presume that Borowczyk wisely stayed back at the harem – or Paris – while it was being filmed). You will lose the will to live watching it.

Another aspect of *Emmanuelle 5* that ensures it's awful is the crude use of dubbing. There isn't enough coverage of each scene, or even basic shots (every shot looks like a first take, grabbed on the run, not rehearsed), so the film is cobbled together with voices dubbed on it to fuse over the cracks (the giveaway is that every time you hear a character speak, it's over another shot). And shots are repeated to add more padding. And as the shots are *so bad* in the first place, it's like adding more shit to a pile of shit.

There is one film director who was a genius at doing this – at making footage spread over into scenes with additional sounds, and that was Orson Welles. His *Othello* (1952) is a masterpiece of a movie that was shot over a very long period (three years), on a low budget and employed a number of actresses playing Desdemona. And the sound is entirely looped in *Othello*, and entirely brilliant.

But if you handed Orson Welles the footage of *Emmanuelle 5* I don't think even he would've been able to patch a 90-minute feature film out of it (though he did a genius job with found and bought footage in 1973's *F For Fake*).[87] Nor would he want to – aside from Walerian Borowczyk's eye for perverse detail and art direction, there's very little to like in *Emmanuelle 5*.

87 Actually, in mentioning *F For Fake*, the Howard Hughes character in *Emmanuelle 5* is called Charles Foster, a reference to *Citizen Kane*, of course. And an early idea for *Citizen Kane*, as Orson Welles explained in *F For Fake*, was to base it on Hughes.

10

LOVE RITES

Love Rites (*Cérémonie d'Amour*, 1988, a.k.a. *Rites of Love*, and *Queen of the Night* in the U.S.A.) had Walerian Borowczyk returning to the very familiar territory of erotic desire in a European setting (this time contemporary Paris, a Paris of the Métro, and the old streets around St Germain). It was made in French. André Pieyre de Mandiargues again provided the story (from *Tout disparaitra*). Alain Sarde, no less, was producer (Sarde's best known for working with Jean-Luc Godard).[88] Philippe Guez co-produced; the cameramen were Gérard Monceau, Jean-Paul Sergent, and Michel Zolat; costumes were by Valérie Adda; hair by Nathalie Blanc; Catherine Mazières was production manager; Gérard Grégory was AD; Alain Muslin was sound mixer; Thierry Godard did the sound; and Jean-Paul Imbert played the organ music.

Love Rites is a strange, allegorical film of power, sexual relations, sadomasochism, *fin-de-siècle* luxury and *mise-en-scène*, and high art imagery and allusions. It's a piece of classy, intellectual erotic story-telling. The film refers to Giuseppe Giachino Belli, André Gide, Abu Hamid Mohammed ibn Mohammed Al-Ghazzali and Charles Baudelaire.

I like *Love Rites* a lot. When it was released in 1988, Walerian Borowczyk was 65, but the movie has the energy and enthusiasm of someone fresh out of film school: he goes into the Métro and has his DPs aim the camera at anything that attracts him: subway trains reflected in mirrors; long lens shots through moving trains, so they appear as abstract patterns; people scurrying to and fro. There's a loose, improvized feel to the film, as if it's been grabbed on the hoof on the streets of Paris. And Marina Pierro has never looked better.

Love Rites wasn't Walerian Borowczyk's last work – he directed some episodes of the TV show *Série Rose*, and continued to make and exhibit art.

Love Rites seems to me more successful and convincing as a portrait of an obsessive and sadomasochistic erotic relationship than many other films that explore similar territory – like *Damage*, *9 1/2 Weeks*, *Fatal Attraction*, etc. Yes, and even *Last Tango In Paris*.

Love Rites focussed wholly on two people, a fashion designer, Hugo

88 Alain Sarde produced *Prénom Carmen*, *Sauve Qui Peut (La Vie)*, *Passion*, *Détective*, *Hélas Pour Moi* and *Éloge de L'Amour*.

Arnold (Mathieu Carrière), and a prostitute, Miriam Gwen (Marina Pierro). Hugo is at first fascinated by Miriam when he encounters her on the Métro; they talk, on opposite platforms in the subway, as the trains rattle back and forth between them (echoes of Jean-Luc Godard's *Masculin/ Féminine,* and *Last Tango In Paris*); their relationship becomes physical when they embrace on the steps of the Métro. Subsequent scenes take in a visit to a church, then walking the streets, and finally to Sarah Sand's boudoir, where they make love.

The sexual games of bondage and desire begin – Hugo kneels before Miriam; butterflies adorn her body; he ties her hands behind her back; she sucks him until he comes; they fuck. Finally, Miriam puts long metal claws on her fingers, mounts Hugo, and tortures him, cutting his skin as she rides him, all the time berating him.

It might be the plot to a run-of-the-mill softcore European porn flick, but *Love Rites* is nothing like that. Sure, there's nudity, there's simulated sex, there's the modern Parisian setting, but this is a very different sort of movie. There's plenty of Johann Sebastian Bach's music, for instance. There are extensive complex montages involving trains, passengers, buildings, and so on. Borowczyk shoots the couple in extended close-ups, often dimly backlit, or framed through windows and plants, or with objects covering the screen.

The first scene of *Cérémonie d'Amour* includes some voiceover to describe Hugo's character. Walerian Borowczyk is not particularly interested in Hugo, really: the evocation of Hugo as a fashion designer is fairly dull; more pertinent is the montage of imagery found in Hugo's apartment, all meticulously art directed by Borowczyk, of course. Hugo is just a guy, but making him a fashion designer does mean he's part of an educated, intellectual culture. But he could be anybody. The emphasis on clothes does I suppose play into the fetishization of the film of clothing and the accoutrements of erotic desire. There's also a woman who works in a store who telephones Hugo a few times and gets no reply – maybe she's a girlfriend or work colleague; they discuss the Fortuny fashion range. (As Hugo leaves his apartment, down an endless flight of stairs, the film includes what feels like ten b-o-r-i-n-g shots of Hugo walking down where one would suffice. In fact, that sequence lasts for 55 seconds! It's a moment when Borowczyk's flair for montage seems to desert him. But that does happen in Borowczyk's cinema quite often – there are rather many shots of characters wandering about where many another film editor – encouraged by the producer and distributor – would prune, prune, prune. And to have 55 seconds of nothing but a guy walking down some stairs is a minor mistake, true, but Borowczyk as an animator knows that you have to make every second count in a movie).

The voiceover says that a famous brothel used to exist on this Parisian street (there's a cut to the carved doors of Hugo's apartment, a *fin-de-siècle* design that shows that the bordello was there). A montage of early erotic photographs is also included.

The first part of *Love Rites* is a lengthy seduction set entirely in the Métro: first Hugo Arnold sits next to Miriam Gwen while she 'plays' at making up her face (as she puts it later); he then pursues her, jumping on and off subway trains, until he finds her at Saint Germain Métro station. Their first (idiosyncratic) conversation takes place (inevitably) on separate platforms, in lengthy telephoto shots through the passing trains, amidst Parisian commuters.[89]

An example of how far *Love Rites* is from standard movies (or porn flicks), is the scene where Hugo and Miriam first encounter each other, sitting next to each other on the subway train. Walerian Borowczyk extends the scene far, far beyond standard (or even arthouse) movies. The encounter contains no dialogue; instead, Borowczyk turns the scene into a lengthy montage of close-ups (and without music – just with the sounds of the subway trains).

Miriam is attractive, early thirties, with her black hair tied up, a bunch at the back, large earrings, pink lipstick, stockings, a black skirt, and a black veil. Marina Pierro, the star of Walerian Borowczyk's later movies, is certainly as luminous as any of her European contemporaries (Juliette Binoche, Irène Jacob, Ornella Mutti, Monica Bellucci, etc). And *Love Rites* is a gift of a role, an incredible role!.

There are images of Miriam making herself up, her reflection in a mirror, a close-up of her bag, close-ups of Hugo looking at her,

89 *Love Rites* takes place within a few hours on one day, and also a timeless time.

medium shots of Miriam's legs beside Hugo's, different angles of Miriam's bag, and so on. The close-ups climax with a shot in Miriam's mirror of her licking her lips repeatedly. The scene runs on and on, way beyond the dramatic requirements of such a scene (especially as there's hardly any dialogue, no back-story exchanged about the characters, no exposition, none of the stuff of the usual first meeting scene in a typical movie).

When Miriam exits the train, Hugo is galvanized into following her (as if he only desires her when she's left him). There are classic images of pursuit in the Paris Métro which recall many another film (filmmakers can't resist staging chases in subways). Eventually, he discovers her on an opposite platform at Saint-Germain, under a poster which has the line 'everything must go' (that *avant garde*, modernist sentiment is one of the mantras of *Love Rites*. The title of the story by André Pieyre de Mandiargues was *Tout disparaître*).

Eventually, Hugo and Miriam meet again, face to face (the film has delayed this meeting for some 30 minutes); they sit on the steps to the Métro and talk (Hugo conjures up images of the animals that live in the underground railway system, the rats and serpents. Miriam, typically, says she doesn't have a problem with snakes – it's Adam and Eve again).

Again, Walerian Borowczyk shoots this scene with a very long lens, framing the soon-to-be-lovers in a medium close-up two shot. As they talk, the man starts caressing the prostitute's thighs (she wears a black semi-transparent veil, a favourite Borowczyk item of clothing). When they kiss passionately, the soundtrack brings up very loud train sounds – the metallic, machine heart of the city.

Some of Walerian Borowczyk's best montages in his later work occur in *Love Rites* in the Métro scenes – where the film cuts away from the couple talking on the platforms or the steps to concentrate on lengthy sequences of images of subway trains and commuters, turning the everyday into the abstract. In another context, these montages would be celebrated as pinnacles of European art cinema – like the subway train montages in *Sunless* (1982) by Chris Marker (an early collaborator of Borowczyk's), for instance, or in *Bande à Part* (1964).[90] Borowczyk reprises the sounds of the trains during the heated, agonized lovemaking in the St Germain boudoir, when Miriam is slicing up Hugo.

What's striking is just how far Walerian Borowczyk extends the duologue in the Métro – it goes on way beyond a typical scene in a movie. Much of the first part is covered with a close-up of Marina Pierro in profile (as if the film is happy to look at Pierro, and not bother with the reverse angle of Mathieu Carrière). Sometimes a C.U. of Miriam's skirt riding up her thighs is included. And these shots are held for the usual length, without Borowczyk using any coverage. When he does cut away, it is to introduce montage elements of the Métro, as if *Love Rites* is also a documentary about the Paris subway system. Also very notable in these dense montages are the *sounds*: many loud train sounds, sounds of doors opening, the crowds, and buskers echoing down the corridors. A final element is a brief inclusion of some drawings (very likely by Borowczyk) to illustrate Miriam's back-story (which she's telling Hugo).

As so often in his films, Walerian Borowczyk carefully obscures faces and bodies, always denying the viewer full access to his characters. There isn't a single full-body nude shot in *Love Rites*, even though it's all about sex (Miriam, for instance, is dressed in a black basque throughout much of the lovemaking, as well as a filmy black dress). The way Walerian Borowczyk shoots bodies in *Love Rites* goes beyond titillation or being coy because of censorship. He's not playing with the audience in that respect (although *Love Rites is* erotic). When he wants to shoot the eroticized parts of the human body – pudenda, nipples, buttocks – he does. But often he's just as interested in the shapes that limbs make, pale in semi-darkness, or the compositions, or the way the human forms intercut with the interior, or how light falls on them.

In other respects *Love Rites* departs from conventional cinema or

90 The subway sequence in the middle of *Bande à Part* is a marvellous scene: it moves into a montage sequence, with Odile singing unaccompanied over images of underground trains and the city streets. It is a truly incredible sequence: like the night of love in *Alphaville*, it's one of those sequences you forget are in the film, but when you come upon them you realize that they are pure cinema magic.

pornography: the music, for instance, is by Borowczyk's beloved Bach (I can't think of a skin flick that has Johann Sebastian Bach has its soundtrack (!) – cheesy disco, cheap jazz and sax, yes, but not Bach). Then there are the montages of images from the history of art and erotica. Line drawings of people making love; 18th century nudes; paintings, etc. These seem to form a continuum with the Fortuny fashion plates from the magazines and books (introduced in the opening scene, when Hugo talks on the phone), as if fashion design is a modern form of high art painting (and the erotic prints which Borowczyk prizes).

Walerian Borowczyk art directs Sarah Sand's boudoir in St Germain as a jungle of the soul, all plants, leaves, windows, glass and wooden frames. He also introduces an exotic element: butterflies. One of the key images of *Love Rites* is a large Brazilian butterfly nestling on Miriam's naked pussy, while Hugo caresses it or blows on it, and Miriam laughs. The butterflies alighting on Miriam's nipples, toes or mound are part of Borowczyk's idiosyncratic cinematic eroticism.

Miriam is weaving all sorts of stories around Hugo from the moment she's met him. It's one of the major elements of *Love Rites*, and you're never sure how much of them is true. They're all relevant to Miriam's psychology and situation, though. In the Métro she talks about her childhood, how her father disowned her. Her storytelling continues on the steps of the subway, in the church, and in the brothel.

Miriam seems to be the classic abused prostitute of literature: one story she tells is how her two brothers tied her to a tree when she young and raped her repeatedly. In the brothel she tells Hugo about one of the masters of the brothel, called Ping (I wonder if that name refers to Samuel Beckett's story *Ping*?). The story of Ping includes more images of erotic illustrations. Miriam says that the madame, Sands, found Ping in Marseilles with his vocal cords and thorax torn out. She took him in and looked after him, but he turned out to be an arch sadist, straight out of the Marquis de Sade, inflicting unmentionable acts on a variety of whores, including Miriam. (How the French love their sexual sadists and the whole cult of sadomasochism! You can see it everywhere when you visit Paris. Whips, masks, chains, leather,

Georges Bataille, *The Story of O* – they love it). *Love Rites*, needless to say, is very much in the tradition of *The Story of O*, or Bataille's *The Story of the Eye*, or Jean de Berg's *The Image*.

The stories of Ping, or Madame Sands, enhance the sadomasochism of the 1988 film, and of Hugo's and Miriam's situation. But it's also part of the game, the acting out. There's no evidence of the existence of any of these people, like the sadist Ping or the brothel madame. They might be figments of Miriam's imagination. She might be making up these stories to enhance the S/M games she's playing with Hugo, her client. If so, Miriam turns out to be a great writer, inventing colourful fictions to enhance her life.

As in Samuel Beckett's later work, like the *Company* trilogy (Beckett being one of the literary gods who lived in Paris when Walerian Borowczyk was making movies), everything in *Love Rites* may turn out to be a figment of the imagination (including Miriam herself).

Religion is a key feature, as so often in Walerian Borowczyk's cinema: the first place the couple visit after meeting in the Métro is a dark (and empty) church (it's a Catholic church, of course). Borowczyk concentrates on religious imagery as much as on the lovers. And when he does film the people, he deliberately cuts off their heads, and focusses on Miriam's legs, while Hugo caresses between them. (As with other scenes in *Love Rites*, the lovemaking goes on a lot longer than the usual scene in drama or film).

The eroticism is increased: in another long lens shot, but much darker, the man caresses the woman between her legs as she talks at length (throughout most of the scene). The conversation veers around subjects such as the *Bible* (and the story of Abraham); Miriam also quotes from André Gide: 'I hate families' (in Gide's fiction, the line is 'familes, je vous haie' – that phrase was often used by the French New Wave filmmakers).

Walerian Borowczyk cuts from shots of paintings in the church, to candles, then back to the lovers again, the woman's thighs spread. There is far more going on here than a simple sexual assignation in a church. For a start, Borowczyk hardly shows anything of the lovers' bodies, which are cast in shadow so dense only Miriam's pale thighs can be made out clearly (many a producer would order a re-shoot). He also uses inserts from paintings, including Leonardo da Vinci's famous drawing of Vitruvius's proportions, the plans of the church, an illuminated mediæval manuscript, and other high art imagery. Through-out, Johann Sebastian Bach organ music plays (Bach's *Toccata, Adagio* and *Fugue*, BWV 564, were used).

After the church visit, the couple wander through the streets of Paris, Miriam leading Hugo like a blind man, so he won't know where her boudoir is located (Miriam is talking continuously; there's a low angle long shot of a narrow Parisian street that's held for ages as they walk into the distance. It's the kind of shot that Orson Welles hated – he would be saying 'cut, cut, cut!' to the editor).

All the way up the stairs of Sarah Sands' boudoir Miriam is talking (and Hugo is listening). It's as if they are going into another world, along passageways, up staircases: when they reach the boudoir, they're in a mythic, timeless place.

When they finally reach the threshold of the secret room (after climbing endless stairs), Miriam announces 'let the orgy begin', and Hugo says 'act two!' and throws the file he's been carrying down over the camera, in a pure Godardian moment (as if throwing away the film script, or abandoning his former life). And as soon as they enter the room, the rituals of undressing occur. And the man worshipping the woman's body, like the camera – dwelling on her breasts, belly, vulva, with the butterflies used a trope to enhance Miriam's exoticism. And in comes the organ music again.

The lovemaking is largely shot in Walerian Borowczyk's customary style of lengthy takes using long lenses; a series of shadowy images of parts of bodies. This is one of Borowczyk's signature shots: a partially-naked body, overlaid with semi-transparent gauzes and veils, the camera a long way back, with plants, blinds and screens in between the camera and the subject, to the sound of Borowczyk's beloved organ music.

Through the sex scene Miriam can't stop speaking. First she sucks Hugo; a voiceover (the voice of the book by André de Mandiargues on which *Love Rites* is based) describes in the language of pornography what's happening (his huge cock at the back of her throat, the usual stuff).

As Hugo is fucking Miriam from behind, the phone rings and Miriam answers it, with Hugo still inside her. As Walerian Borowczyk and de Mandiargues knew well, this is one of the standard scenes in pornography. Usually it's a husband or lover on the other end of the line. Sometimes it's a mother-in-law or friend and the woman has to pretend she's just sitting around watching TV.

In *Love Rites*, Miriam says 'oui... oui... oui' repeatedly (and quietly), clearly in response to the caller's questions. It might be the sadist Ping on the line, or it might be the brothel madame, Sarah Sands. The narrator describes how Hugo keeps tupping Miriam while she's on the phone. One can imagine the conversation, which isn't heard:

> 'Are you with someone?' 'Oui'
> 'Is it a man?' 'Oui'
> 'Are you making love?' 'Oui'
> 'Is he inside you, right now?' 'Oui'
> 'Does it feel good? Is he deep?' 'Oui'

And so on and on.

There's yet another level of narrative to Borowczyk's *Love Rites* which separates it from run-of-the-mill media, and that's a voiceover, which turns out to be even more sexually explicit than the imagery or dialogue. It's one way of getting explicit stuff into a movie, and bypassing the censor.

A lot of Miriam's dialogue constitutes voiceover – because the movie employs Walerian Borowczyk's montage approach, and is cutting to all sorts of images, including fragments of Miriam's body, as well as close-ups of her face as she talks. Miriam is very much the narrator of *Love Rites*, much more than the narrator himself (who's voiced by Jean Negroni). The film is commenting upon the erotic encounter between Hugo and Miriam all the time: not only in the obvious way of the narration, but also with Miriam's continuous dialogue: she's commenting upon the narrative throughout. And for her, the encounter with Hugo is an act, a game, a story played on a stage.

Critics, considering Walerian Borowczyk's cinema, rarely note his talent for editing, but it's always been a vital element in his films. The visual splendour, the art direction, the painterly imagery, the art historical allusions, are often remarked upon, and no viewer can miss the eroticism and love of female nudes. But Borowczyk has his own editing style that's as distinctive as everything else in his movies. *Love Rites* contains some outstanding examples of montages (the editors *Love Rites* were Florence Poulain, Guila Salama, Lili Sonnet and Marie-Hélène Zirisch). Very often Borowczyk and his editors will construct scenes in terms of lengthy close-ups of objects or parts of bodies while one of the characters talks, so the dialogue is essentially a voiceover (or he'll intercut imagery to a voiceover). In *Love Rites*, characters are so often talking off-camera you don't really notice it, but it's very rare in conventional movies.

I do think that at times *Love Rites* does get swallowed by its darkness and shadows. Often there's no fill light, just a pale rim light or back light. One wonders if Walerian Borowczyk from time to time argued with his cinematographers (who often like to over-light scenes – at least you know you're going to get something on celluloid). But Borowczyk often pushes to the limit what film stock (and the audience) can handle, and he goes dark, dark, dark.[91] But in *Love Rites* it's not wholly successful. More effective is the continuous use of layers or veils between the camera and the actors – they are obscured by blinds, by glass, by window frames, by plants.

After Hugo has come twice inside Miriam, she takes over; the tables are reversed; Miriam becomes Sarah Sand, a dominatrix who dons steel claws, rides on top of Hugo and scratches him, drawing blood. Throughout the scene, Miriam/ Sarah berates Hugo at length, for being inadequate, a useless lover and man. The S/M scene goes on and on; Miriam really gets into it; the camera lingers over Miriam's face, again in profile, as she rides Hugo, cutting away to depict her ass, breasts, and torso; the film also concentrates on poor old Hugo, lying on his

91 Gérard Monceau, Jean-Paul Sergent and Michel Zolat were credited as DPs.

back, lit from behind, and Miriam's claws raking his chest, neck and face.

During this extraordinary sadomasochistic scene, Hugo's cries of pain are heard, but everything's dominated by Miriam's stream of invective. She humiliates him in countless ways – and he is taking it all. It's classic S and M, the master and the slave, the spider and the fly (and also, somehow, very French). And when you think it'll finish, Borowczyk keeps the scene going – he's going to shoot all of the script, and then he's going to add twenty pages of his own monologue written for Marina Pierro.

It's completely predictable, and wonderfully naïve, and so dumb, that when the bout of S/M is over, Hugo, blood-stained and exhausted, maintains that he didn't expect this, that he is a simple man. He tries to come across as the regular Joe who just wanted a good fuck with a woman (Miriam berates him for those pathetically meagre desires: a fuck and a bottle of wine). And during the diatribe, the film now concentrates very much on Hugo's response, rather than Miriam delivering her monologue.

Note that one of the insults that Miriam throws at Hugo when she attacks him is that he's a bad actor who can't deliver and has been fired (there must have been actors in Borowczyk's film career who couldn't or wouldn't deliver what he wanted).

Eventually, Hugo staggers barefoot out of the boudoir onto the streets of Paris, dazed, a broken man, with no identity papers, wallet, or money. And he does exactly what Miriam told him to do: he goes down to the River Seine, wandering along the antique stalls and *bouquinistes* next to the river.

The 1988 film is now wholly in a mythical realm (actually, it has been since the beginning of act two, the lovemaking in the boudoir, and maybe all the way through). On the banks of the River Seine Hugo meets a naked woman who emerges from the river; she says she is Miriem (Josy Bernard), a prostitute from the River Jordan who liked pleasuring men ('another prostitute!' Hugo remarks). Miriem is a wholly mythological figure, an incarnation of the 'holy whores' of the ancient world (the Seine becomes the Jordan). Boats pass behind the actors as they talk under the trees on the embankment (as they do every day of the year in gay Paree).

Hugo, now stripped of his name, his identity, and his purpose, helps her dress, then watches stunned when Miriem stabs herself in the chest and dies. Just before that Miriem offers Hugo a piece of advice straight out of the European *avant garde*: say yes to every question you are asked. It's a method of changing his life, which's what this coda to *Love Rites* is about: losing identities, and goals, and even desires. As if to prove to Miriem that he's not going back to his old life, he throws the keys to his apartment into the Seine.

A hobo is on hand to witness Miriem's suicide, which turns instantly into murder: when the police arrive and handcuff him, Hugo doesn't struggle; the bearded, grizzled hobo is eager to denounce Hugo (yes of course the scene replays the Agony in Gethsame with the soldiers coming to take Christ away, and other scenes from the Passion). A crowd gathers behind the railings on the embankment. Hugo's led away to the jeers of the crowd that shouts 'kill the bastard'.

The coda to *Love Rites* is certainly odd. It has the feeling of a rewrite and reshoot scene. What is Hugo's crime? (his punishment is severe). Was is because he broke the rules in Sarah Sands' boudoir? To not play the game? To step out of character and reveal the game to be a sham? Was it that his desires were too banal, too simple, as Miriam says? Was it because he wasn't willing to give up everything? ('everything must go', Miriam tells him).

11

BLANCHE AND *LA MARGE*

There are a number of films directed by Walerian Borowczyk that have been difficult to get hold of.[92] So I've decided not to write lengthy studies of movies I haven't seen for a long time. A great pity, because *Blanche* and *La Marge* are wonderful movies, and *Blanche* is regarded widely as Walerian Borowczyk's masterpiece, alongside *Goto: Island of Love*. I made a few notes after seeing them years ago, and have included them here.

It's just that Walerian Borowczyk's films are difficult to track down (at least in Europe and the U.S.A.). Classics such as *Immoral Tales* are very elusive, while *The Art of Love, Blanche, La Marge, Bloodbath of Dr Jeckyll* and *Lulu* are really tough to obtain. It's such a loss, really, because films such as *Immoral Tales* and *Blanche* really should be readily available. And it's ironic that a movie such as *Emmanuelle 5* is easy to buy from retailers, but not *Blanche* or *The Art of Love*.

BLANCHE

Blanche (1971)[93] was instantly recognizable as a Walerian Borowczyk film; no one else could have made it. Borowczyk was one of the very few filmmakers who could put 'un film de' or 'a film by' or 'a Walerian Borowczyk film' in the opening credits and be totally credible. Borowczyk was very much the *auteur* of his films.

> All stages of a film's creation are in me at one and the same time. My temperament does not allow me to create only part of a work and then to entrust the rest to specialists... I... eliminate the collaborators who dare to try and barter my own ideas with me. *I know everything*. And that very often drives members of my crew to tears. (J. Gerber, 171).

In doing everything himself, meant that Borowczyk worked alone,

92 Some of them I've seen – *Blanche* and *La Marge*, and really enjoyed – but some I haven't seen: *Bloodbath of Dr Jeckyll* and *Lulu*.
93 Not to be confused with *Blanche* (Bernier Banvoisin, 2002) or *Blanche* (2001) or *Blanche* (Eric du Bellay, 2008).

too. 'Filmmakers are lonely people,' Borowczyk once said.

Set in the 13th century in a castle (and mostly shot in interiors), *Blanche* starred Ligia Branice as a Baron's wife, at the centre of a web of erotic fascination. It was based on *Mazepa* by Juliusz Slowacki.[94] The usual Walerian Borowczyk eccentrics – a lustful page, a dumb, handsome lover, a possessive old man, and the beautiful Branice – played out a bizarre fairy tale of desire which ends in tragedy.

Visually, *Blanche* was remarkable: again, it employed Borowczyk's penchant for flattened perspective, the dissolution between foreground and background, a pictorial sense that recalled not only theatre but Italian Renaissance fresco (the early Quattrocento painters, such as Giotto and Duccio, and the mystical planar geometry of Piero della Francesca). Actors were shot (by DPs André Dubreuil and Guy Durban) against doors and walls for most of the film, with long lenses, always moving parallel to walls, moving only on the right angle axis to the camera, hardly ever approaching the camera. There were also few close-ups: most of the shots in *Blanche* were medium or long shots (Branice, with her large eyes, could consume the lens).

LA MARGE

In *La Marge* (a.k.a. *Emmanuelle '77, The Margin,* or *The Streetwalker*), Walerian Borowczyk worked with two prominent stars of the era: Sylvia Kristel, whose *Emmanuelle* film is one of the most successful porn flicks in history, and Joe Dallesandro, most known at the time for appearing in Paul Morrissey and Andy Warhol's films (though he appeared in later pictures such as 1984's *The Cotton Club*). In *La Marge*, Kristel brings the *Emmanuelle* aura with her. Kristel played Diana, the prostitute of the title. So *La Marge* is intriguing simply because its two lead roles are taken by two internationally

94 One of the inspirations for *Blanche* was Borowczyk's short film *Gavotte* (1967).

recognizable actors, unlike most of the rest of Borowczyk's cinema.

The story, by André Pieyre de Mandiargues, had been set in Barcelona, but the Spanish authorities had apparently refused the production to be shot there (due to Borowczyk's reputation as a pornographer). The Hakim brothers produced; Boro scripted; Bernard Daillencourt was DP; Louisette Hautecoeur was editor; Marie-Françoise Perochon was costume designer; Jacques D'Ovidio was production designer; Jacky Bouban did the make-up; sound was by Maurice Gilbert and Louis Hochet.

Walerian Borowczyk should be celebrated as one of cinema's true originals, a filmmaker with a vision wilfully eccentric, determinedly personal and individual, indulgently lyrical, boundlessly imaginative, and shamelessly erotic. You have to admire someone who said, fuck it, I'm going to do what *I* want, I'm going to create mesmerizing hallucinations, entire worlds. Borowczyk's was a cinema of magical spaces, a surreal city of dreams...

...somewhere on earth a partially-clothed and beautiful woman (who looks a lot like Leda) is washing herself in an antique bathtub in a *fin-de-siècle* apartment art-directed to perfection by a Renaissance master to the strains of Handel and Scarlatti.

ILLUSTRATIONS

Illustrations include:

✤ Some of Walerian Borowczyk's movies, including early short films. Plus artwork from home entertainment releases.

✤ Also, some of Borowczyk's own art.

✤ Some painters and art that have appeared in Borowczyk's films.

✤ And images from classic erotica, some of which's been featured in Borowczyk's cinema.

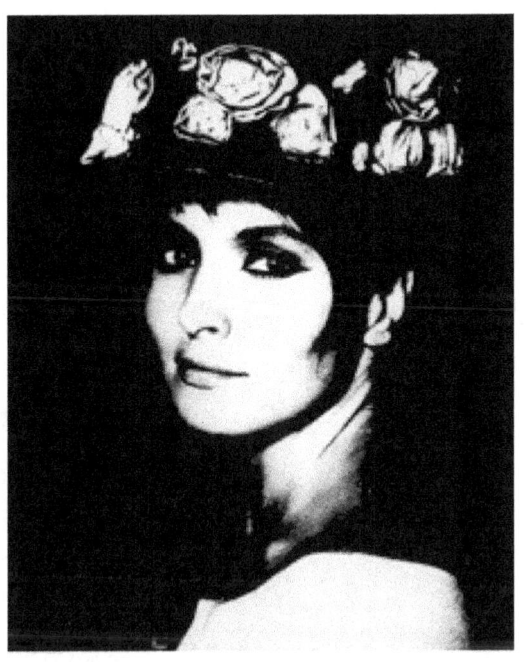

The wonderful Ligia Branice
in two images by her husband, Walerian Borowcyk.
A portrait, above, and from Goto: Island of Love, below

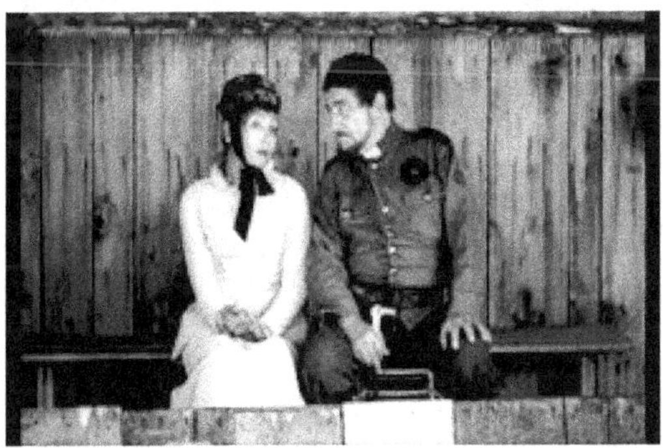

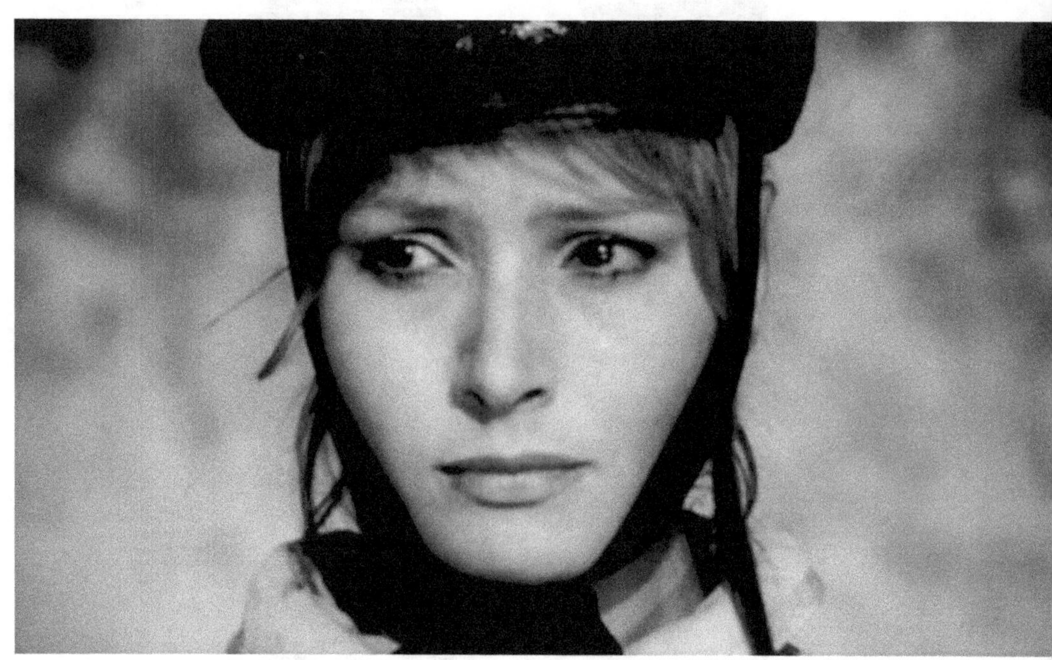

One of the finest moments in Walerian Borowczyk's cinema – when Glossia (Ligia Branice) looks out from the island in Goto: Island of Love and sees her hopes of escaping dashed. Borowczyk and Branice were never better than here.

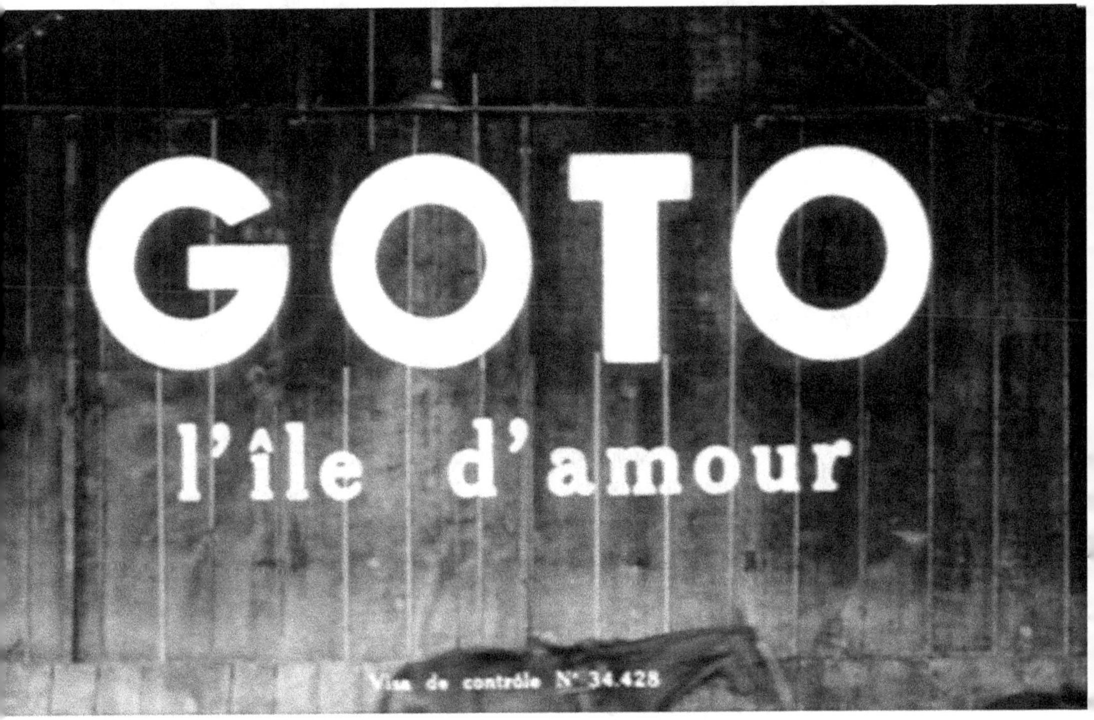

GOTO

l'île d'amour

Visa de contrôle N° 34.428

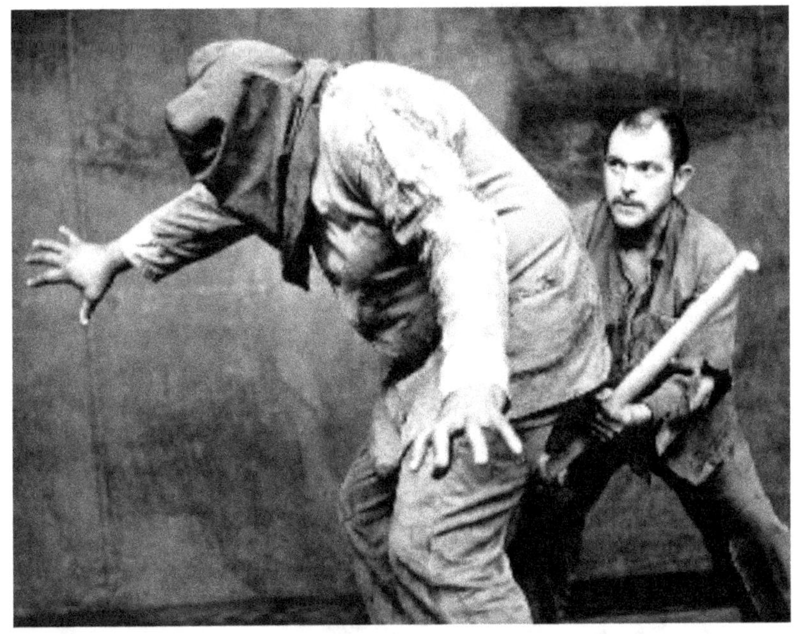

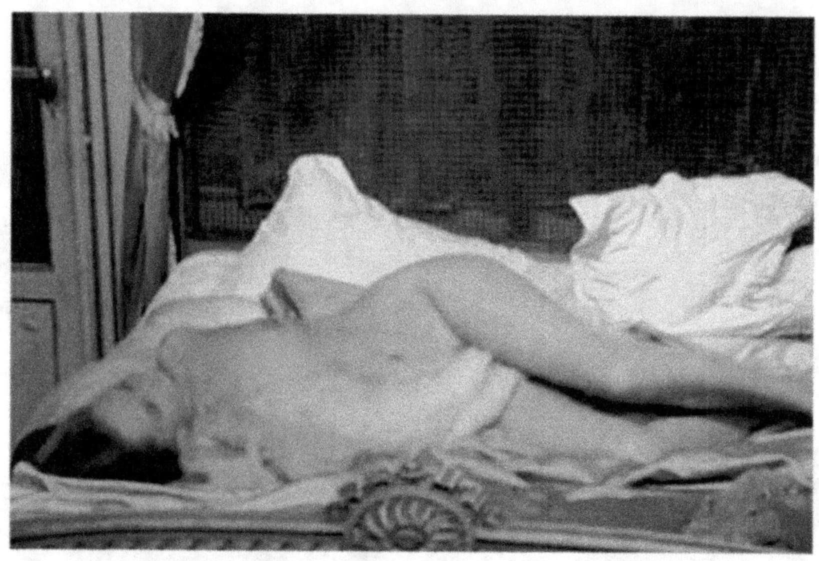

Classic images of Borowcykian erotica:
Lucy masturbating with her clothes in The Beast, above,
and women being fucked from behind at a table,
in Three Immoral Women, middle, and Immoral Tales, bottom.

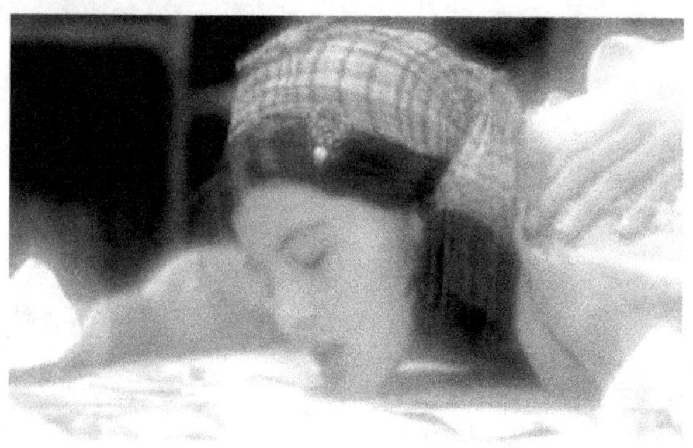

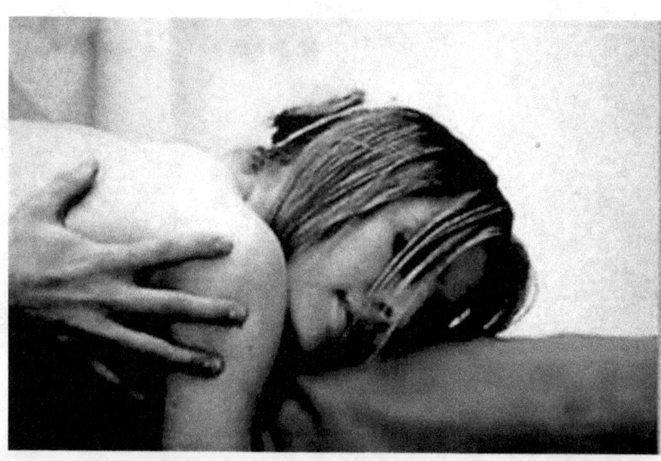

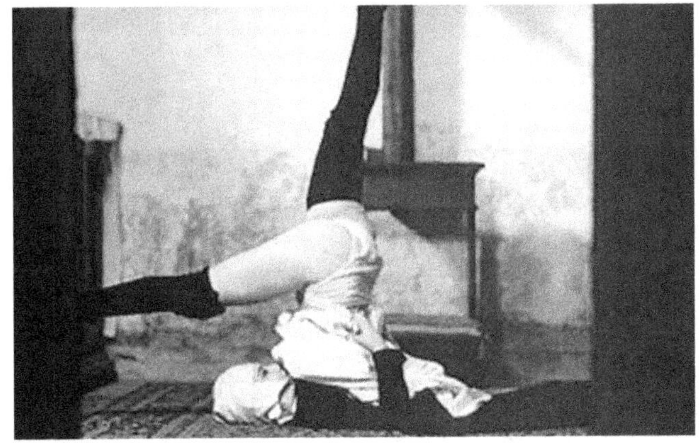

Sex, death and religion in Borowczyk's films:
exercising nuns in Behind Convent Walls, above.
Naked virgins moments before they're slaughtered in Immoral Tales, below.
And the Pope making out with his daughter in Immoral Tales, bottom.

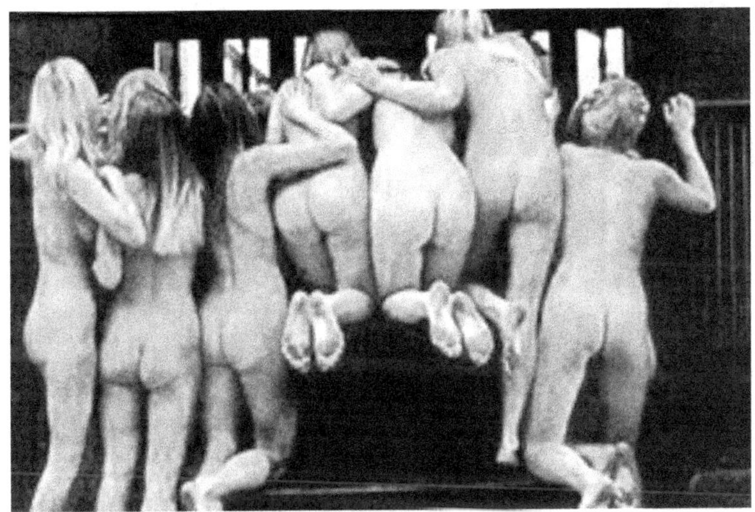

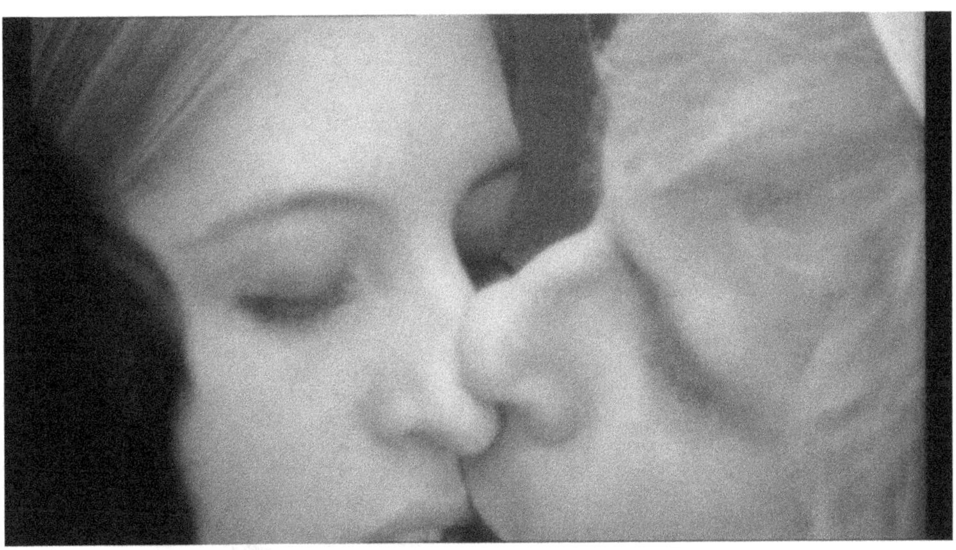

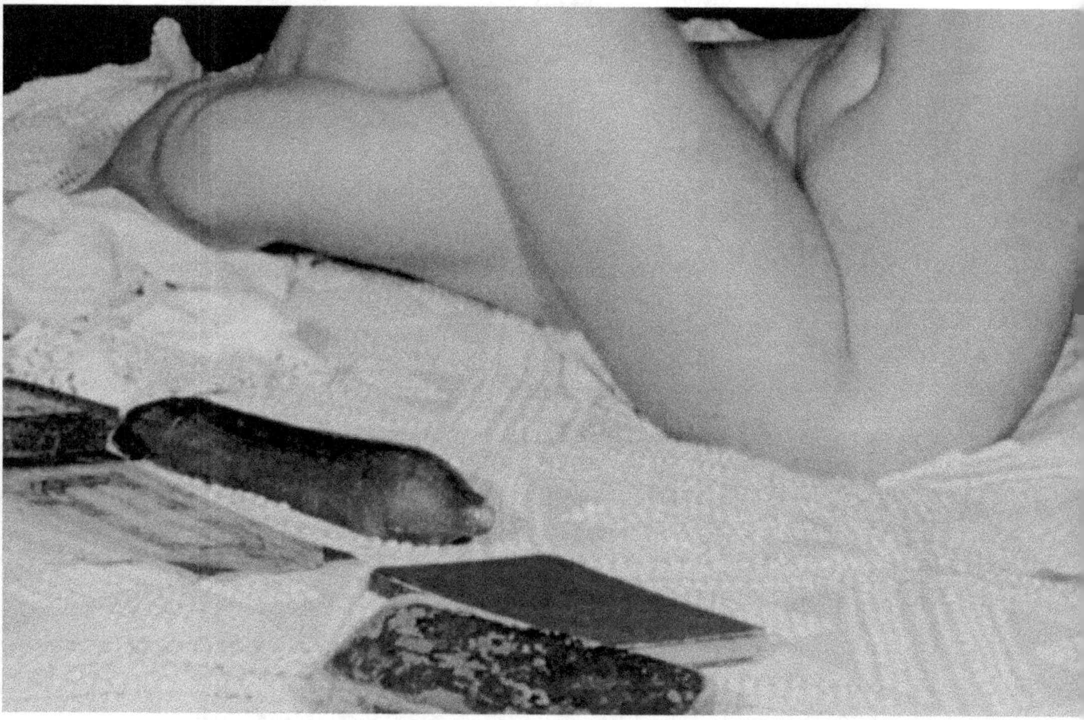

Women masturbating is one of the specialities of Walerian Borowczyk's cinema.
In Thérèse Philosophe from Immoral Tales (1974), above, a young women has everything ready: erotic books, a print, and a cucumber.
Behind Convent Walls (1977) featured plenty of scenes of nuns masturbating, below right.
Most outrageous, perhaps, was Marceline playing with her pet bunny rabbit in Three Immoral Women (1979), below left.

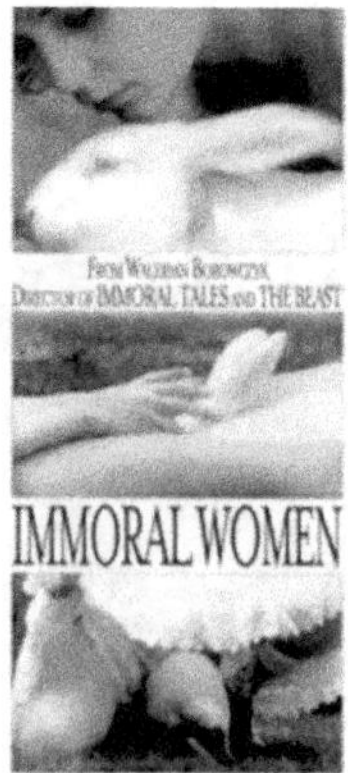

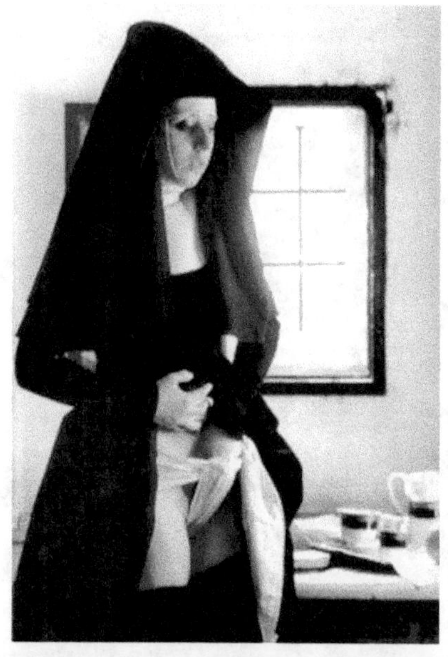

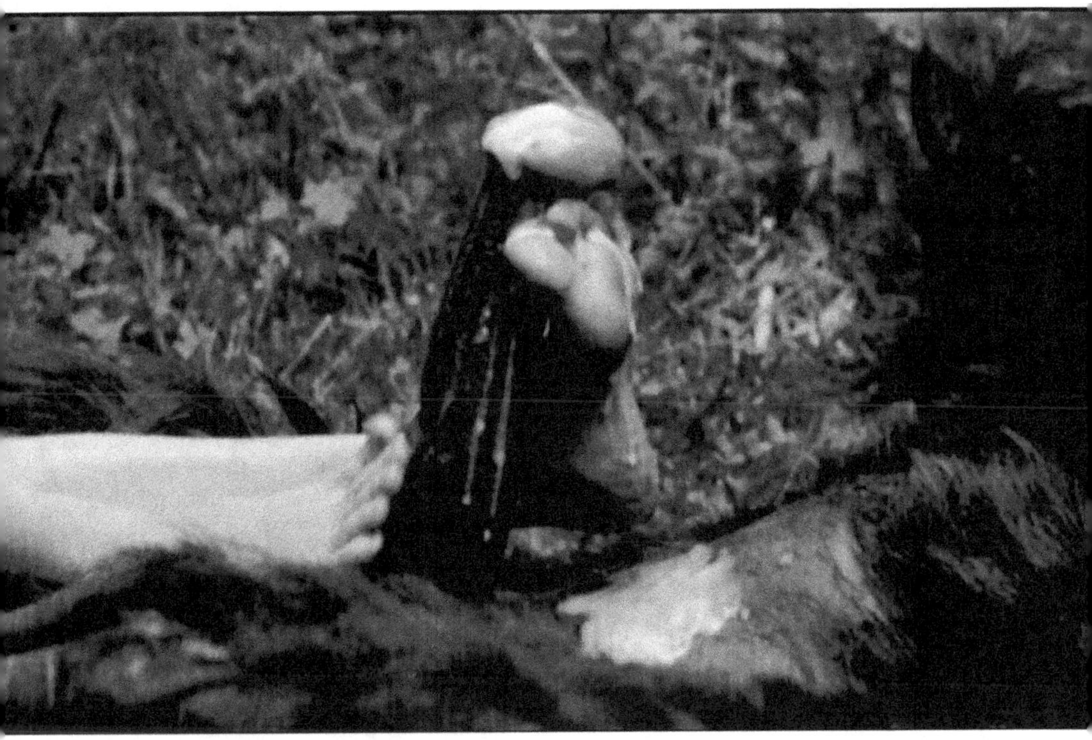

Sex in The Beast (1975)

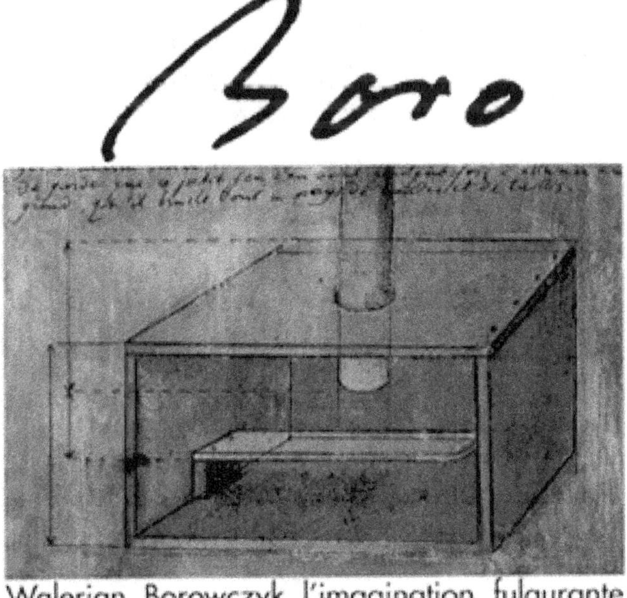

Some of Borowczyk's art

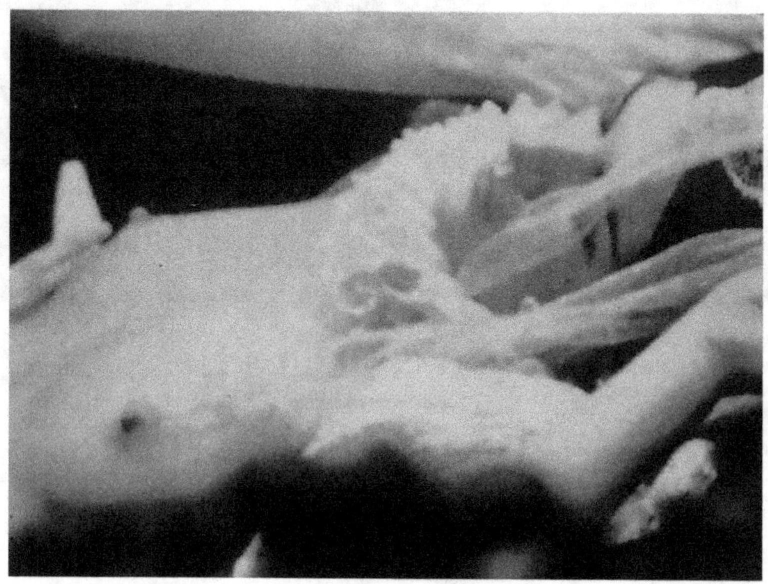

Pablo Picasso's daughter Paloma as 'Countess Dracula' in Immoral Tales

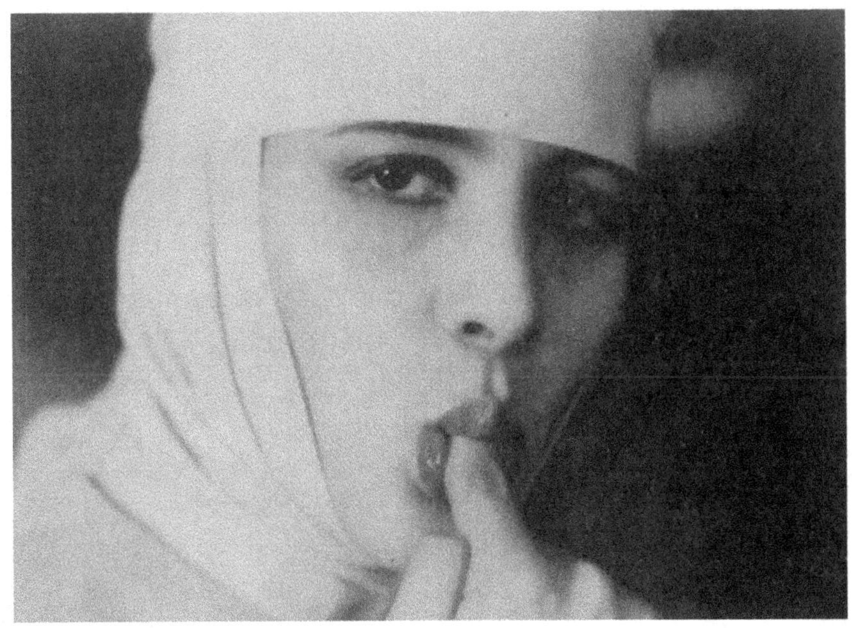

Nuns at play in Walerian Borowczyk's Behind Convent Walls:
a finger pricked on a rose, above, and carving a dildo from wood and glass, below.

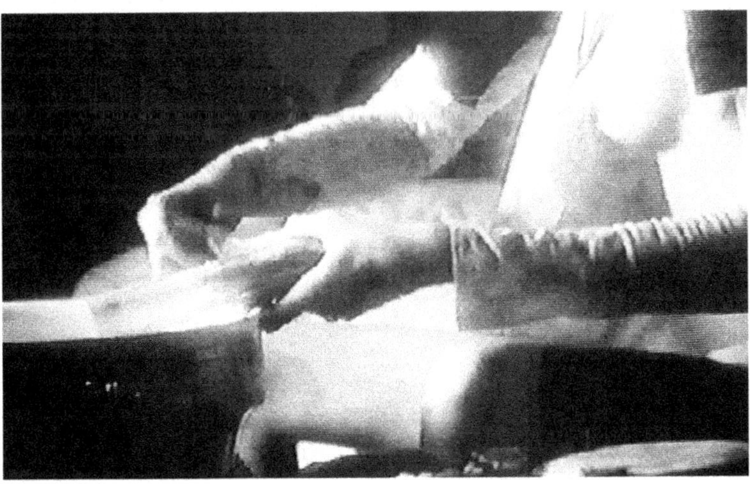

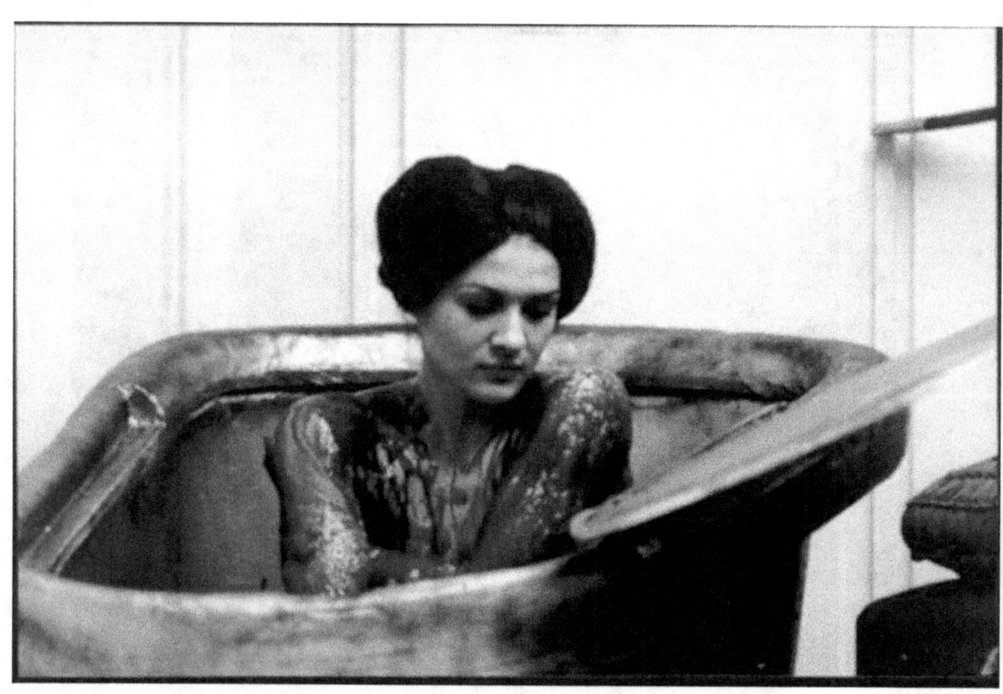

One of the most grotesque images in contemporary cinema:
Pablo Picasso's daughter Paloma bathing in the blood of thirty young women in Walerian Borowcyk's Immoral Tales (1974).
It's a literal bloodbath. The film calmly washes over the mechanics of extermination, and focusses on the pleasure the Countess gleans from bathing.
Isn't it a marvellous idea of Walerian Borowczyk's to have Paloma Picasso play this mass murderer with a quiet, dignified charm? One can imagine many another filmmaker and actor being unable to resist an obscene leer or two, a lick of the lips, some evil-eyed stare, or some other Movie Villain Business. But there's nothing at all: Báthory just goes about her bath as if it's the most normal thing in the world. It's as if she's been doing it everyday.

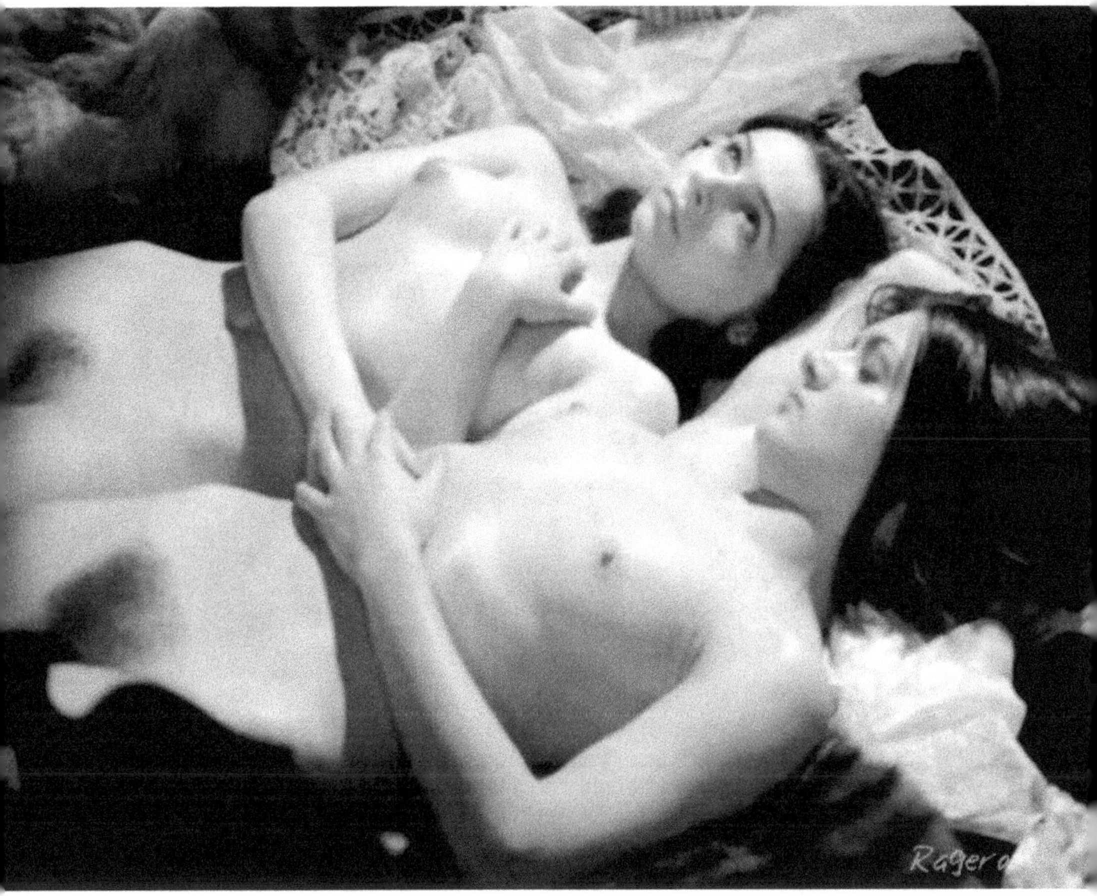

Paloma Picasso in Immoral Tales

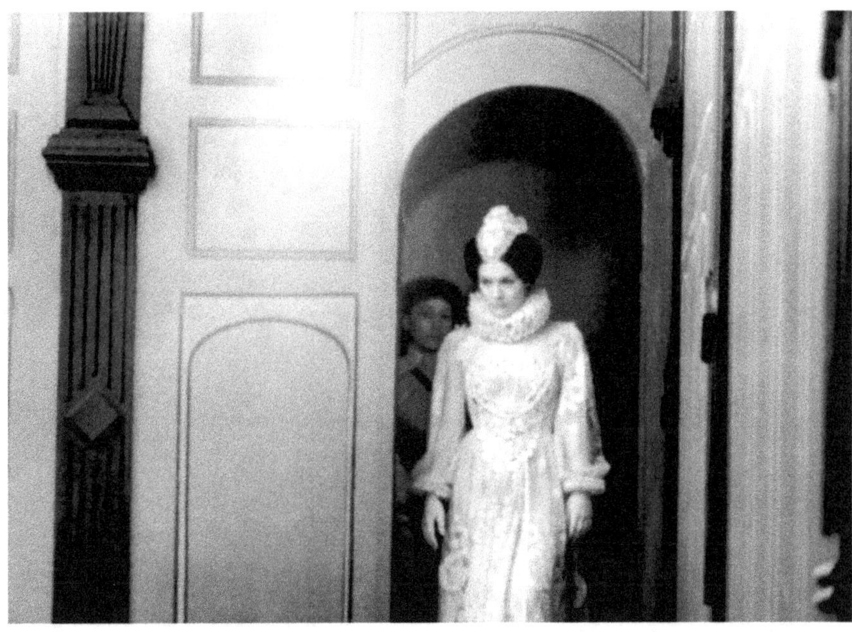

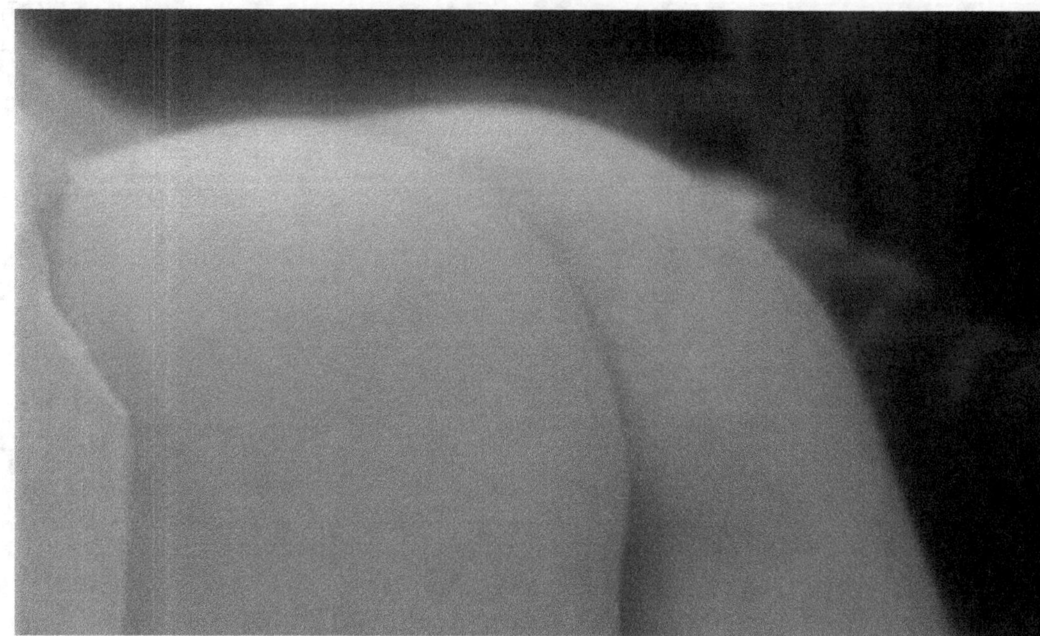

The two extremes of Walerian Borowczyk's cinema: sex and high art (which also illustrate Borowcyk's eye for detail): a close-up of Margherita Lutti's cute butt in Three Immoral Women (1979), which Raphael worships and kisses (in a lengthy shot), above.

And a carving of an ancient diety in The Beast (1975), below.

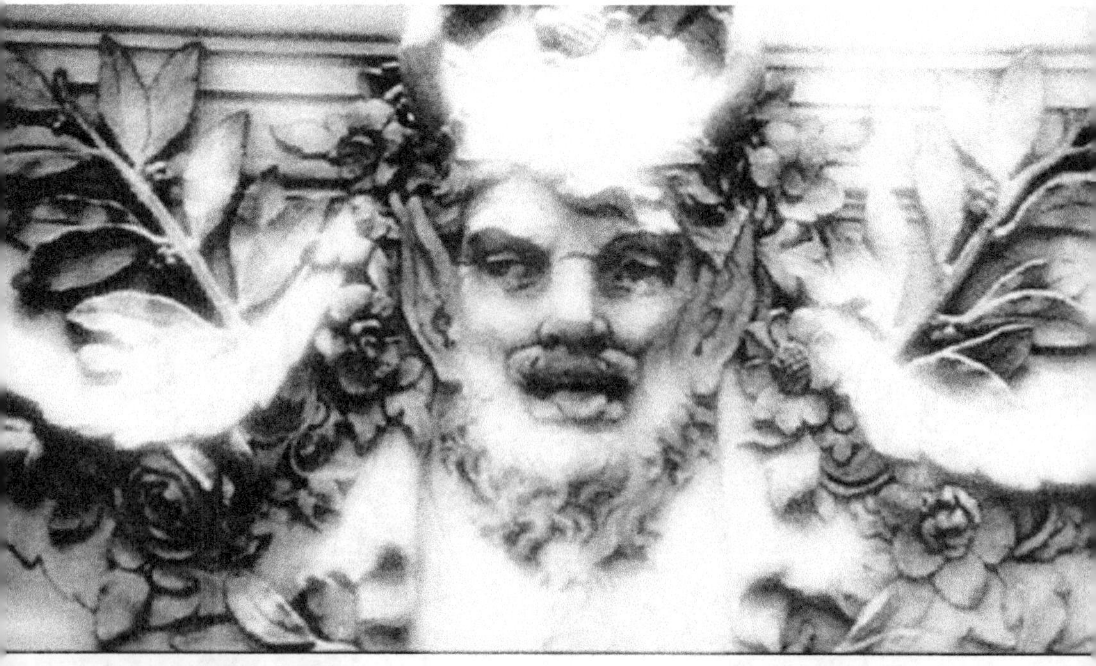

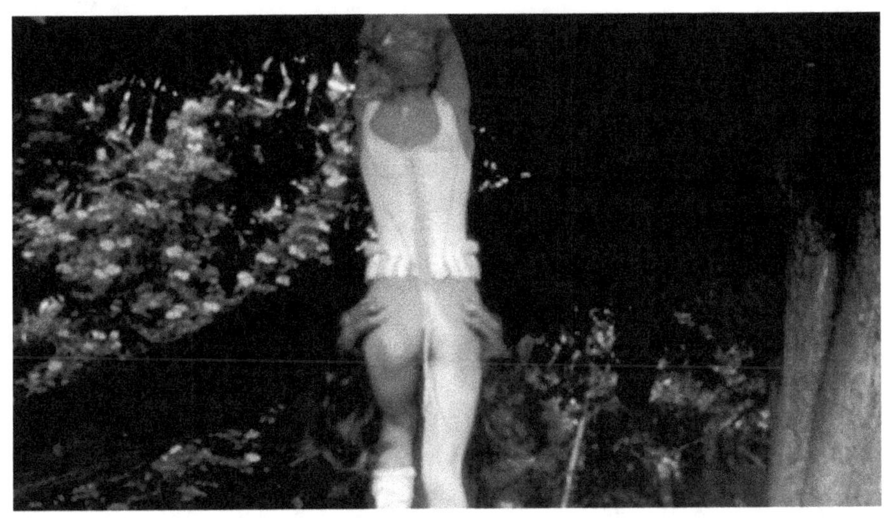

Beauty and the Beast, Borowczyk-style.

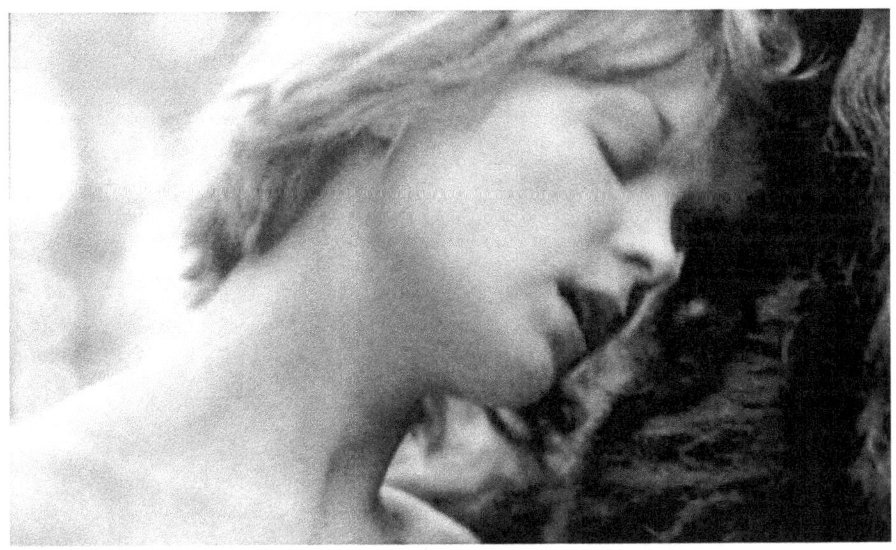

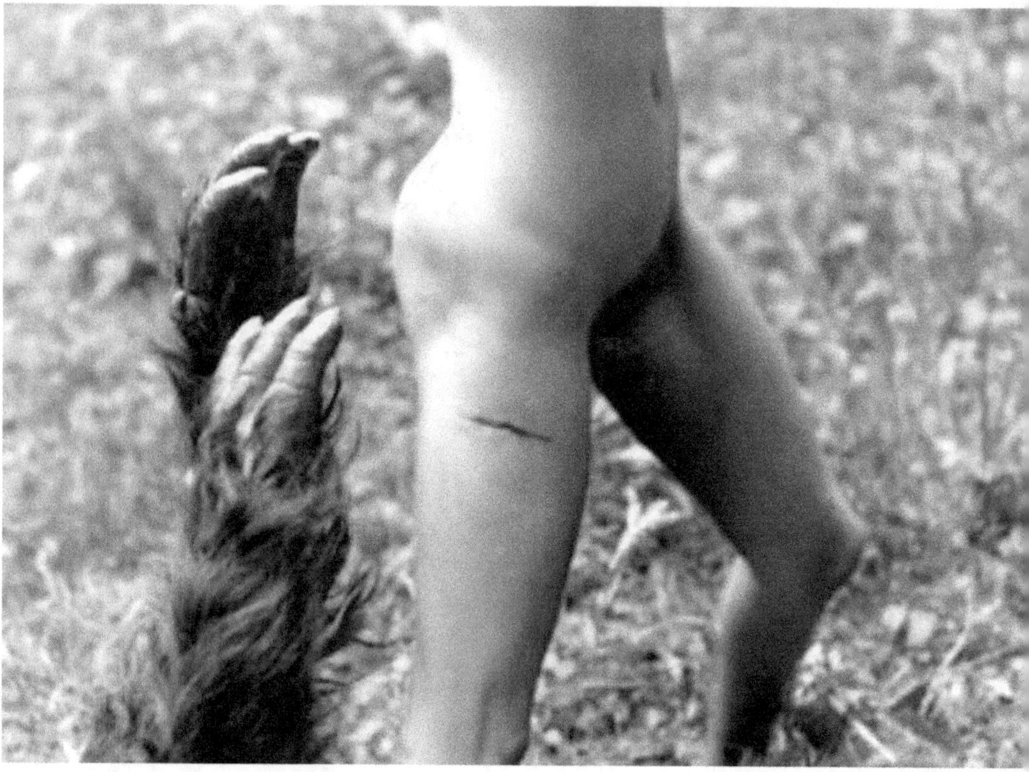

The Beast (above). La Marge (below).

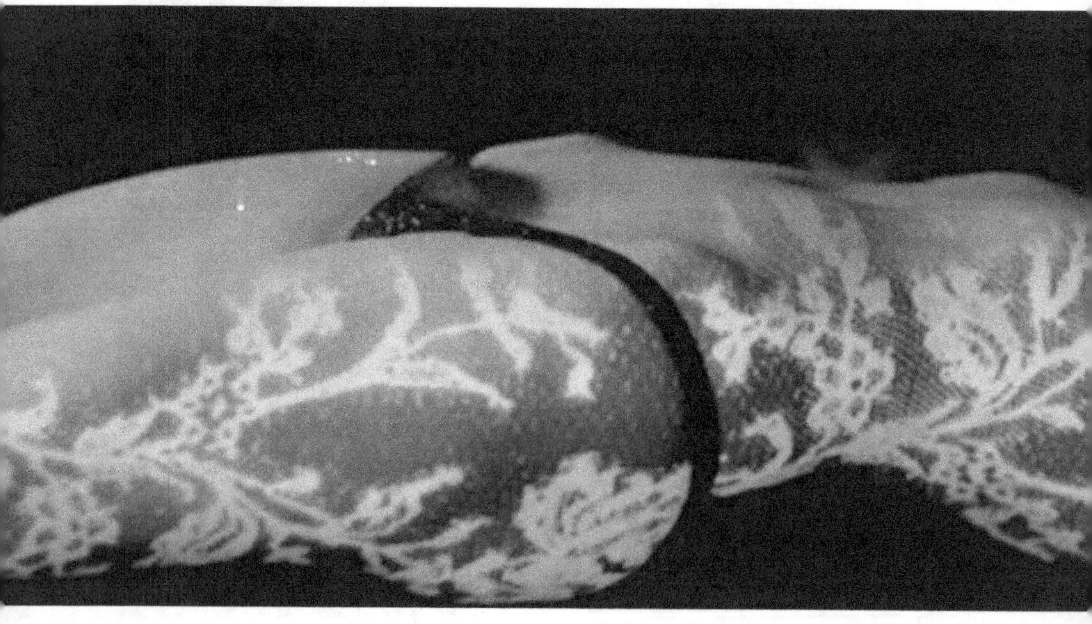

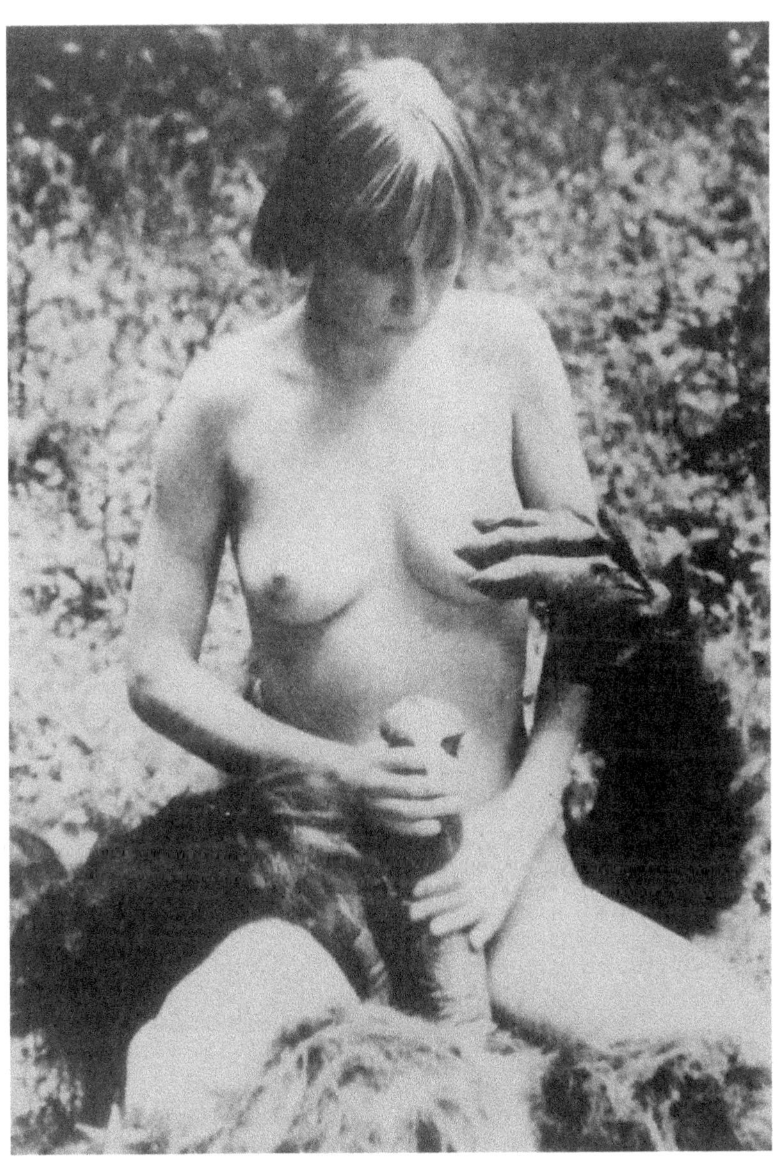

A naked young woman, a beast, a forest and an enormous cock:
it could only be Walerian Borowczyk's The Beast (1975)

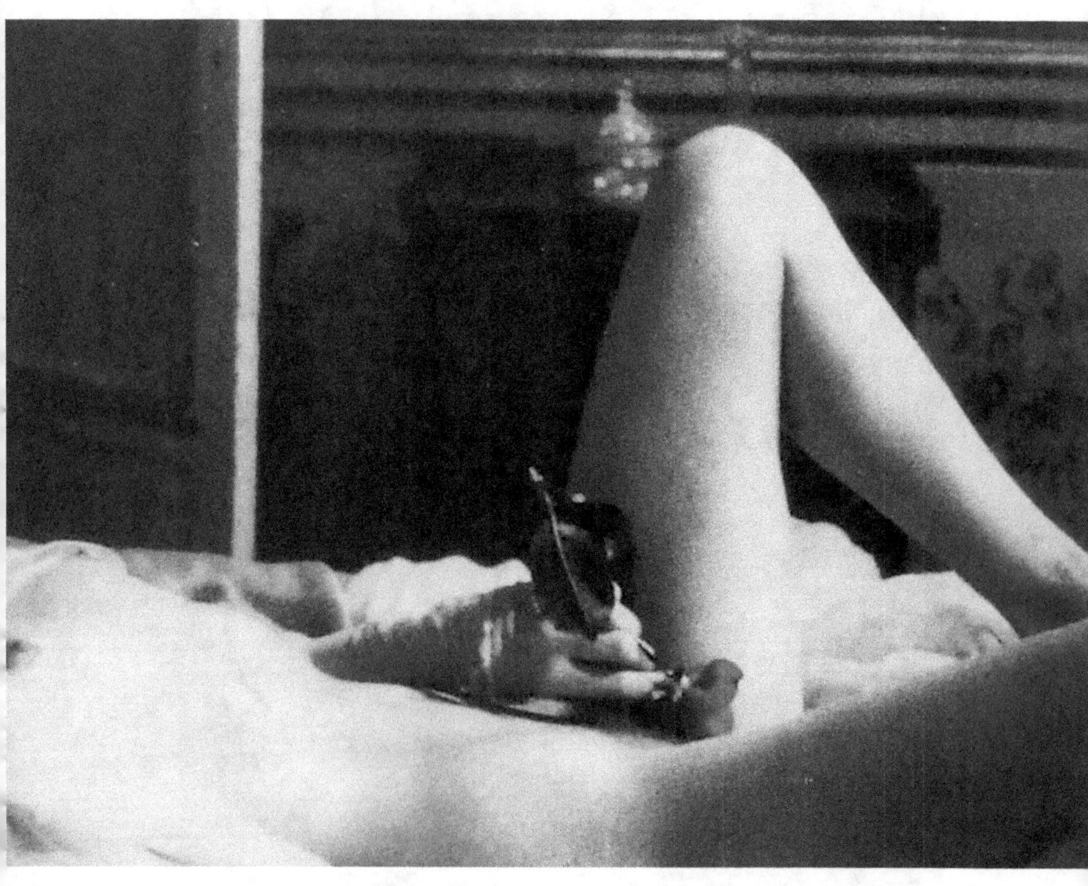

The camera pans down Lucy's body in Walerian Borowczyk's The Beast, in the famous masturbation with a red rose scene.

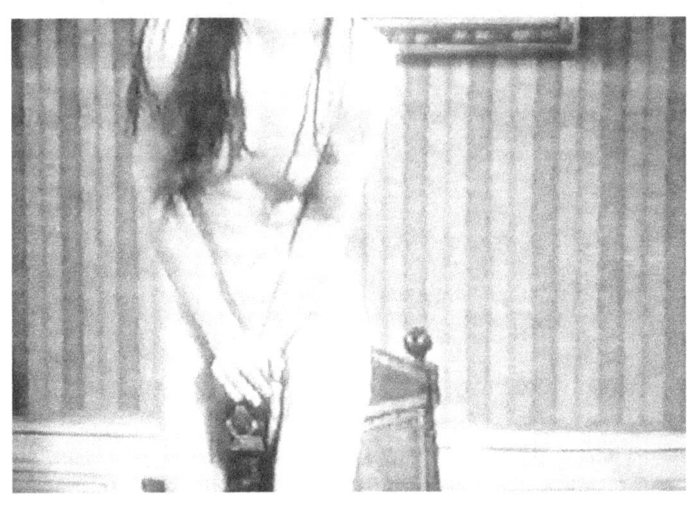

Clarisse (Pascale Rivault) in Walerian Borowczyk's La Bête:
indulging in some interracial fucking with Ifany (below),
and when he's called away, masturbating
on the headboard.

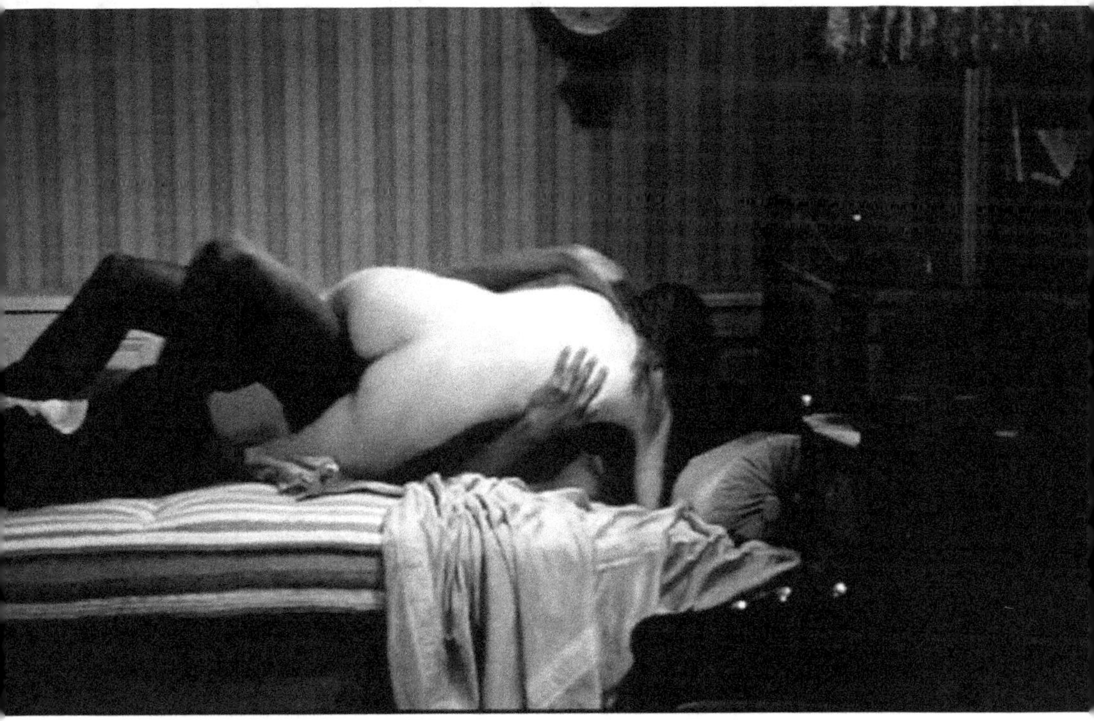

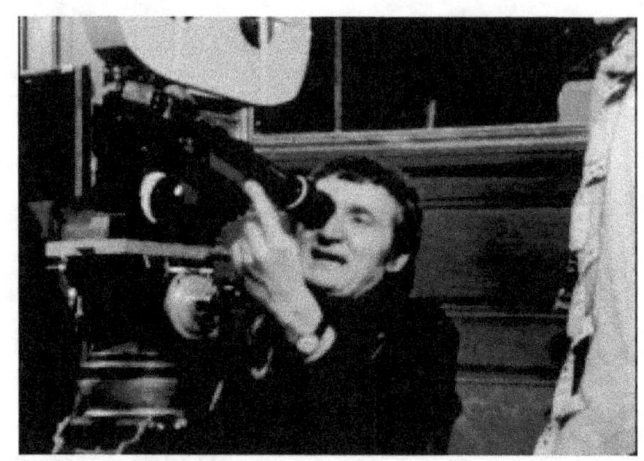

The maestro at work on The Beast, above.
And a classic Borowczykian image: a snail on a shoe in The Beast.
As Borowczyk says, The Beast is more a comedy than an erotic film. This isn't just a dumb-ass movie: no silly film would include in the middle of a sex scene sudden cuts to the trees, to a lake, to a snail crawling on a shoe. Something else is going on here.

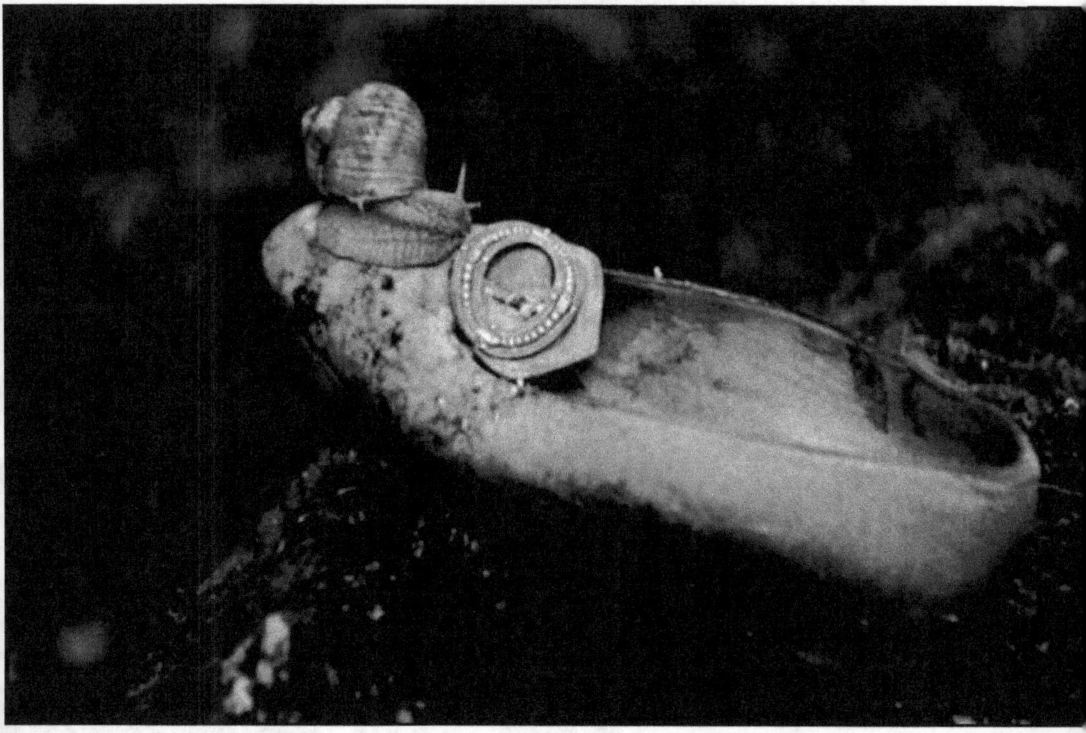

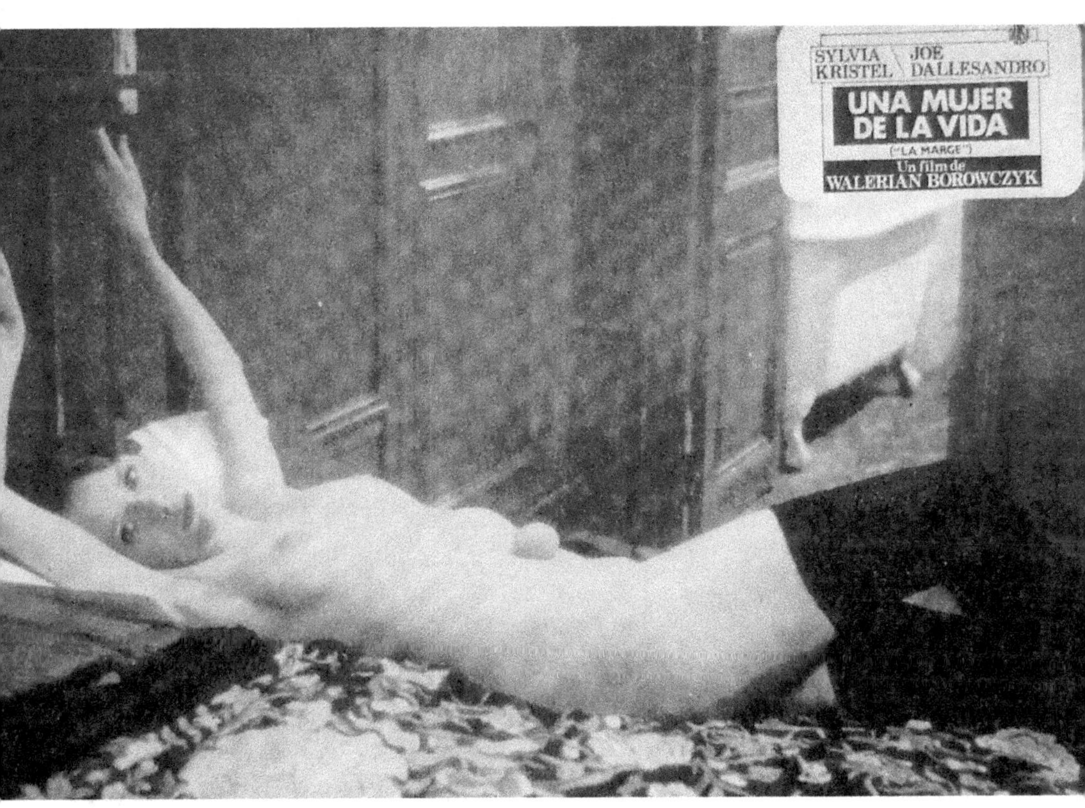

Sylvia Kristel in Walerian Borowczyk's La Marge

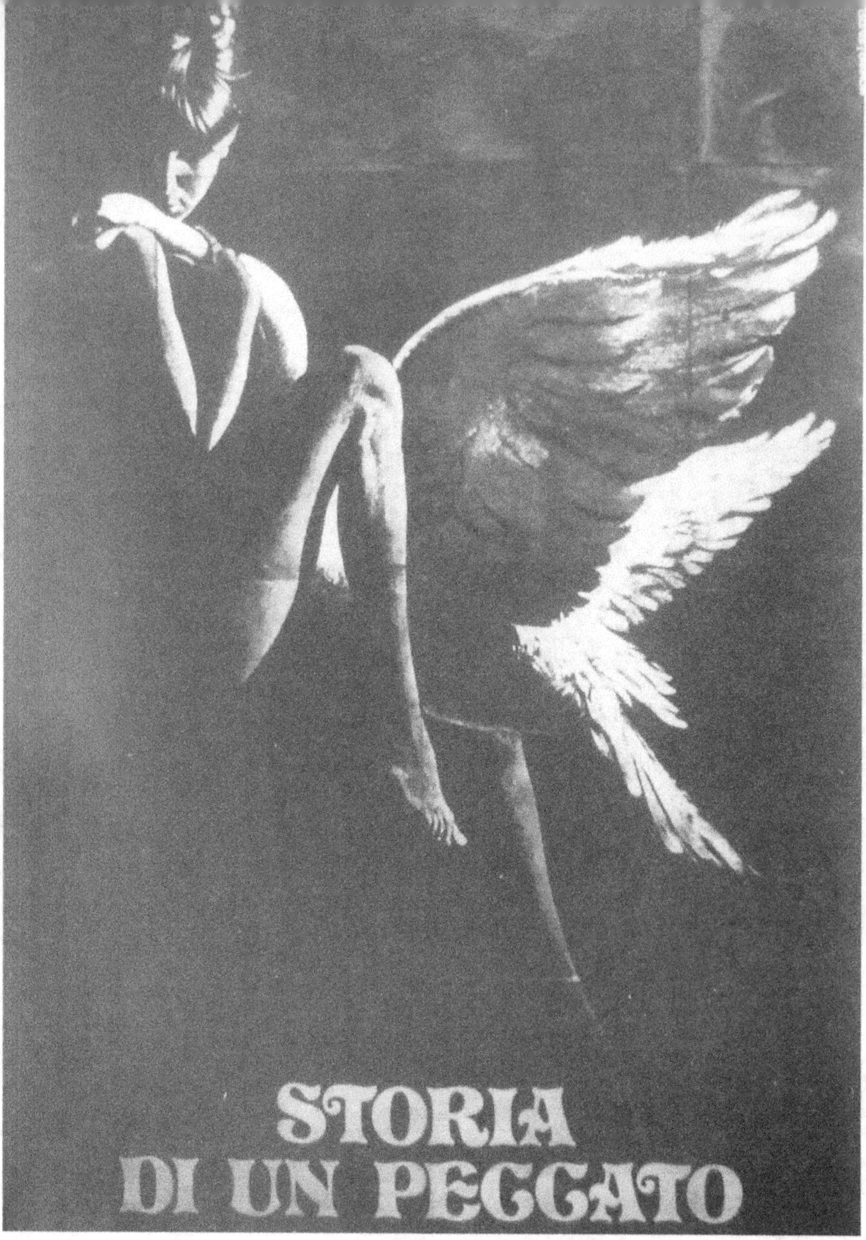

STORIA
DI UN PECCATO

Borowczyk's Story of Sin, above, and Love Rites, below.

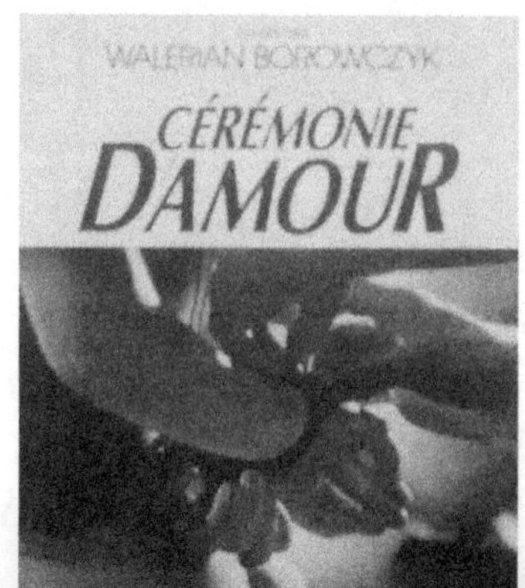

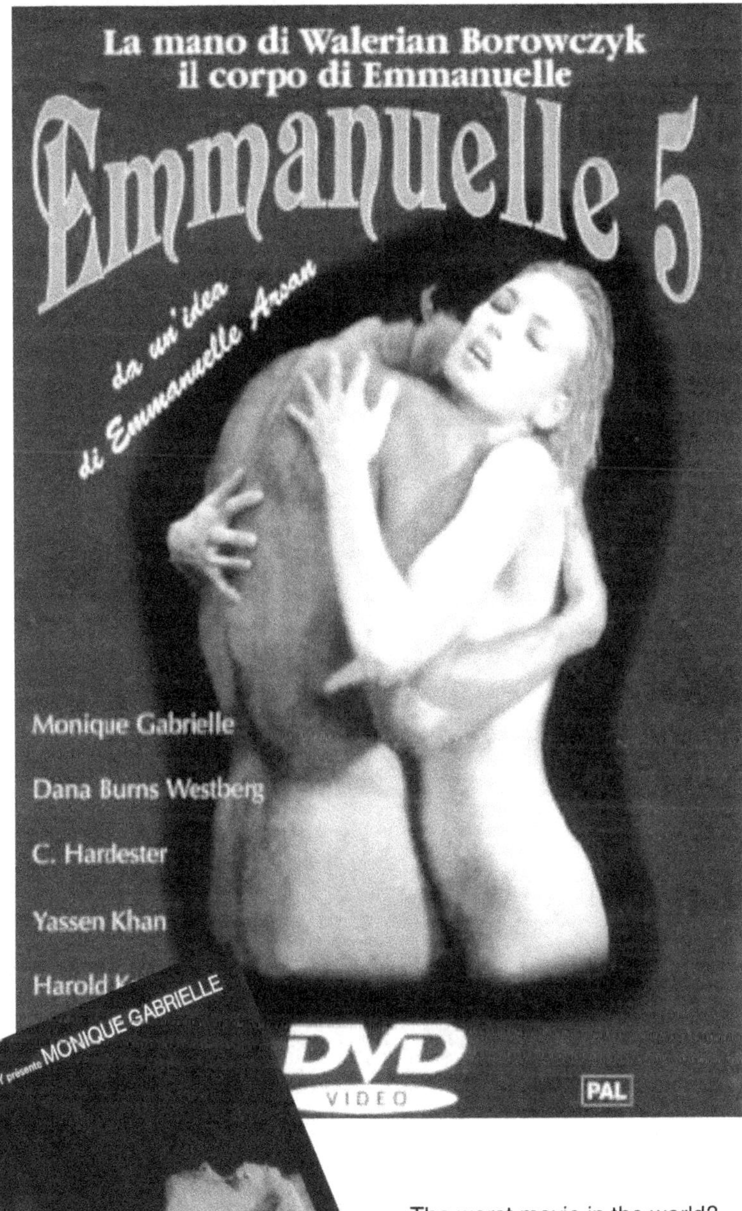

The worst movie in the world?
Pretty close: Emmanuelle 5

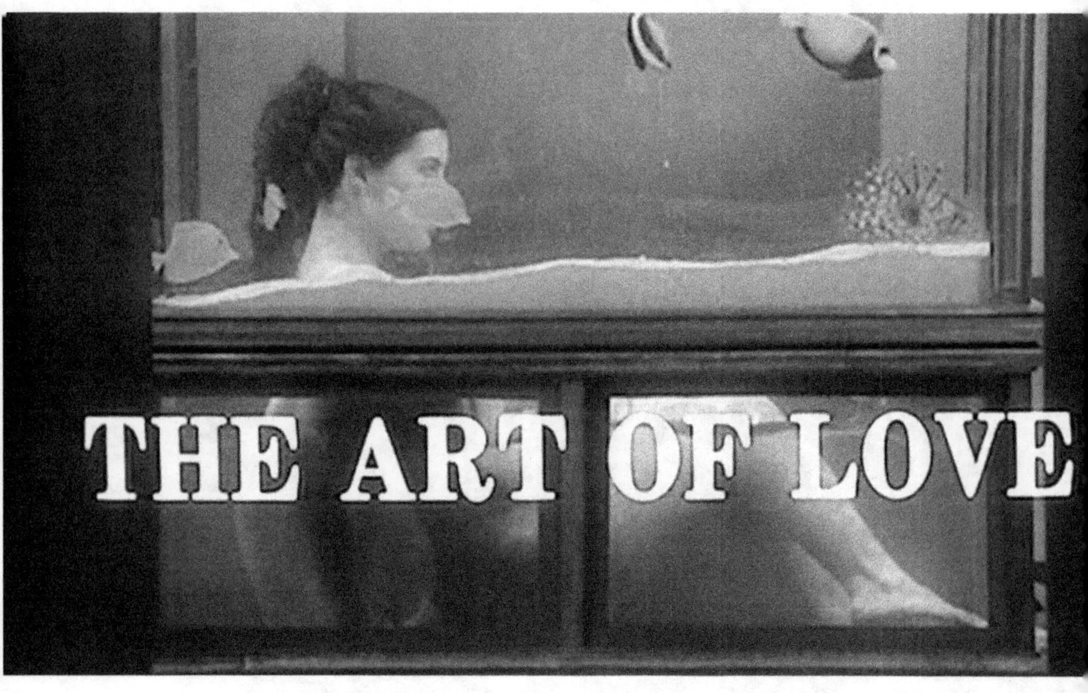

Open with your money: thus, 1983's The Art of Love begins with the star, Marina Pierro – naked, of course, in the proper Borowczyk manner, and bathing in an idiosyncratic ancient Roman prop

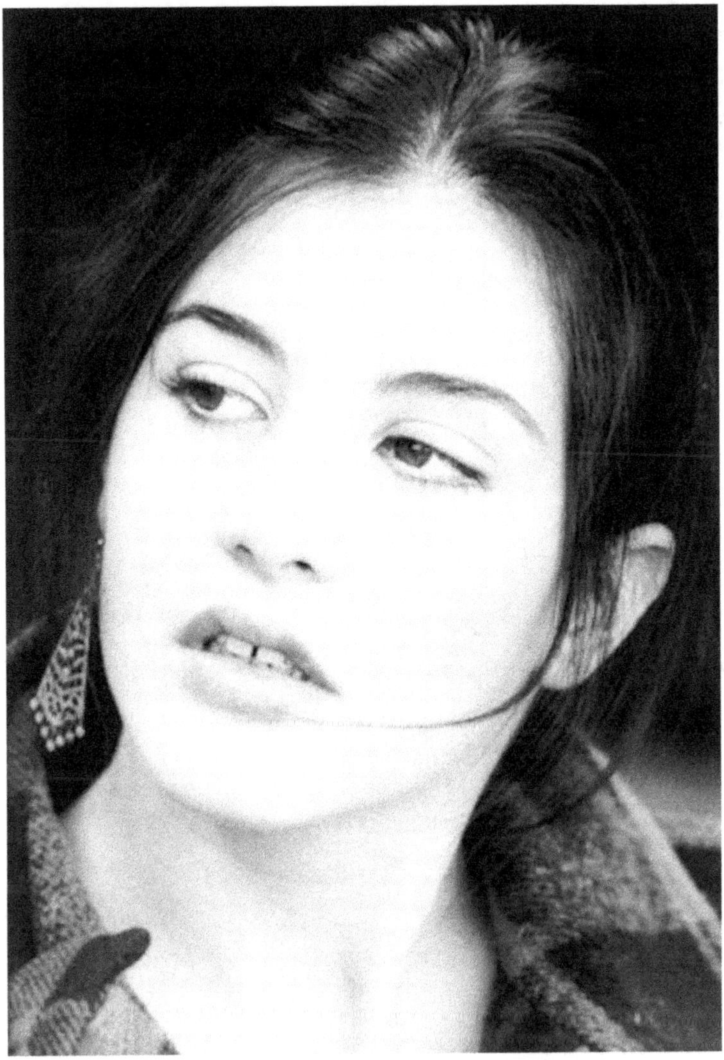

The wonderful Marina Pierro, star of Borowczyk's later films, and easily the equal of her European contemporaries, such as Juliette Binoche, Monica Bellucci, Irène Jacob, etc.
Two of her finest roles – in Three Immoral Women and Love Rites, below.

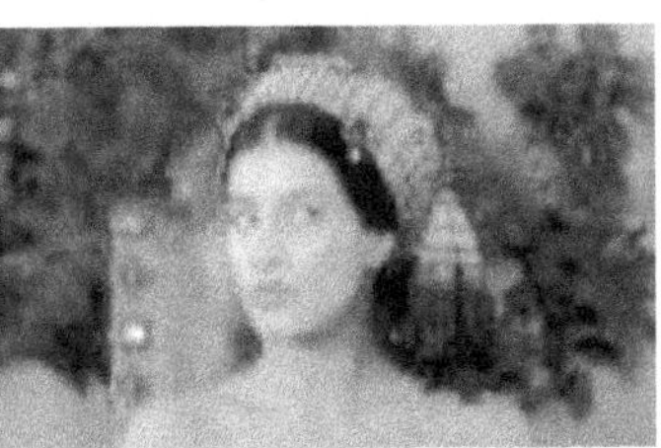

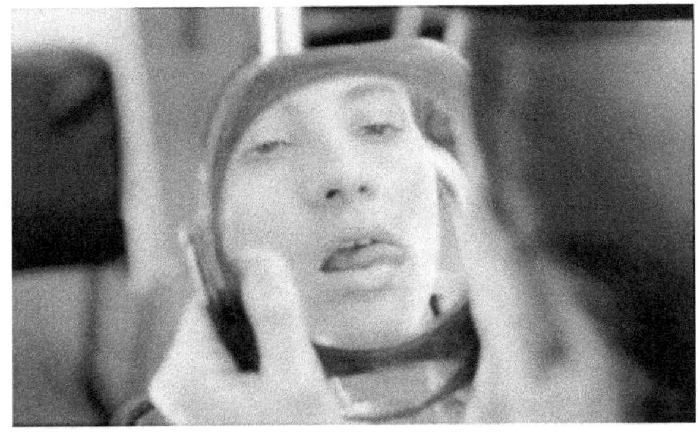

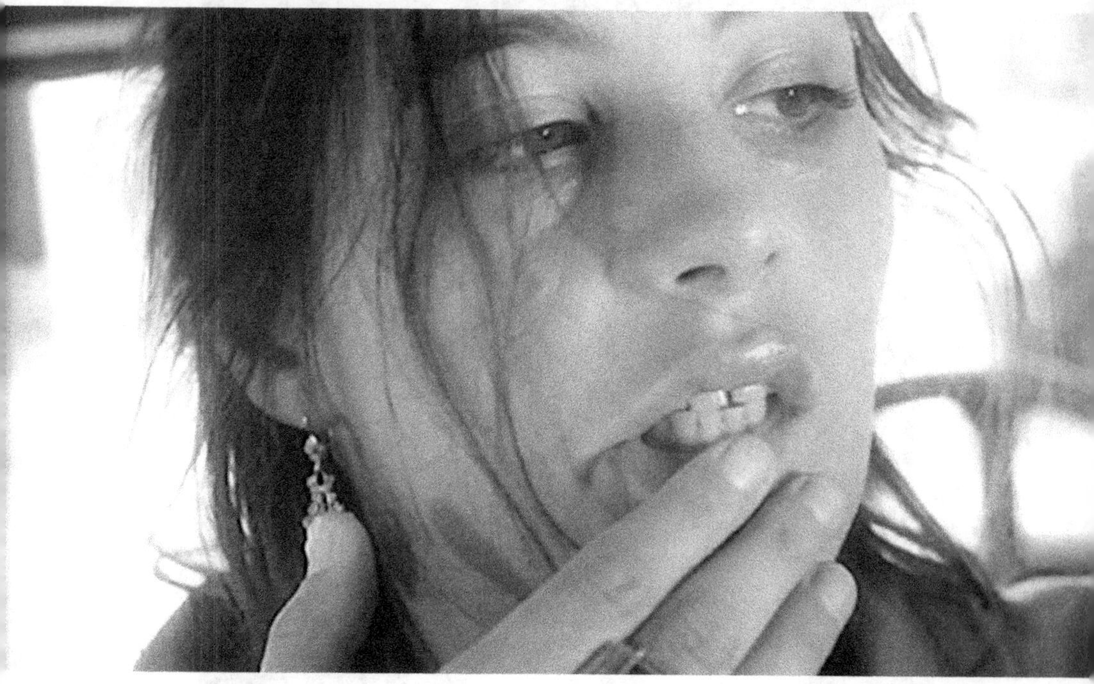

Marina Pierro in the modern-day framing story in The Art of Love (above). Jacopo Berinzini and Florence Bellamy in Immoral Tales (below).

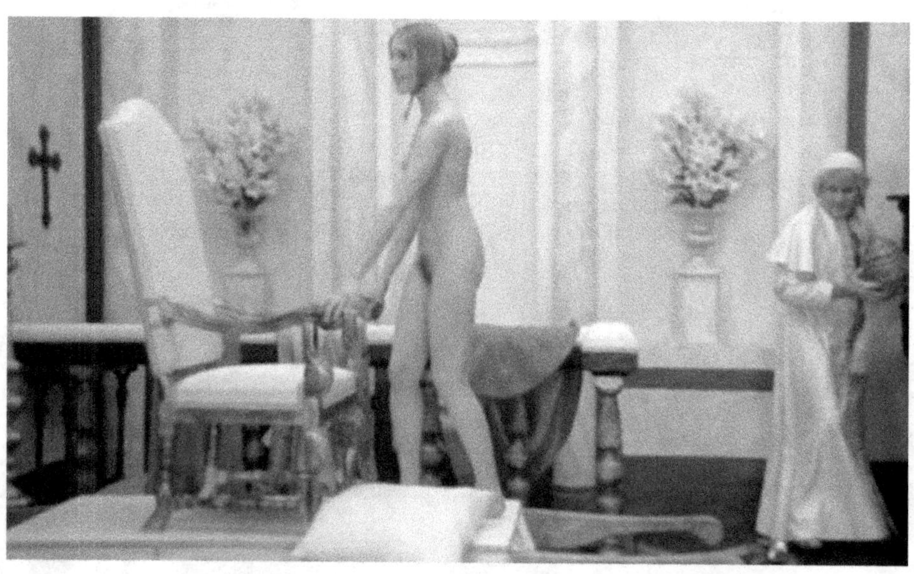

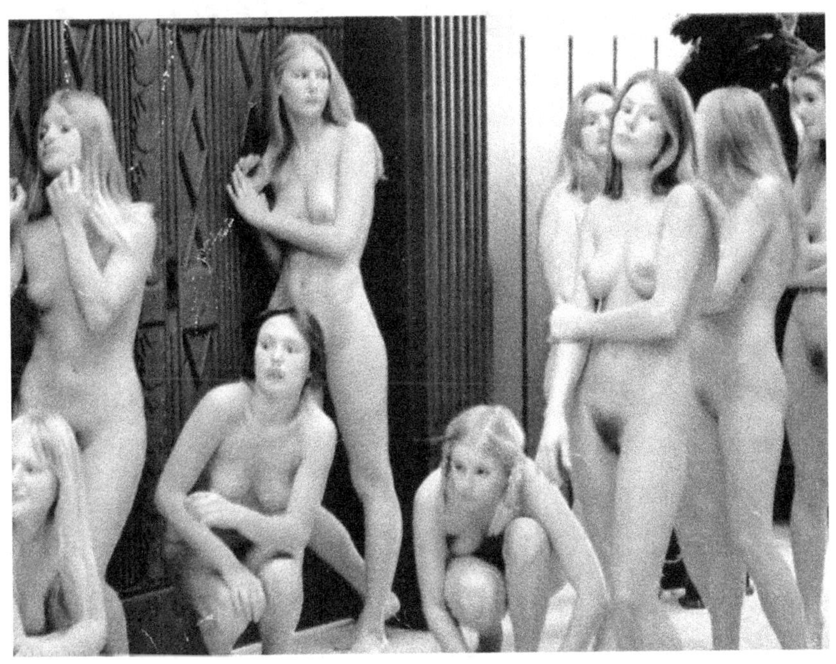

Immoral Tales (above). Behind Convent Walls (below).
Note the mirror, religious art, and roses.

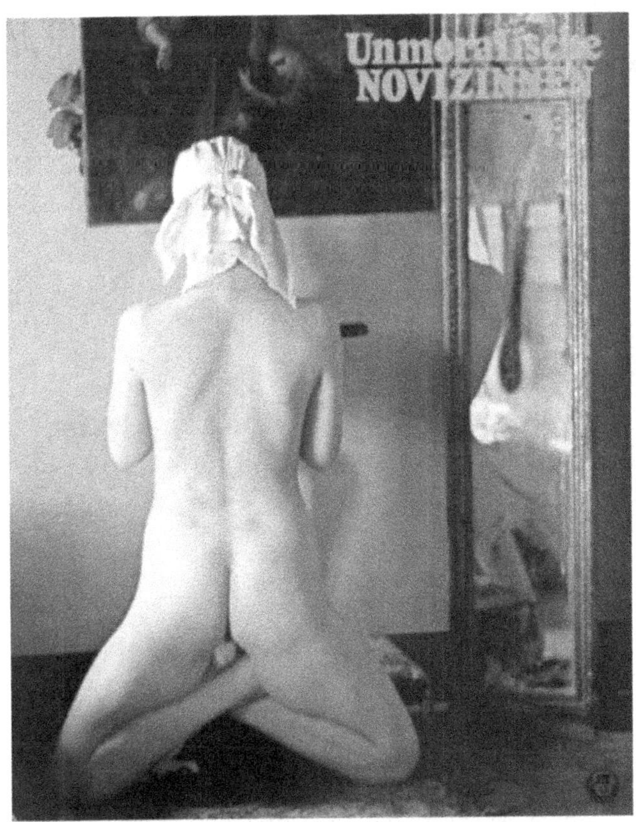

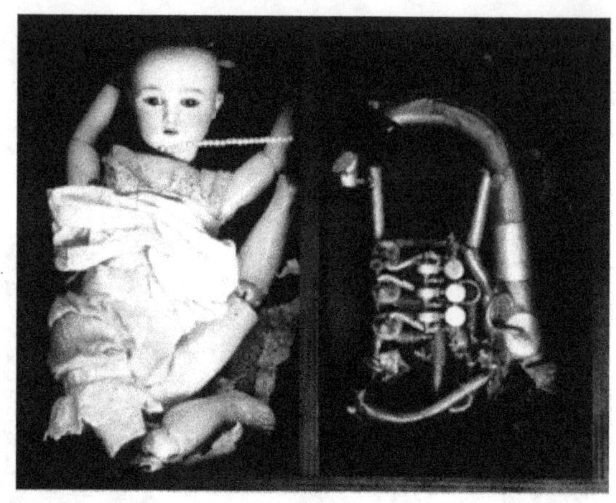

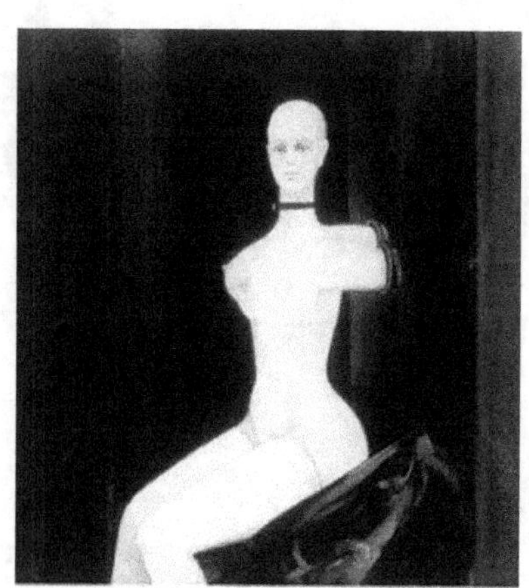

Examples of Walerian Borowczyk's art

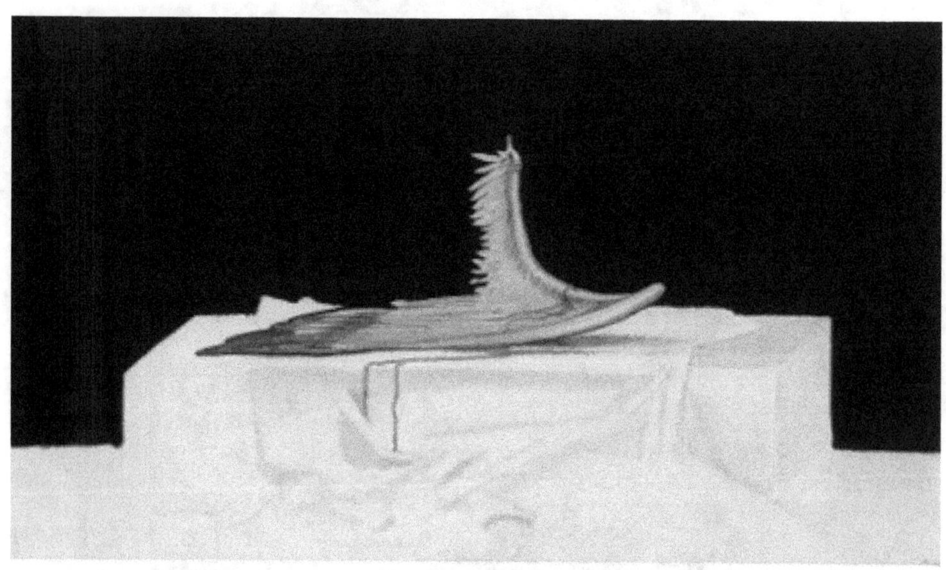

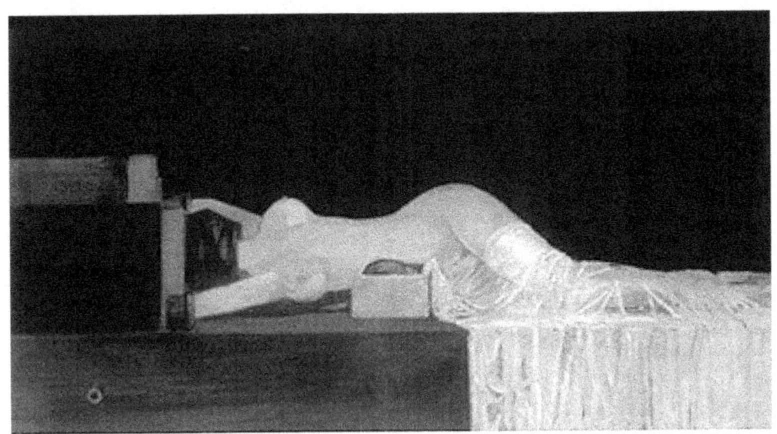

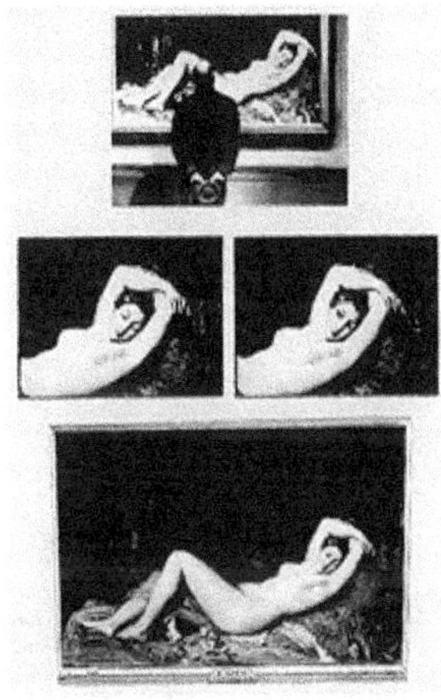

Examples of art by Walerian Borowczyk

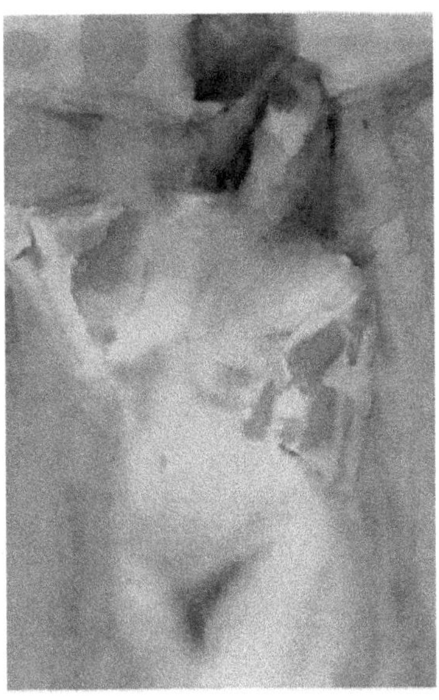

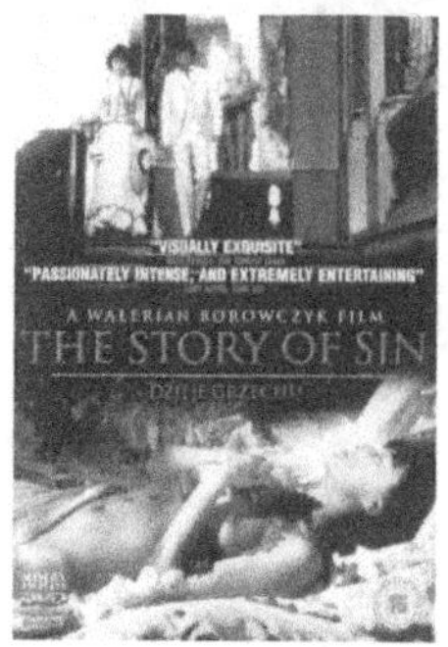

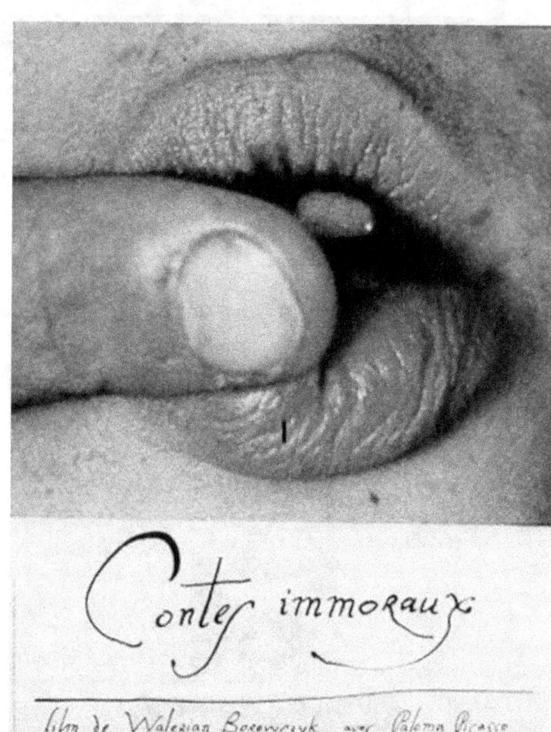

Some posters and artwork from Borowczyk's films

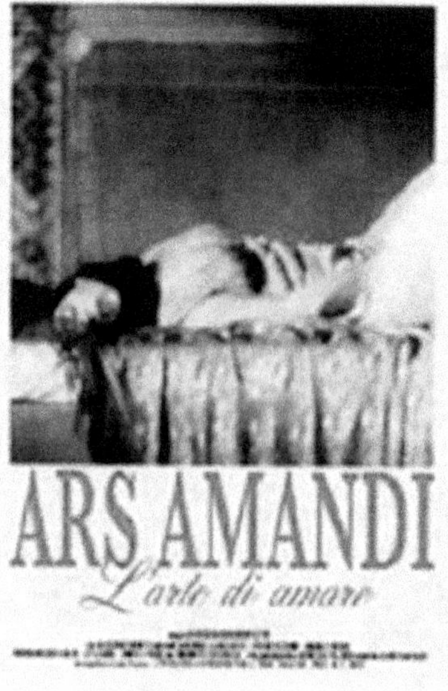

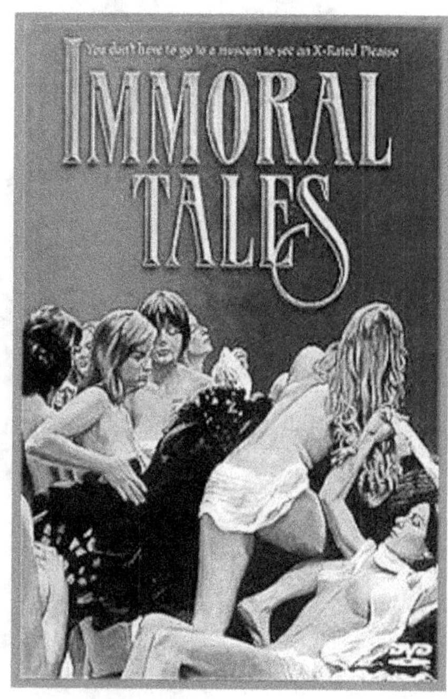

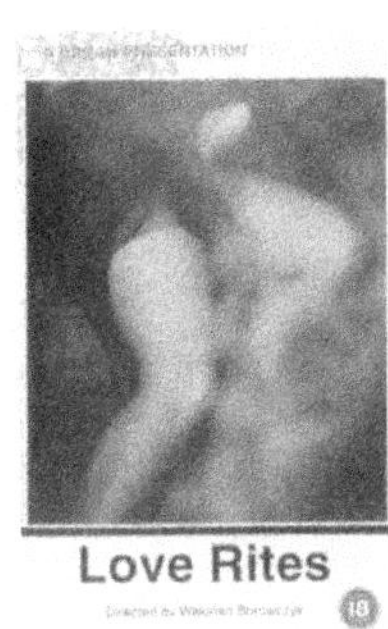

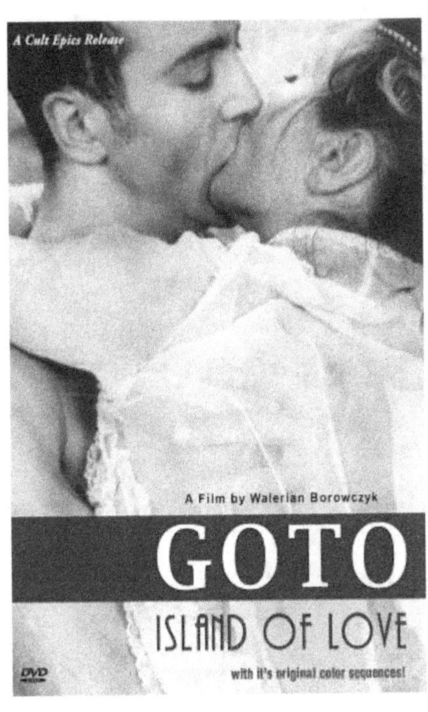

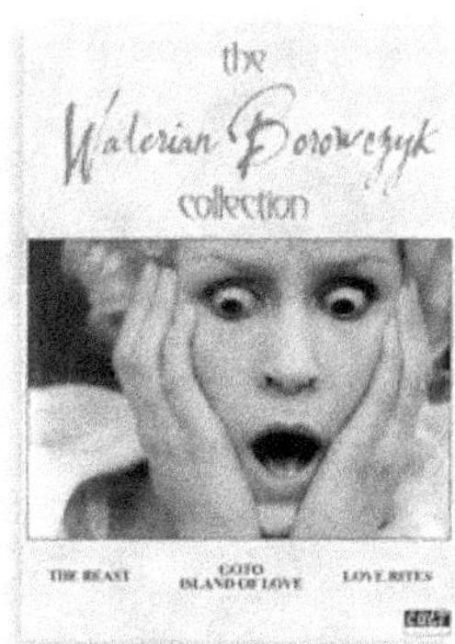

Some artwork for Walerian Borowczyk's films

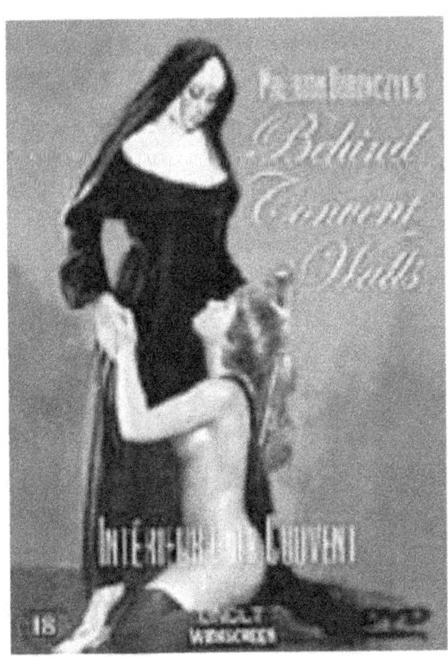

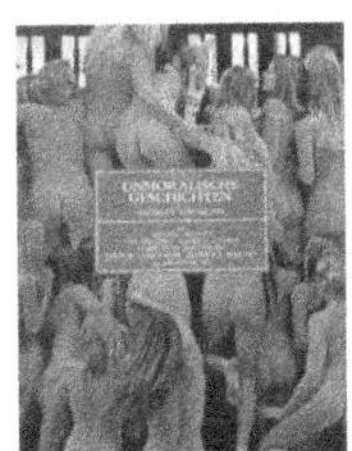

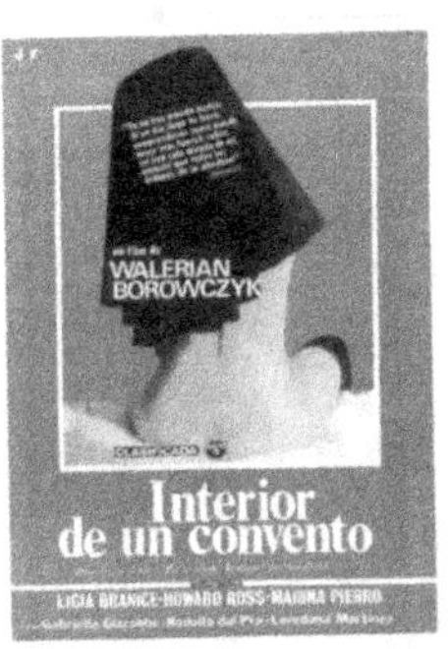

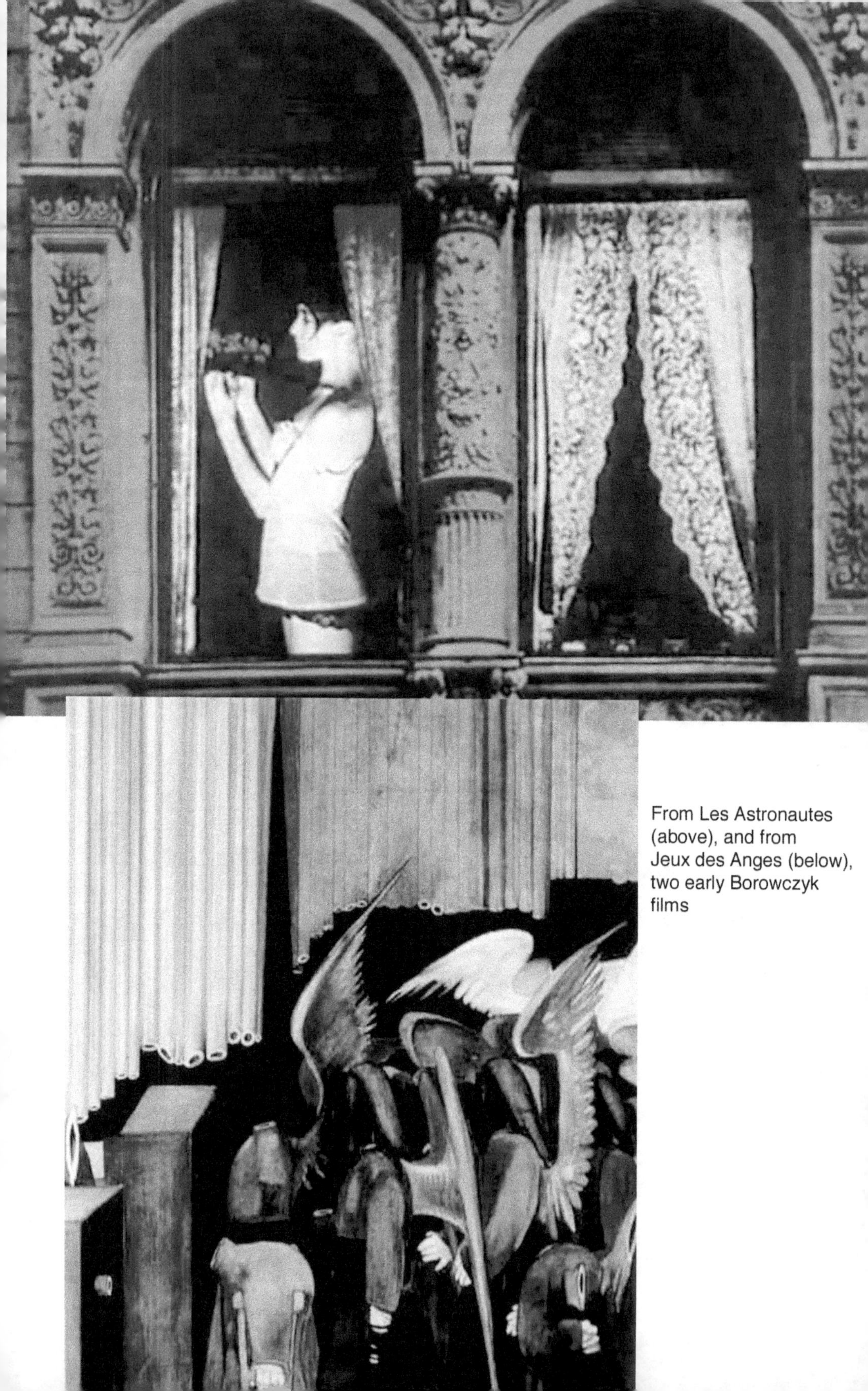

From Les Astronautes (above), and from Jeux des Anges (below), two early Borowczyk films

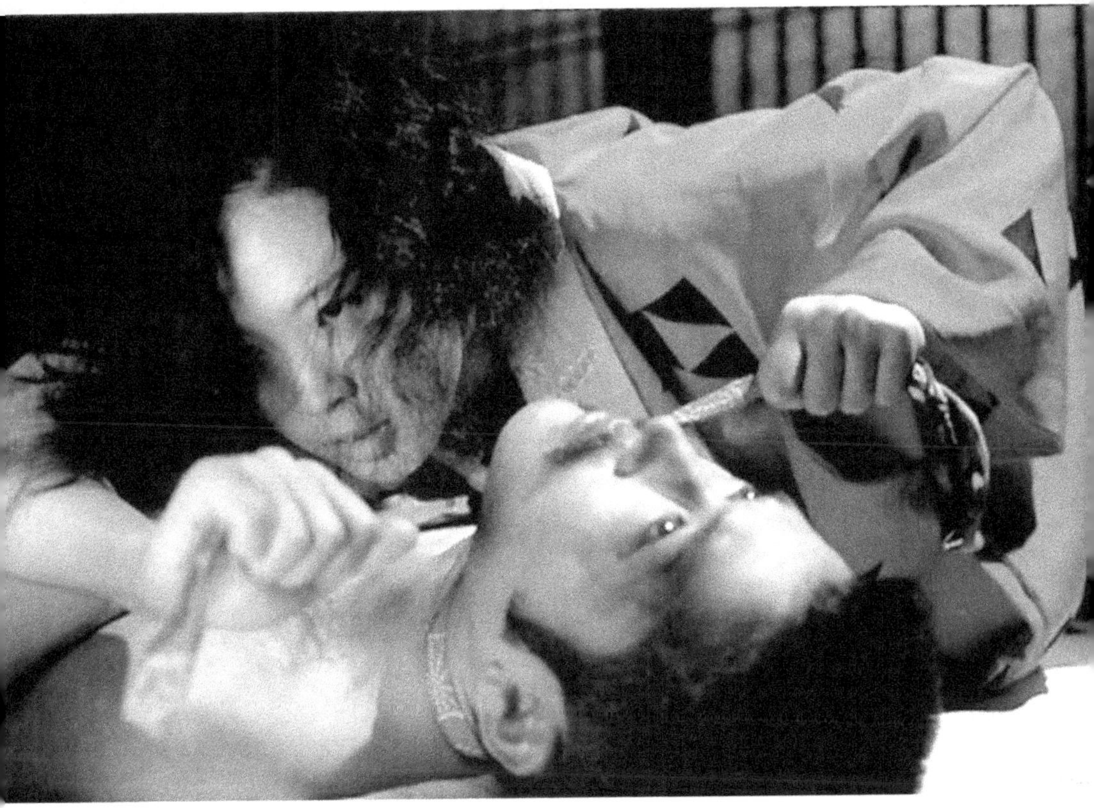

Two classic 'X' rated movies of the 1970s:
In the Realm of the Senses (above), and Last Tango In Paris (below).

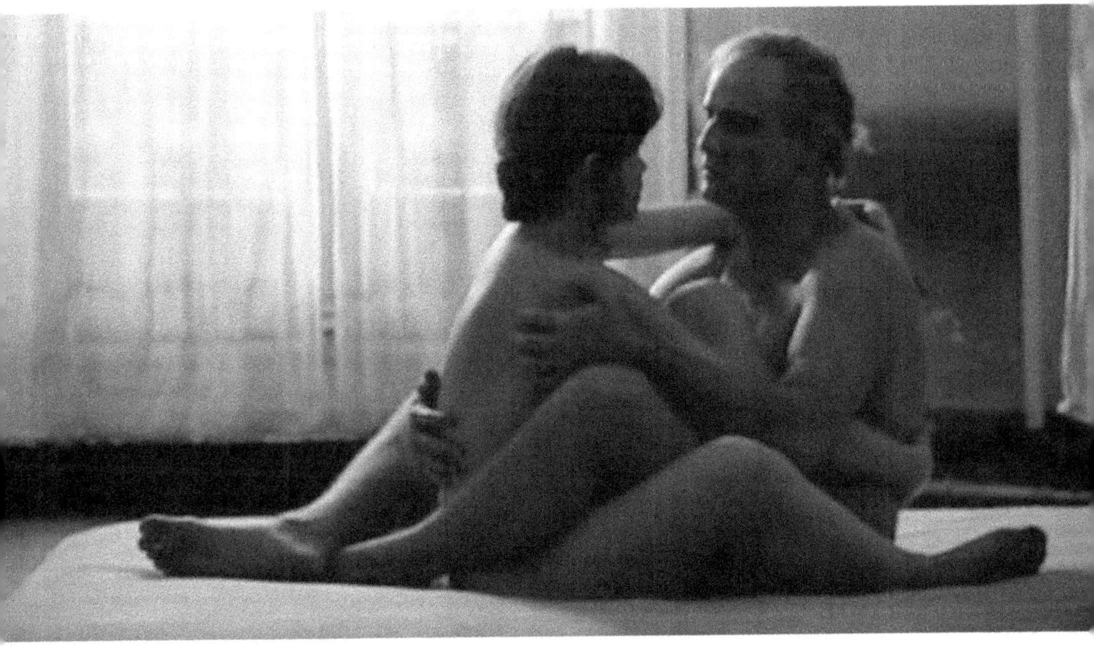

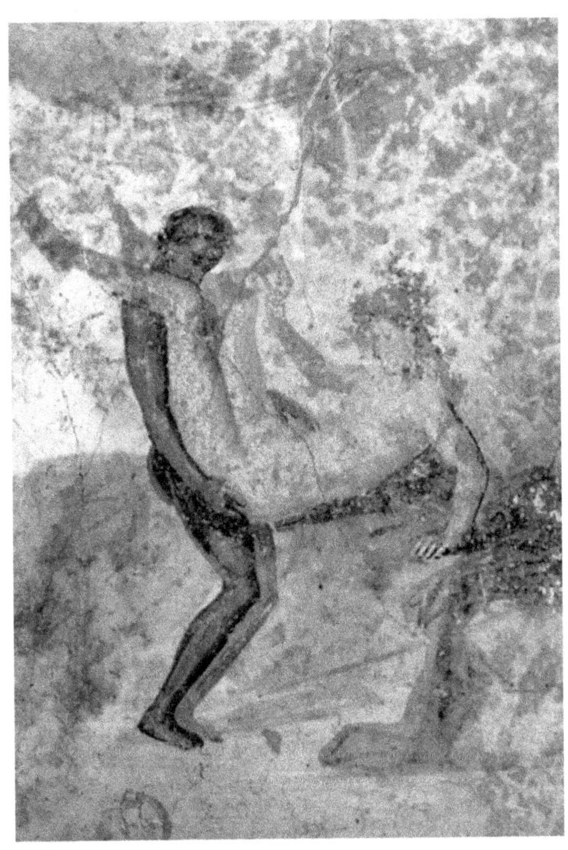

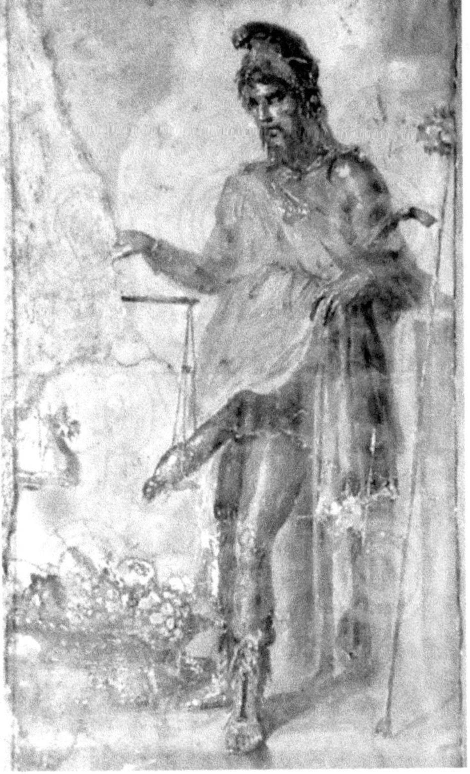

Ancient Roman images used by Borowczk in films such as The Art of Love and Three Immoral Women

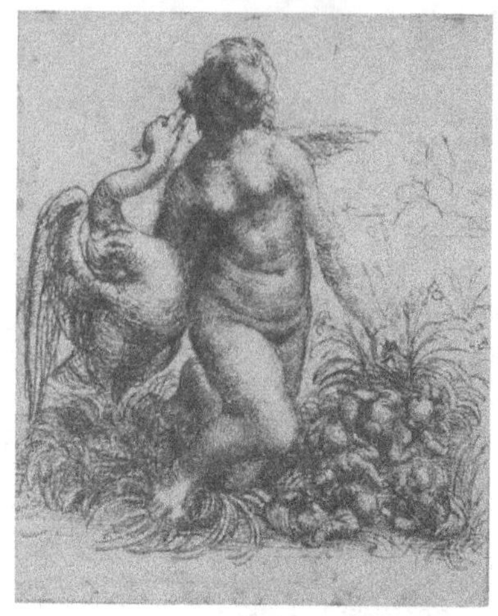

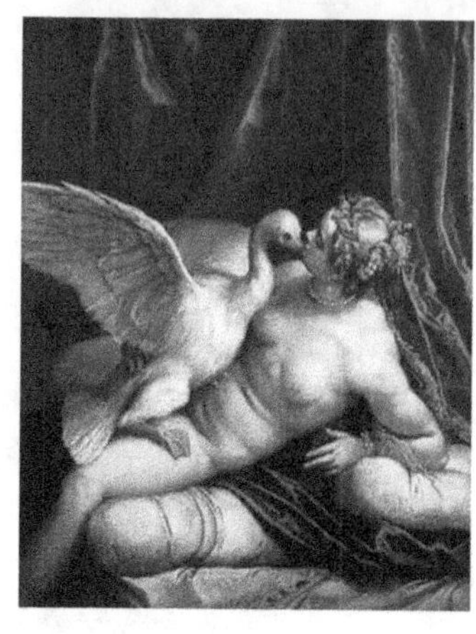

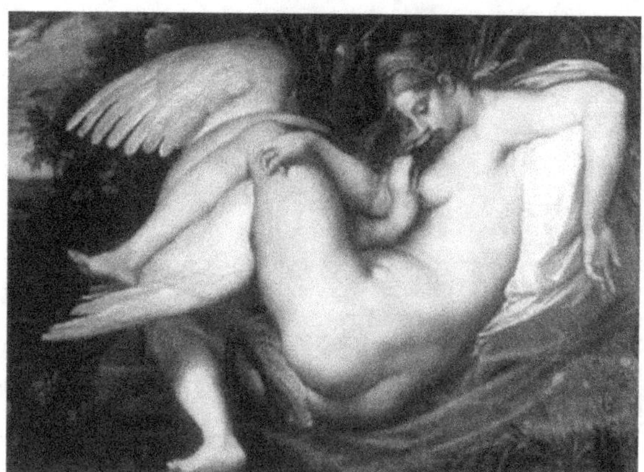

One of Walerian Borowczyk's favourite subjects in art, Leda and the Swan, in versions by Leonardo da Vinci, top, Veronese, top right. Peter Rubens, left, Giovanni Boldini, bottom left, and Luciano Castelli, below.

Asked who'd he like to be in history if he had the choice, Borowczyk said: 'if I have to choose an epoch and an identity, it would be that of Leda's swan in antiquity (if she really was as beautiful as the artists represent her)'.

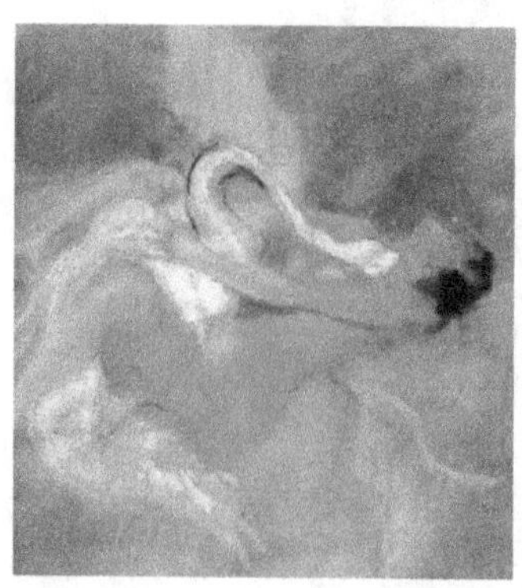

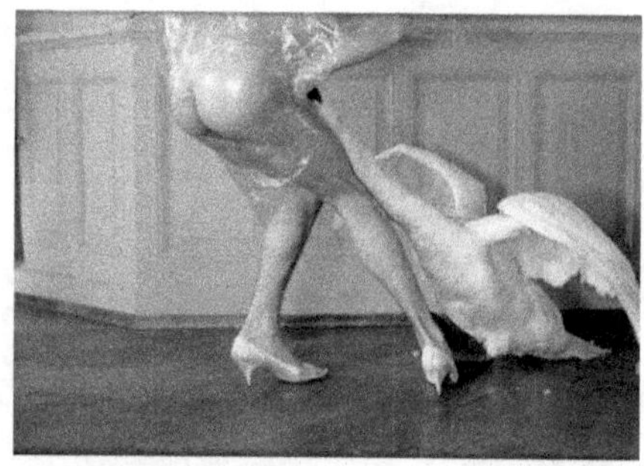

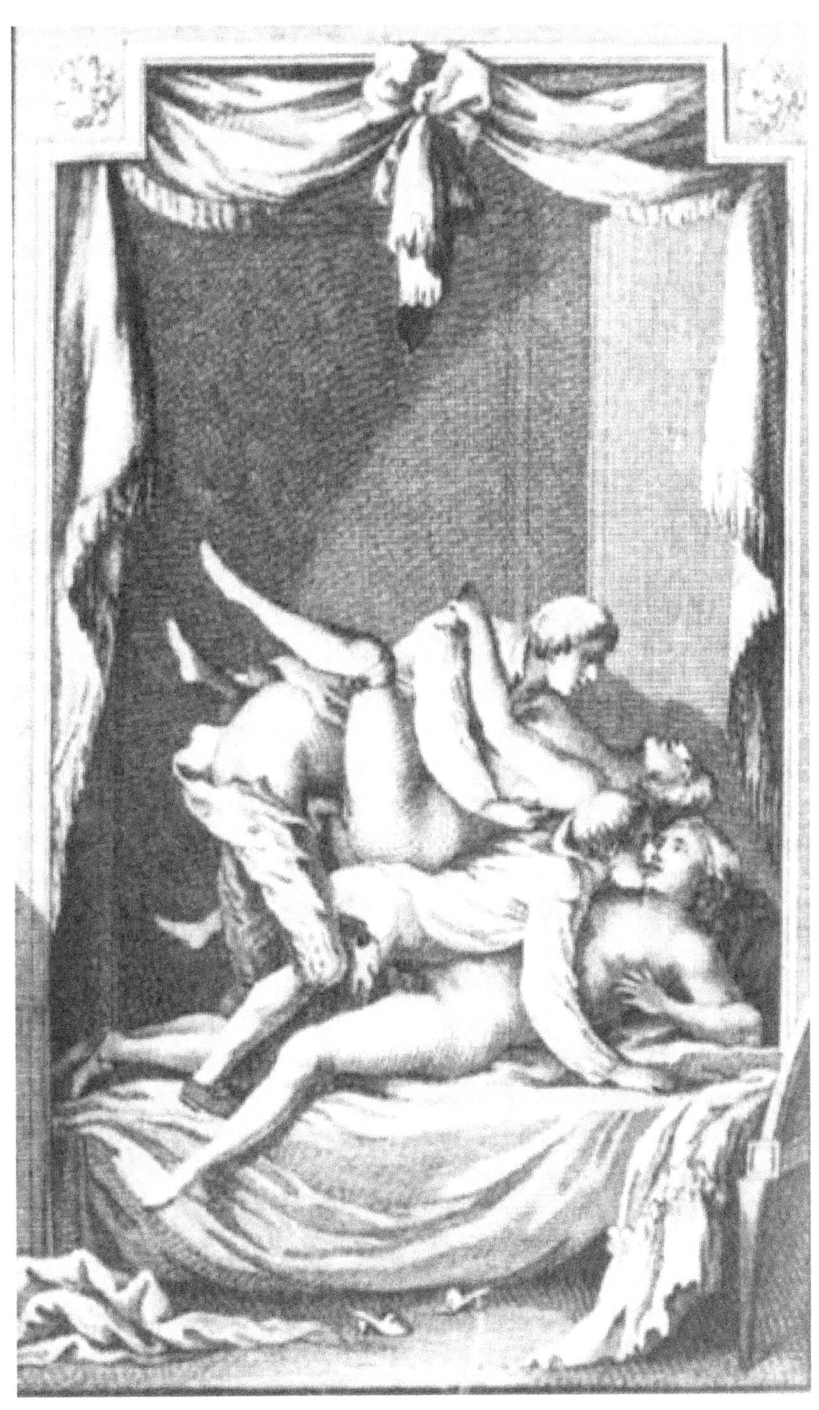

Antoine Borel, illustration for Mémoires de Saturnin,
by Jean-Charles Gervaise, 1787

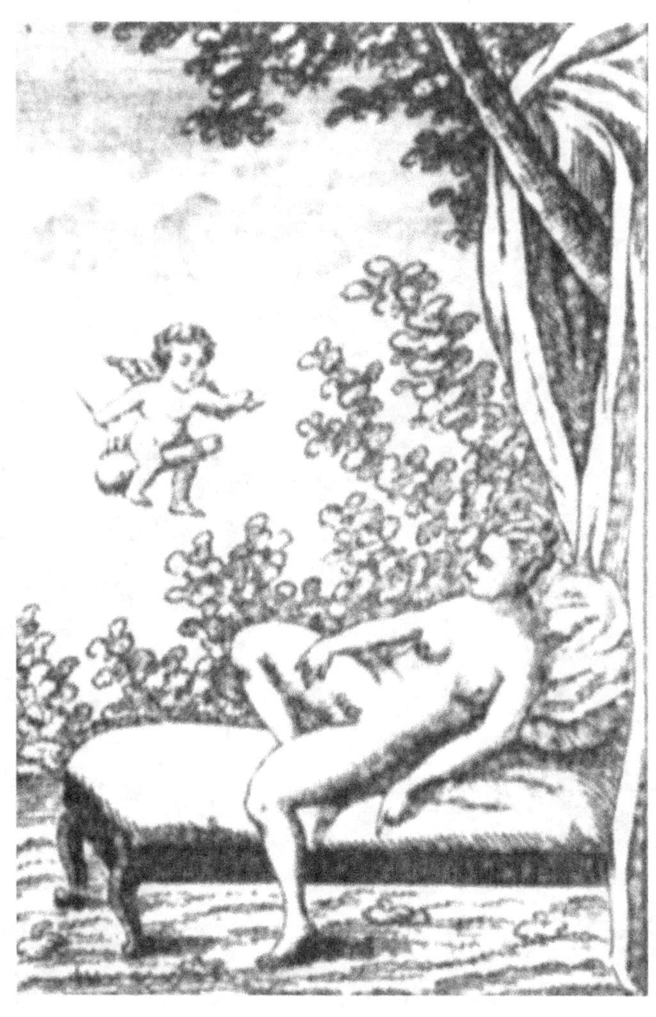

Anonymous, from Memoires de Suzon

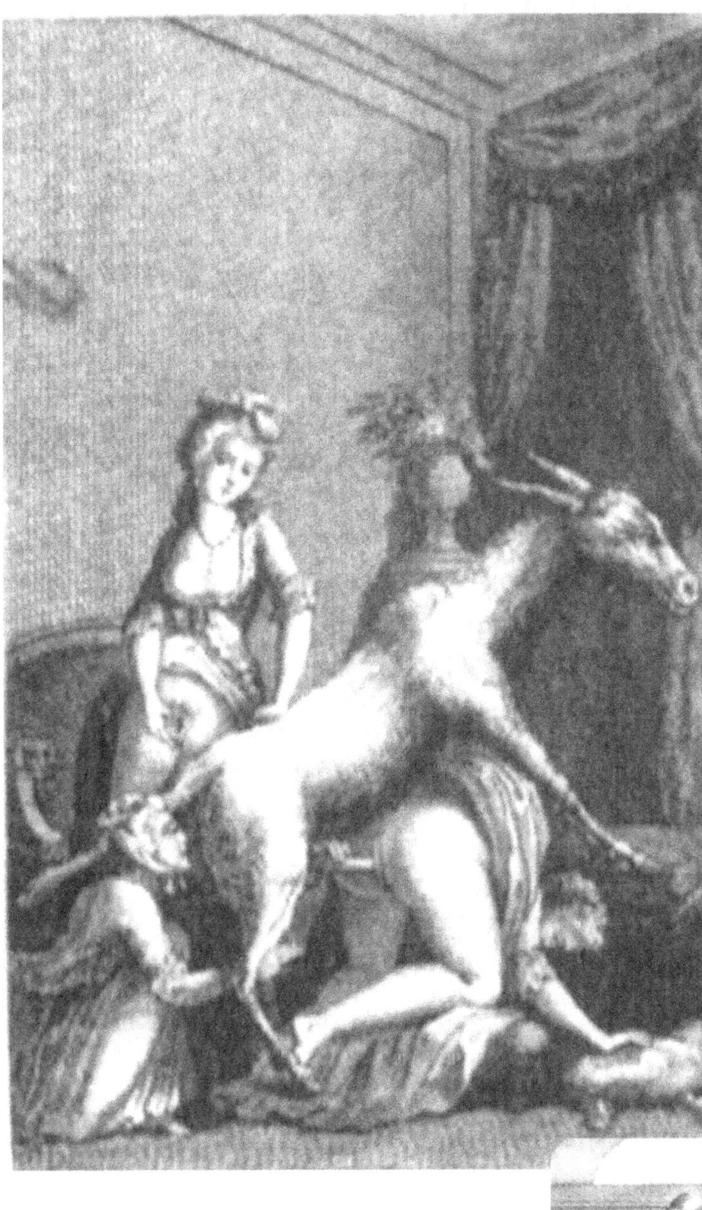

Anonymous, from Le Diable
(this page and over)

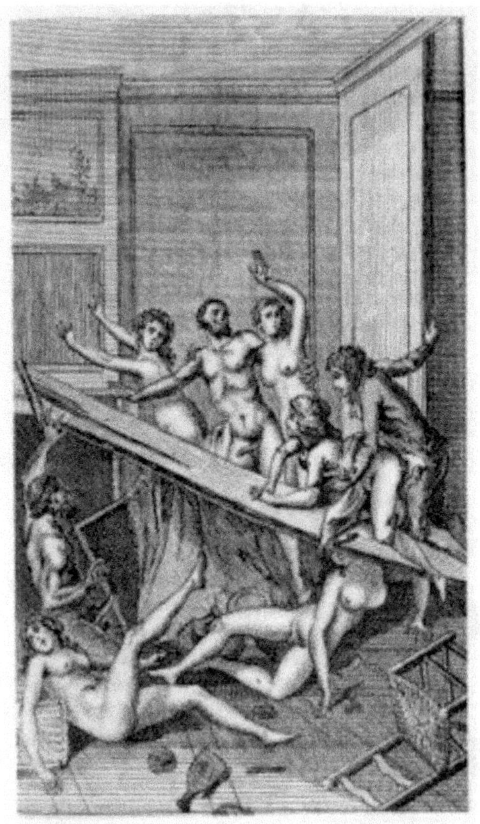

Illustration from Histoire de Juliette,
Marquis de Sade, 1797

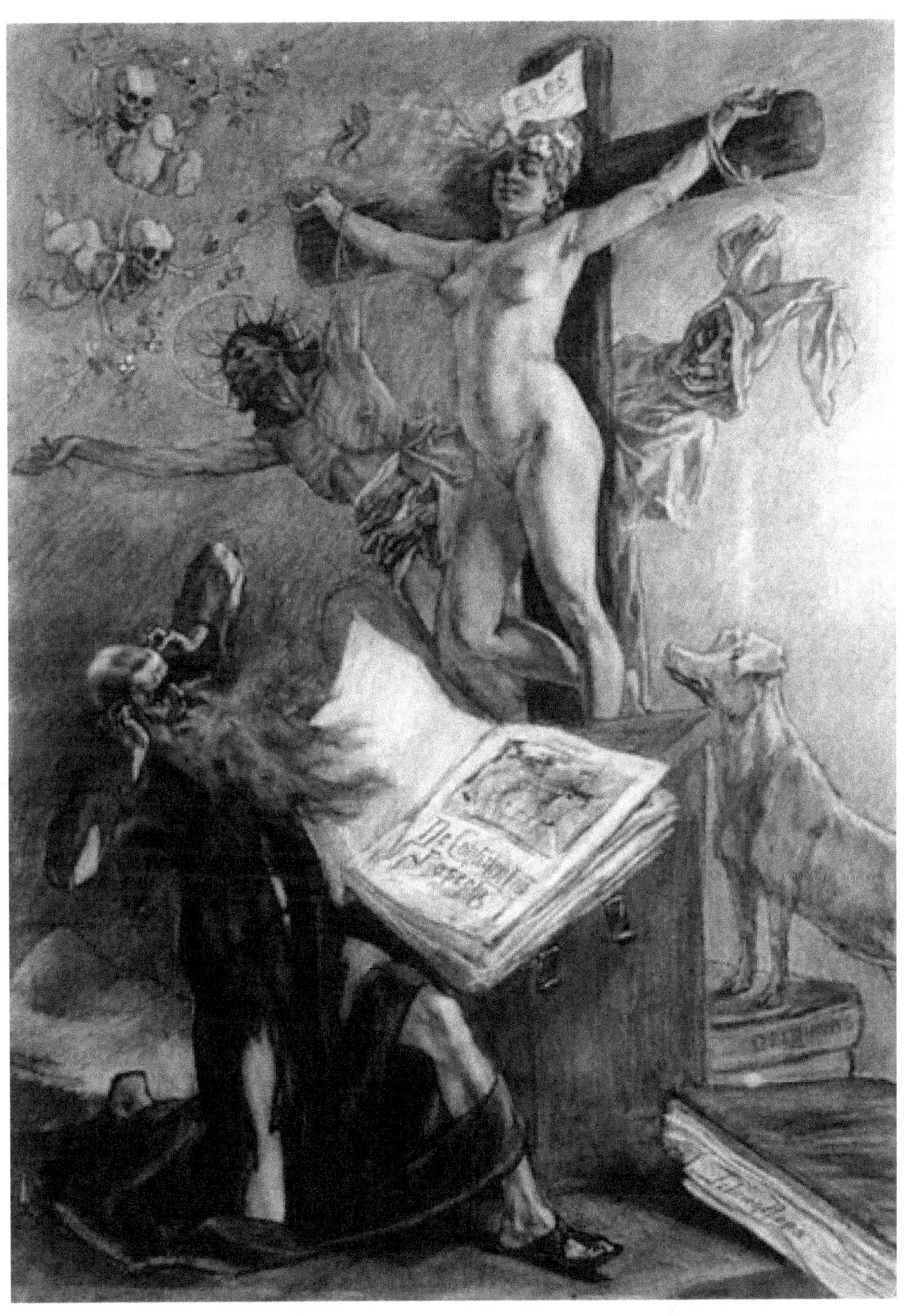

The Temptation of St Anthony, a popular subject of the era, by Félicien Rops

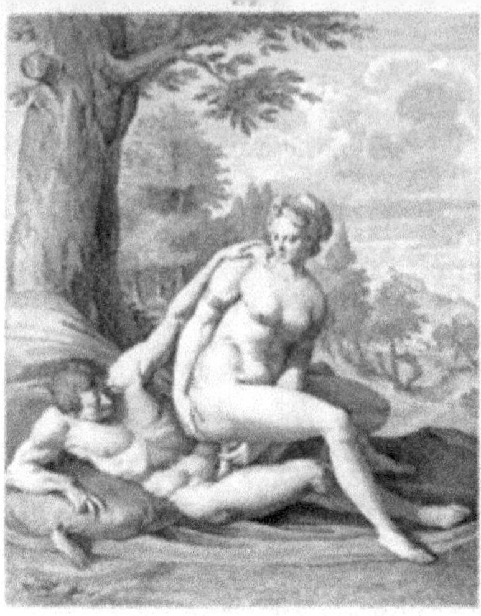

ANGELIQUE ET MEDOR.

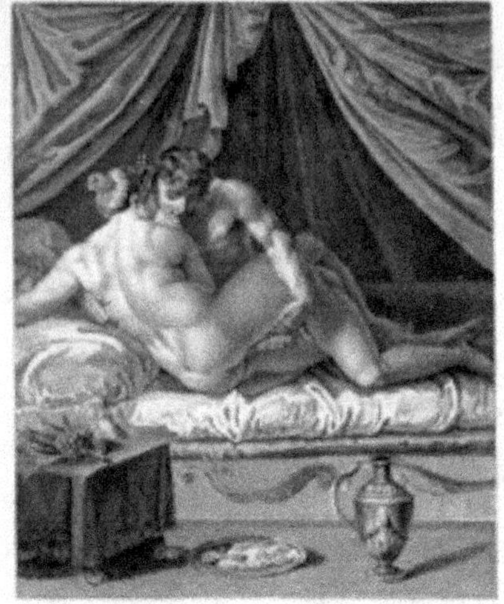

ANTOINE ET CLEOPATRE

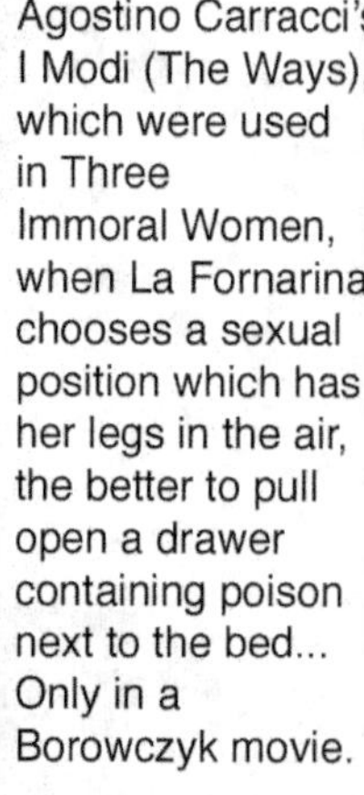

Agostino Carracci's I Modi (The Ways), which were used in Three Immoral Women, when La Fornarina chooses a sexual position which has her legs in the air, the better to pull open a drawer containing poison next to the bed... Only in a Borowczyk movie.

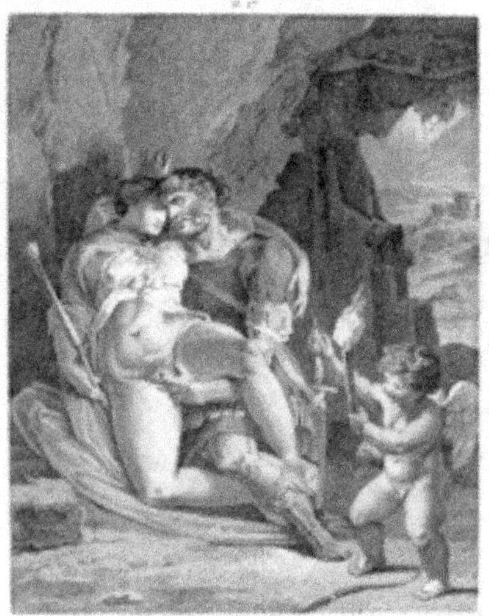

ENEE ET DIDON

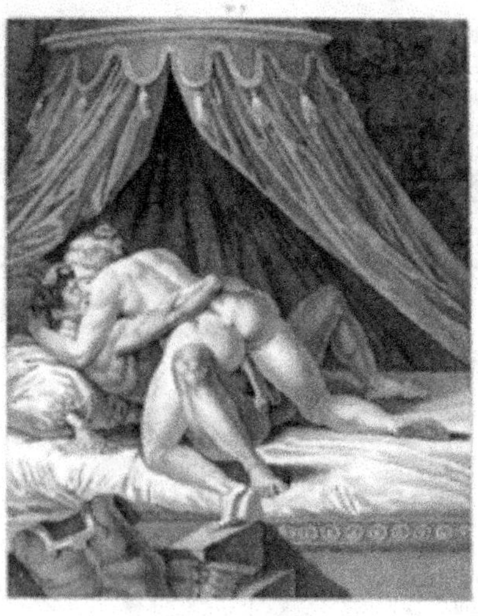

MARS ET VENUS

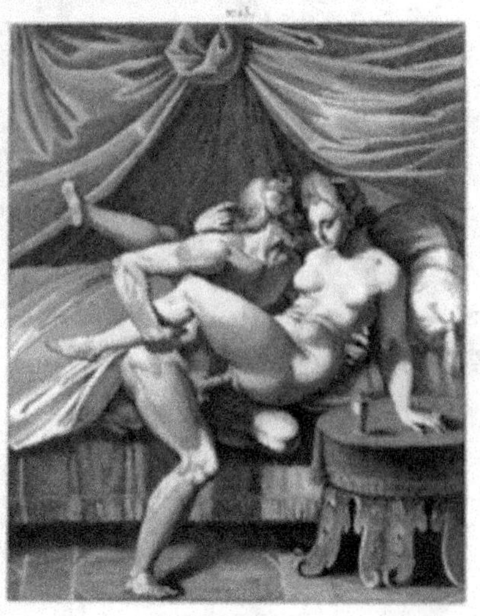

JUPITER ET JUNON

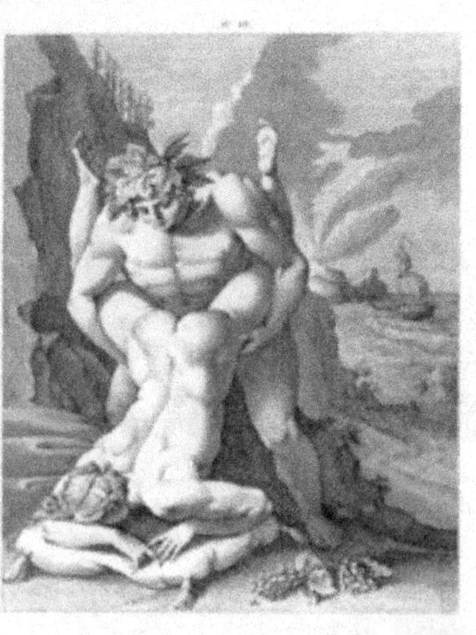

BACHUS ET ARIANE

N° II

POLYENOS ET CHRISIS

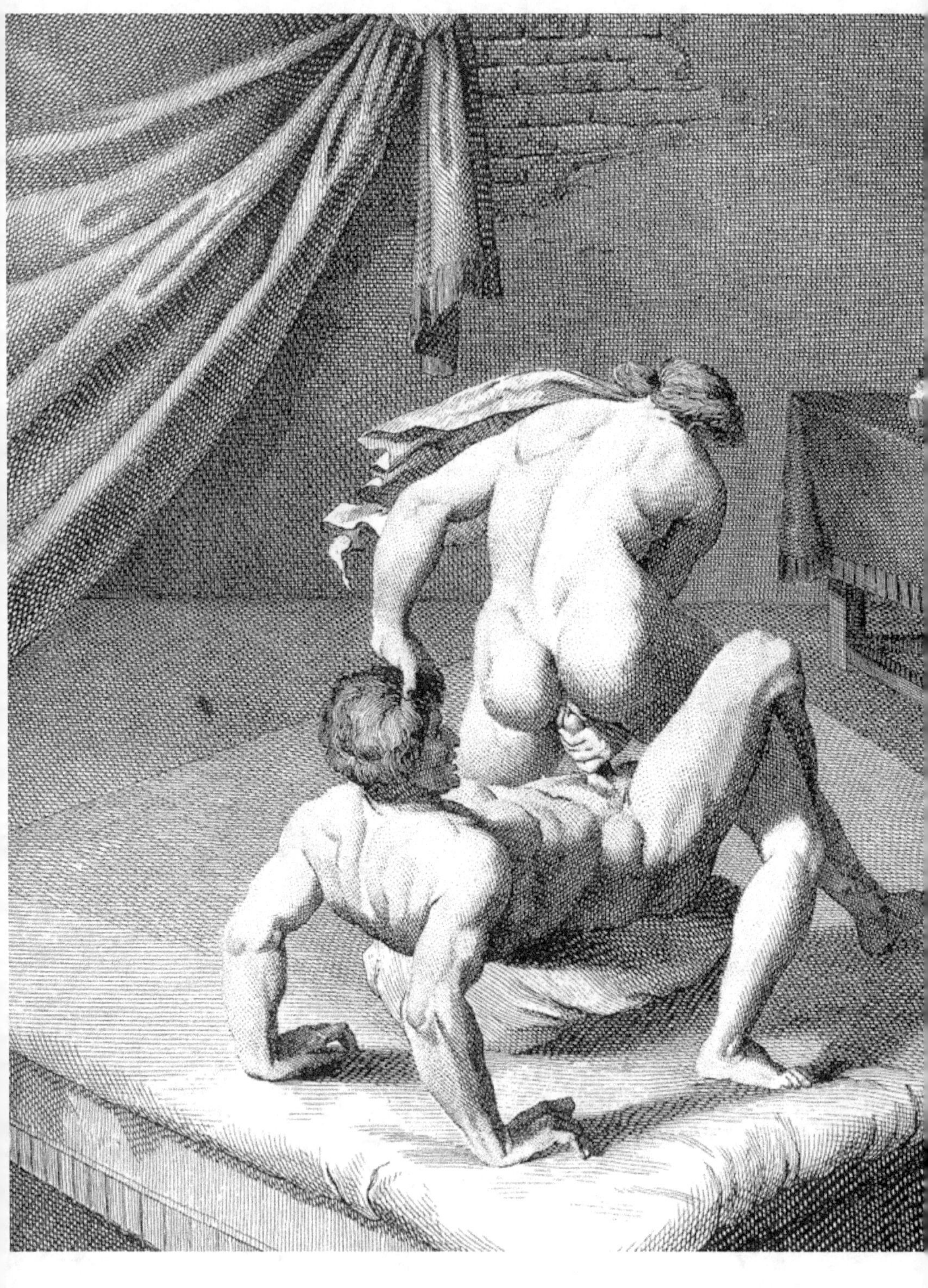

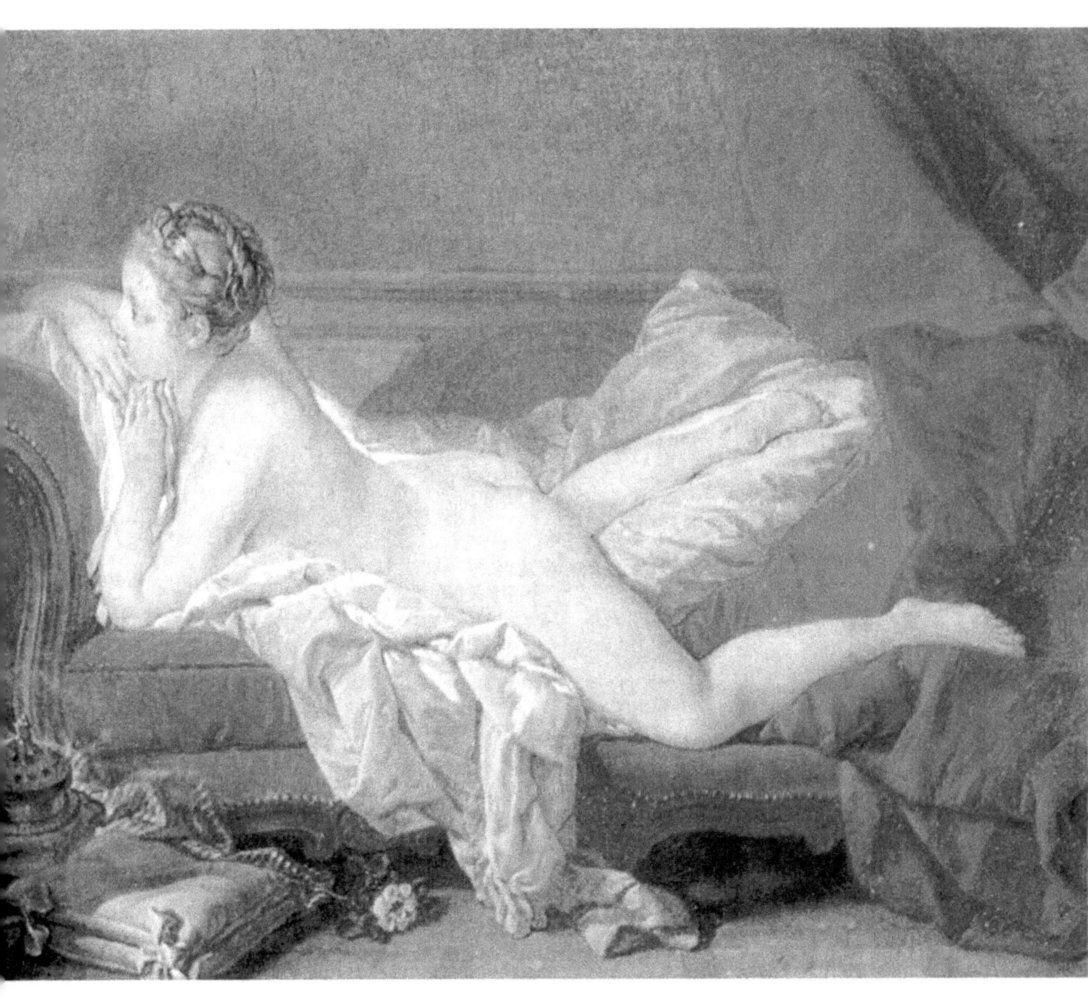

François Boucher, Madamoiselle O'Murphy, 1751

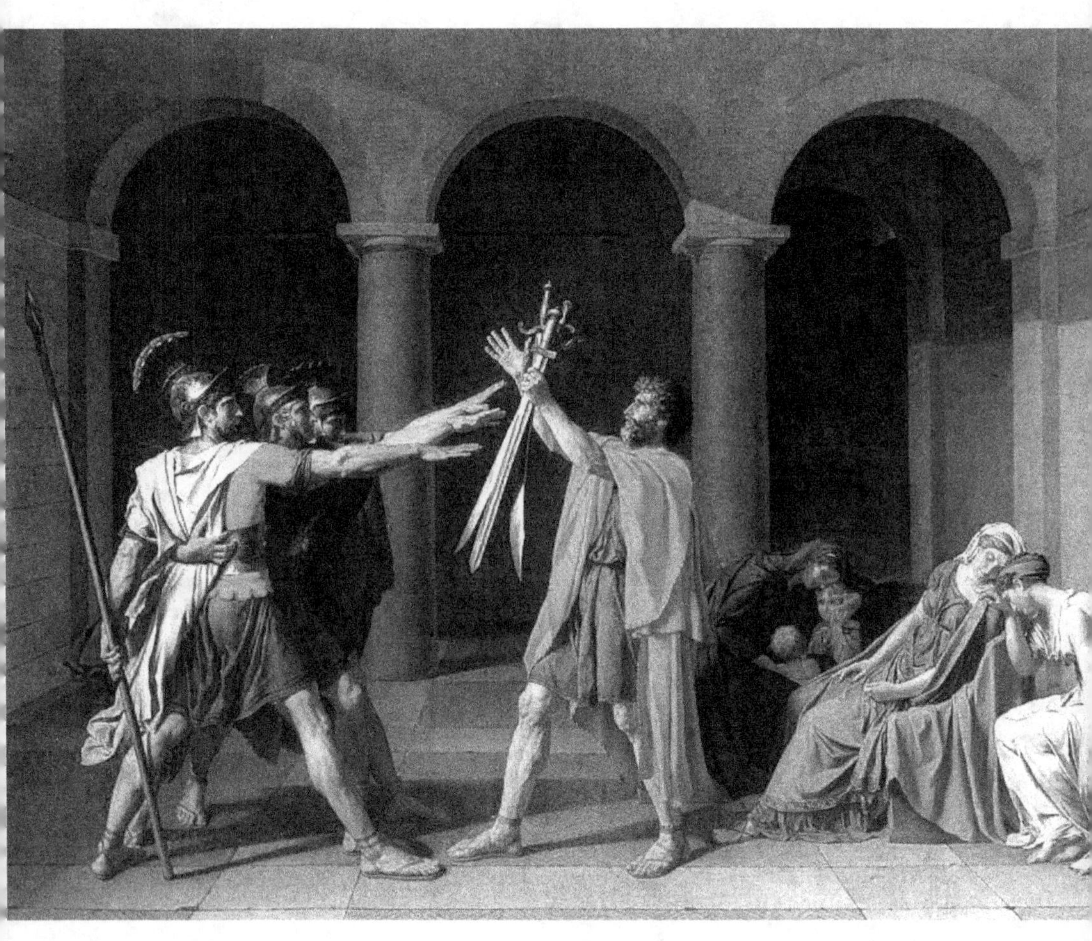

Jacques-Louis David, The Oath of Horatii, 1784, Louvre, Paris

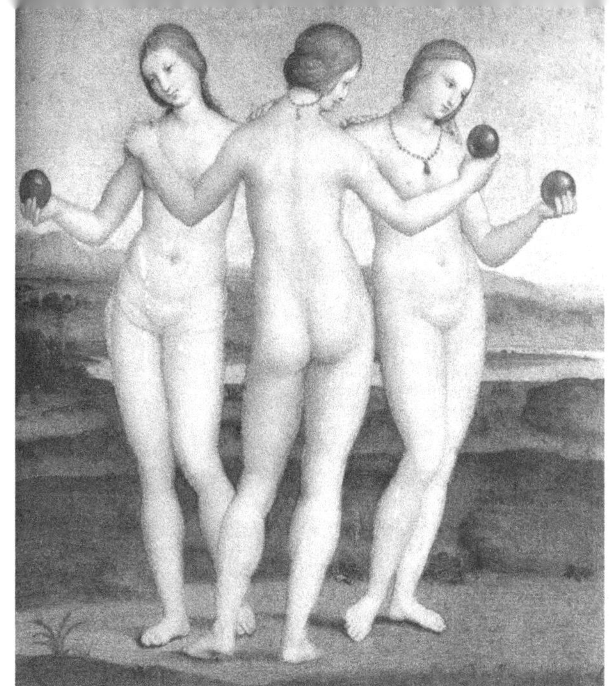

Two of Raphael's paintings recreated in
Three Immoral Women: The Three Graces (1504)
and The Liberation of St Peter (1512-14)

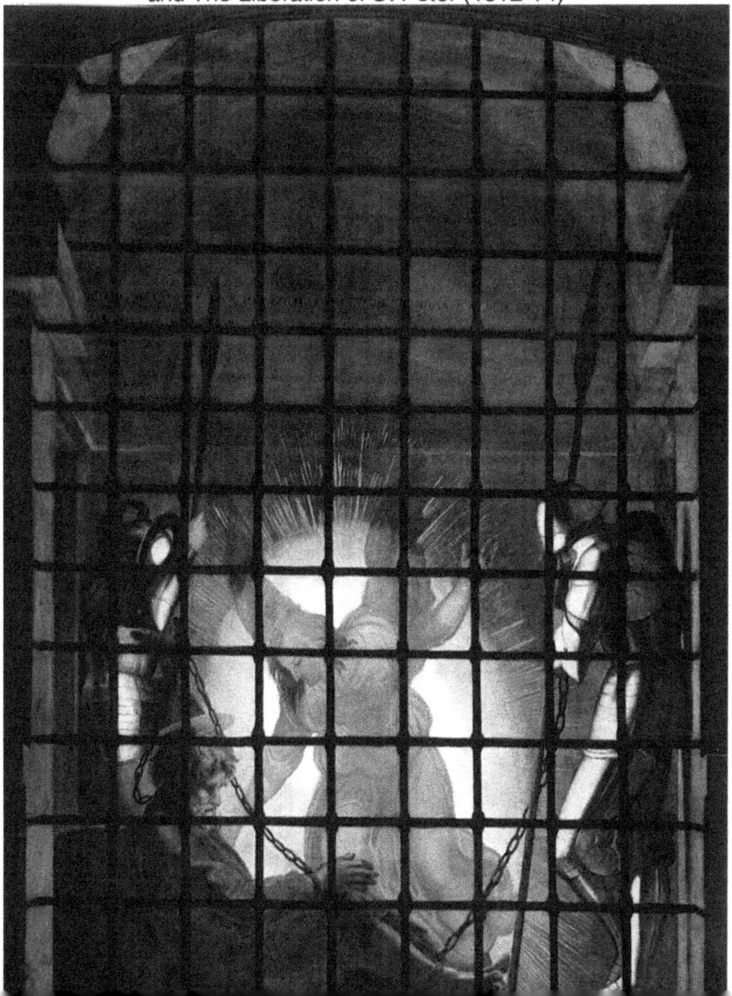

QUOTES BY WALERIAN BOROWCZYK

All stages of a film's creation are in me at one and the same time. My temperament does not allow me to create only part of a work and then to entrust the rest to specialists... I... eliminate the collaborators who dare to try and barter my own ideas with me. *I know everything*. And that very often drives members of my crew to tears.

⚜

I attach a great deal of importance to details

⚜

I conceive all my films in an instant, and only objective means prevent me from making them in that instant.

⚜

La Bête is a fantasy film and especially an 'adult film'. But first of all it is a film about dream mechanisms. Dreams translate our deepest desires. Why then cover with a veil of silence the temptation of an intimate relationship with an animal?

⚜

Eroticism, sex, is one of the most moral parts of life. Eroticism does not kill, exterminate, encourage evil, lead to crime. On the contrary, it makes people gentler, brings joy, gives fulfilment, leads to selfless pleasure.

⚜

If I have to choose an epoch and an identity, it would be that of Leda's swan in antiquity (if she really was as beautiful as the artists represent her).

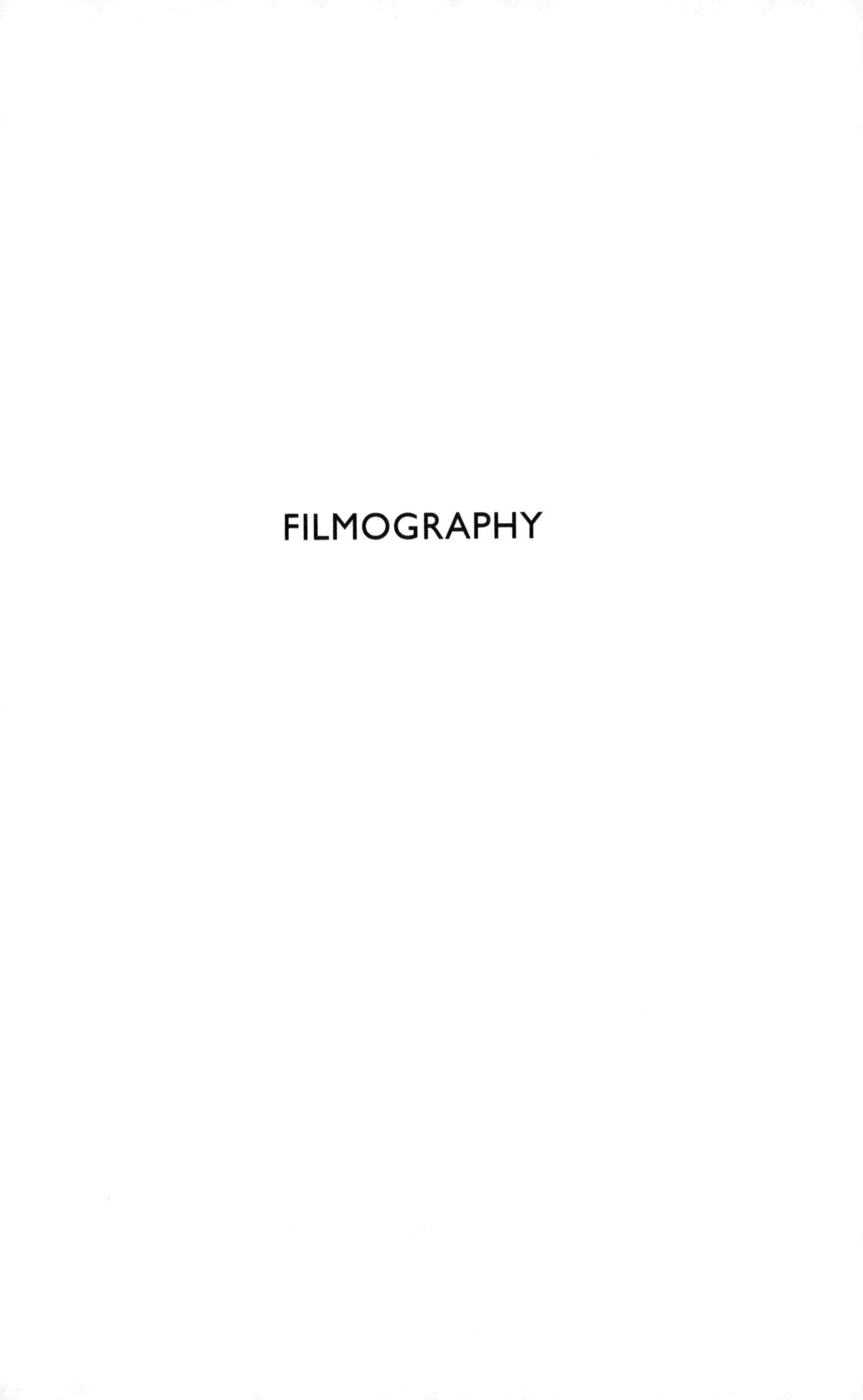

FILMOGRAPHY

FILMS DIRECTED BY WALERIAN BOROWCZYK

Goto, Island of Love (1968)

A.k.a. *Goto, l'île d'amour*

CAST

Jean-Pierre Andréani - Gono.
Fernand Berchet - Professor.
Ligia Branice - Glossia.
Pierre Brasseur - Goto.
Michel Charrel - Grymp.
Raoul Darblay - General Gwino.
René Dary - Gomor.
Ginette Leclerc - Gonasta.
Guy Saint-Jean - Grozo.
Michel Thomas - Gra.
Ari Arcadi - L'éxecuteur de chiens
Colette Régis - La directrice.
Percival Russel - Gotudo.
Pascale Brouillard - Gauda.

CREW

Producers - Louis Duchesne, René Thévenet
Script - Walerian Borowczyk, Dominique Duvergé
Cinematography - Guy Durban
Editing - Charles Bretoneiche
Makeup - Serge Groffe
Production Manager - Claude Cheutin
Assistant Director - Patrick Saglio
Sound - Gérard de Lagarde, Norbert Gernolle
Sound mixer - Jacques-Clément Duval
Editorial - Colette Cueille
Script supervisor - Suzanne Ohanessian

Blanche (1971)

CAST

Michel Simon - Master.
Georges Wilson - The King.
Jacques Perrin - Bartolomeo.
Ligia Branice - Blanche.
Denise Péronne - Madame d'Harcourt.

Lawrence Trimble - Nicolas.
Roberto - The Dwarf.
Jean Gras.
Michel Delahaye.
Genevieve Graves.
Stanley Barry.
Guy Bonnafoux.

CREW

Producer - Philippe d'Argila, Dominique Duvergé
Script - Walerian Borowczyk
Original Music - Christian Boissonnade, Annie Challan, Agnès Faucheux, Maurice-Pierre Gourrier, Florence Lassailly
Cinematography - André Dubreuil, Guy Durban
Editing - Walerian Borowczyk, Charles Bretoneiche
Production Design - Walerian Borowczyk, Jacques D'Ovidio
Art Direction - Jacques D'Ovidio
Costume Design - Piet Bolscher

Immoral Tales (1974)
A.k.a. *Contes Immoraux*

CAST

Lise Danvers - Julie.
Fabrice Luchini - Andre.
Charlotte Alexandra - Therese.
Florence Bellamy - Lucrezia Borgia.
Jacopo Berinzini - Pope Alexander VI.
G. Lorenzo Bernini - Cesare Borgia.
Pascale Christophe - Istvan.
Marie Forså - Close-up girl.
Paloma Picasso - Elisabeth Báthory.
Philippe Desboeuf - Giralomo Savonarola.
Robert Capia.
Kjell Gustavsson.
Tomas Hnevsa.
Nicole Karen.
Mathieu Rivollier.
Gerard Tcherka

CREW

Producer - Anatole Dauman
Script - Walerian Borowczyk, André Pieyre de Mandiargues
Original Music - Maurice Leroux

Cinematography - Bernard Daillencourt, Guy Durban, Noël Véry, Michel Zolat
Editing - Walerian Borowczyk
Production Design - Walerian Borowczyk
Costume Design - Piet Bolscher
Assistant Director - Dominique Duvergé

Story of Sin (1975)

CAST

Grazyna Dlugolecka - Ewa.
Jerzy Zelnik - Lukasz Niepolomski.
Olgierd Lukaszewicz - Count Szczerbic.
Roman Wilhelmi - Pochron.
Marek Walczewski - Plaza-Splawski.
Karolina Lubienska - Ewa's mother.
Zdzislaw Mrozewski - Ewa's father.
Mieczyslaw Voit - Cyprian Bodzanta.
Marek Bargielowski - Horst.
Jolanta Szemberg - Aniela.
Zbigniew Zapasiewicz - Priest.
Wladyslaw Hancza - Dr. Wilgosinski.
Jadwiga Chojnacka - Leoska.
Janusz Zakrzenski - Editor.
Zbigniew Koczanowicz - Chief clerk

CREW

Script - Walerian Borowczyk
Cinematography - Zygmunt Samosiuk
Editing - Lidia Pacewicz
Art Direction - Teresa Barska
Set Decoration - Marek Iwaszkiewicz
Costume Design - Jerzy Szeski, Roswita Stern
Makeup - Zbigniew Dobracki
Art Dept - Felicja Blaszynska
Production Manager - Helena Nowicka
Assistant Director - Ewa Smal
Sound - Jan Czerwinski

La Bête (1975)
A.k.a. *The Beast in Heat. The Beast. Death's Ecstasy*

CAST

Sirpa Lane - Romilda de l'Esperance.
Lisbeth Hummel - Lucy Broadhurst.
Elisabeth Kaza - Virginia Broadhurst.
Pierre Benedetti - Mathurin de l'Esperance.
Guy Tréjan - Pierre de l'Esperance.
Roland Armontel - Priest.
Marcel Dalio - Duc De Balo.
Pascale Rivault - Clarisse De l'Esperance.
Hassane Fall - Ifany.
Anna Baldaccini - Théodore.
Thierry Bourdon - Modeste.
Marie Testanière - Marie.
Stéphane Testanière - Stéphane.
Mathieu Rivollier.
Julien Hanany.
Robert Capia.

CREW

Producer - Anatole Dauman
Script - Walerian Borowczyk
Cinematography - Bernard Daillencourt, Marcel Grignon
Music - Domenico Scarlatti
Editing - Walerian Borowczyk
Production Design - Jacques D'Ovidio
Set Decoration - Alain Guillé
Costume Design - Piet Bolscher
Makeup Odette Berroyer
Production Manager Dominique Duvergé
Sound - Michel Laurent, Alex Pront, Jean-Pierre Ruh
Camera operator - Gérard Wurtz
Editorial - Florence Bory
Assistant editors - Alain Cayrade, Florence Dauman, Claude Delon, Jean-Pierre Platel, Monique Prim, Michel Valio

La Marge (1976)
A.k.a. *Emmanuelle '77. The Margin. The Streetwalker*

CAST

Sylvia Kristel – Diana.
Joe Dallesandro – Sigimond Pons.
André Falcon – Antonin Pons.
Mireille Audibert – Sergine Pons.
Denis Manuel – Man with a moustache.
Norma Piccadilly – The stripper.
Louise Chevalier – Feline.
Dominique Marcas.
Camille Larivière.
Luz Laurent.
Karin Albin.
Jean Lara.
Carlo Nell.
Dominique Erlanger.
Sylvaine Charlet

CREW

Producer – Raymond and Robert Hakim
Script – Walerian Borowczyk
Cinematography – Bernard Daillencourt
Editing – Louisette Hautecoeur
Production Design – Jacques D'Ovidio
Costume Design – Marie-Françoise Perochon
Makeup – Jacky Bouban
Production Manager – Henri Baum
Assistant Director – Alain Cayrade
Sound – Maurice Gilbert, Louis Hochet
Assistant camera – Jean-Pierre Platel
Editorial – Khadicha Bariha

Behind Convent Walls (1977)
A.k.a. *Interno di un convento. Sex Life in a Convent. Within a Cloister*

CAST

Ligia Branice – Sister Clara.
Howard Ross – Rodrigo Landriani.
Marina Pierro – Sister Veronica.
Gabriella Giacobbe – Abbess Flavia Orsini.

Rodolfo Dal Pra - Bishop.
Loredana Martínez - Sister Martina.
Mario Maranzana - Father Confessor.
Alessandro Partexano - Silva.
Olivia Pascal.
Gina Rovere.
Dora Calindri.
Francesca Balletta.
Maria Cumani Quasimodo.
Raymonde Carole Fouano.
Miana Merini

CREW

Producer - Giuseppe Vezzani
Script - Walerian Borowczyk
Original Music - Sergio Montori
Cinematography - Luciano Tovoli
Editing - Walerian Borowczyk, Roberto Olivieri
Set Decoration - Francesco Chianese, Luciano Spadoni
Costume Design - Maria Laura Zampacavallo
Makeup - Franco Ruffini
Art dept - Filippo Bufo
Sound - Carlo Palmieri, Alberto Tinebra
Special Effects - Giulio Molinari
Assistant camera - Giuseppe Tinelli

Three Immoral Women (1979)
A.k.a. *Heroines of Evil. Heroines of Pain. Immoral Women*

CAST

Marina Pierro - Margherita Lutti.
Gaëlle Legrand - Marceline Cain.
Pascale Christophe - Marie.
François Guétary - Raphael Sanzio.
Jean-Claude Dreyfus - Bini.
Jean Martinelli - Pope.
Pierre Benedetti - Mad Painter.
Philippe Desboeuf - Doctor.
Noël Simsolo - Julio Romano.
Roger Lefrere - Michelangelo.
Gérard Falconetti - Tomaso.
Hassane Fall - Petrus.
France Rumilly - Madame Cain.
Yves Gourvil - Cain.
Lisbeth Arno - Floka.

Gérard Ismaël - Antoine.
Henri Piégay - Husband.
Mathieu Rivollier.
Robert Capia.
Daniel Marty.
Jacky Baudet.
Sylvain Ramsamy.
Jean Boullu.
Françoise Queré.
Mazouz Ould-Abderrahmane.
Bernard Hiard

CREW

Producers - Pierre Braunberger and Gisèle Braunberger
Executive producers - Jean-Paul De Vidas, Michel de Vidas
Script - Walerian Borowczyk, story - André Pieyre de Mandiargues
Cinematography - Bernard Daillencourt
Editing - Khadicha Bariha
Production design - Jacques D'Ovidio
Production manager - Emilienne Pecqueur
Original Music - Philippe d'Aram, Olivier Dassault
Sound - Eric Rophe

Lulu (1980)

CAST

Anne Bennent - Lulu.
Michele Placido - Schwarz.
Jean-Jacques Delbo - Doctor Goll.
Hans-Jürgen Schatz - Alwa Schoen.
Bruno Hübner - Schigolch.
Beate Kopp - Baroness Geschwitz.
Carlo Enrici - Monsieur Hunidei.
Pierre Saintons - Kungu Poti.
Udo Kier - Jack the Ripper.
Heinz Bennent - Dr. Schoen

CREW

Producers - Robert Kuperberg, Jean-Pierre Labrande
Script - Walerian Borowczyk, Anton Giulio Majano, Géza von Radványi
Original Music - Giancarlo Chiaramello
Cinematography - Michael Steinke
Editing - Khadicha Bariha
Production Design - Walerian Borowczyk

Doctor Jeckyll and His Women (1981)

A.k.a. *Docteur Jekyll et les femmes. The Blood of Doctor Jeckyll. The Bloodbath of Doctor Jeckyll. Bloodlust. Dr. Jeckyll and Miss Osbourne. The Experiment*

CAST

Udo Kier – Dr. Henry Jeckyll.
Marina Pierro – Miss Fanny Osbourne.
Patrick Magee – General.
Gérard Zalcberg – Mr. Hyde.
Howard Vernon – Dr. Lanyon.
Clément Harari – Reverend Donald Regan.
Jean Mylonas. Eugene Braun Munk.
Louis-Michel Colla.
Catherine Coste.
Rita Maiden.
Michèle Maze.
Agnès Daems.
Magali Noaro.
Dominique Andersen.
Isabelle Cagnat.
Gisèle Préville

CREW

Producers – Ralph Baum, Robert Kuperberg, Jean-Pierre Labrande
Script – Walerian Borowczyk, from Robert Louis Stevenson's novel *The Strange Case of Dr. Jeckyll and Mr. Hyde*
Original Music – Bernard Parmegiani
Cinematography – Noël Véry
Editing – Khadicha Bariha
Production Design – Walerian Borowczyk
Costume Design – Piet Bolscher
Makeup – Christine Fornelli
Production Manager – Martine Alleton
Assistant Director – Roland Fruytier
Sound – Gérard Barra, Alex Pront

The Art of Love (1983)
A.k.a. *Ars Amandi. L'arte di amare. L'Art d'aimer*

CAST

Marina Pierro - Claudia.
Michele Placido - Macarius.
Massimo Girotti - Ovid.
Laura Betti - Clio.
Milena Vukotic - Modestina.
Philippe Lemaire - General Laurentius.
Mireille Pame - Sepora.
Philippe Taccini - Cornelius.
Simonetta Stefanelli - Vedova Nero.
Antonio Orlando - Rufus.
Gian Francesco Aiello - Flavius

CREW

Producers - Marcel Albertini, Jacques Nahum, Ugo Tucci
Script - Walerian Borowczyk, Wilhelm Buchheim, Enzo Ungari
Original Music - Luis Enríquez Bacalov
Cinematography - Walerian Borowczyk, Noël Véry
Editing - Walerian Borowczyk
Costume Design - Luciana Marinucci
Assistant Director - Gianni Ricci
Sound - Claudio Oliviero

Emmanuelle 5 (1987)

CAST

Monique Gabrielle - Emmanuelle.
Crofton Hardester - Eric Dana.
Burns Westburg - Charles Foster.
Yaseen Khan - Rajid.
Julie Miklas - Linda.
Pamm Vlastas - Suvi.
Max Strom - Talking Soldier.
Heidi Paine - Girl No. 1.
Roxanna Michaels - Girl No. 2.
Michele Burger - Girl No. 3.
Bryan Shane.
Marie Chocolat.
Marie Vanille.
Isabelle Strawa.
Muriel Catau.

Jessica Stehl.
Michael Rogers.
Peter Lowell.
Noelle Fabiani.
François Clavier.
Paul Ricci.
Katia Valys.
André Kay.
Claude Bruna.
Martine Coudeville

CREW

Producer - Alain Siritzky
Script - Walerian Borowczyk and Alex Cunningham
Original Music - Pierre Bachelet, Bernard LeVitte
Cinematography - Zoran Hochstätter, Max Monteillet
Editing - Nina Gilberti, Kevin Tent
Production Design - Steve Greenberg
Assistant Director - Thierry Bazin
Costume Design - A.C. Lathuilliere, Kimberly Love, Sophie Maret

Love Rites (1988)
A.k.a. *Cérémonie d'amour. Queen of the Night. Rites of Love*

CAST

Marina Pierro - Miriam.
Mathieu Carrière - Hugo Arnold.
Josy Bernard - Miriem.
Jean Négroni - Narrator.
Isabelle Tinard.
Jacques Couderc.
Guy Bonnafoux.
Claudine Berg.
Lucette Gill.
Julian Lee.
Jennifer Ford.
Sabrina Belleval.
Jean-Raphael Sessa.

CREW

Producer - Alain Sarde, Philippe Guez
Script - Walerian Borowczyk, from André Pieyre de Mandiargues' novel *Tout disparaitra*
Cinematography - Gérard Monceau, Jean-Paul Sergent, Michel Zolat

Editing – Florence Poulain, Guila Salama, Lili Sonnet, Marie-Hélène Zirisch

Costume designer – Valérie Adda

Hair – Nathalie Blanc

Production Manager – Catherine Mazières

Assistant Director – Gérard Grégory

Sound – Thierry Godard

Organ – Jean-Paul Imbert

OTHER FILM PROJECTS DIRECTED BY WALERIAN BOROWCZYK

Mois d'août (1946)
Photographies vivantes (1954)
Atelier de Fernand Léger (1954)
Autumn (a.k.a. Jesien, 1955)
Once Upon a Time (1957)
School (1958)
Requited Feelings (a.k.a. Nagrodzone uczucia, 1958)
Dom (1959)
Les astronautes (1959)
Le concert de M. et Mme. Kabal (1962)
L'encyclopedie de grand-maman en 13 volumes (1963)
Holy Smoke (1963)
Renaissance (1964)
Les jeux des anges (1965)
Le dictionnaire de Joachim (1965)
Rosalie (1966)
Diptyque (1967)
Mr. and Mrs. Kabal's Theatre (a.k.a. Théâtre de M. et Mme. Kabal, 1967)
Gavotte (1968)
Le phonographe (1969)
Une collection particulière (1973)
Brief von Paris (1975)
Escargot de Venus (1975)
L'amour monstre de tous les temps (1977)
Private Collections (1979), segment: L'armoire
Scherzo infernal (1984)
Série rose (a.k.a. Softly from Paris, 4 episodes, 1986-1991)
    Le lotus d'or (1986)
    Un traitement mérité (1990)
    Almanach des adresses des demoiselles de Paris (1990)
    L'experte Halima (1991)

BIBLIOGRAPHY

Sue Adler. "Enticements to Voyeurism", *Cinema Papers*, 50, Feb, 1985
W. Borowczyk. *Anatomy of the Devil*, 1992
–. *My Polish Years*, Hypnos Media, Paris, 2001
Borowczyk: Cinéaste Onirique: Le cas étrange du Dr Jekyll et Miss Osbourne, Collection La Vue and B. Diffusion, Paris, 1981
D.A. Cook. *A History of Narrative Film*, W.W. Norton, New York, NY, 1981, 1990, 1996
J. Gerber. *Anatole Dauman: Pictures of a Producer*, British Film Institute, London, 1992
T. Gilliam. *Gilliam on Gilliam*, ed. I. Christie, Faber, London, 1999
S. Jaworzy, ed. *Shock: The Essential Guide to Exploitation Cinema*, Titan Books, London, 1996
C. Kessler. "How You Look at It: The Beastly Art of Walerian Borowczyk", in *Video Watchdog*, Special Edition, 1
–. *Cinema Papers*, 128, 129
Tom Milne. "Héroïnes du mal, Les (Three Immoral Women)", *Monthly Film Bulletin*, July 1981
K. Newman. *Nightmare Movies*, Harmony, New York, NY, 1988
M. Praz. *The Romantic Agony*, tr. Davidson, Oxford University Press, Oxford, 1933
M. Richardson. *Surrealism and Cinema*, Berg, New York, NY, 2006
D. Thomson. "That Hairy Monster" [on Walerian Borowczyk's *The Beast*], *Sight & Sound*, June, 2001
C. Tohill & P. Tombs. *Immoral Tales: Sex and Horror Cinema in Europe 1956-1984*, Titan Books, London, 1995
P. Verlaine. *Selected Poems*, tr. J. Richardson, Penguin, London, 1974
Walerian Borowczyk di Valerio Caprara, La Nuova Italia, Florence, 1981
J. Zipes. *The Brothers Grimm: From Enchanted Forests to the Modern World*, Routledge, New York, NY, 1989,
–. *The Enchanted Screen* Routledge, New York, NY, 2011

CRESCENT MOON PUBLISHING

ARTS, PAINTING, SCULPTURE

The Art of Andy Goldsworthy: Complete Works
Andy Goldsworthy: Touching Nature
Andy Goldsworthy in Close-Up
Andy Goldsworthy: Pocket Guide
Andy Goldsworthy In America
Land Art: A Complete Guide
The Art of Richard Long: Complete Works
Richard Long: Pocket Guide
Land Art In the UK
Land Art in Close-Up
Land Art In the U.S.A.
Land Art: Pocket Guide
Installation Art in Close-Up
Minimal Art and Artists In the 1960s and After
Colourfield Painting
Land Art DVD, TV documentary
Andy Goldsworthy DVD, TV documentary
The Erotic Object: Sexuality in Sculpture From Prehistory to the Present Day
Sex in Art: Pornography and Pleasure in Painting and Sculpture
Postwar Art
Sacred Gardens: The Garden in Myth, Religion and Art
Glorification: Religious Abstraction in Renaissance and 20th Century Art
Early Netherlandish Painting
Leonardo da Vinci
Piero della Francesca
Giovanni Bellini
Fra Angelico: Art and Religion in the Renaissance
Mark Rothko: The Art of Transcendence
Frank Stella: American Abstract Artist
Jasper Johns
Brice Marden
Alison Wilding: The Embrace of Sculpture
Vincent van Gogh: Visionary Landscapes
Eric Gill: Nuptials of God
Constantin Brancusi: Sculpting the Essence of Things
Max Beckmann
Caravaggio
Gustave Moreau
Egon Schiele: Sex and Death In Purple Stockings
Delizioso Fotografico Fervore: Works In Process 1
Sacro Cuore: Works In Process 2
The Light Eternal: J.M.W. Turner
The Madonna Glorified: Karen Arthurs

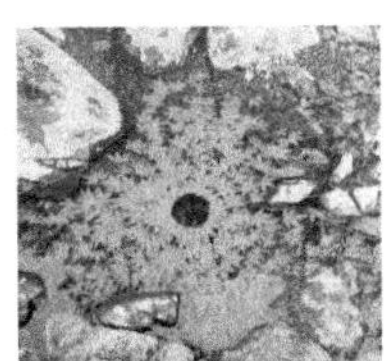
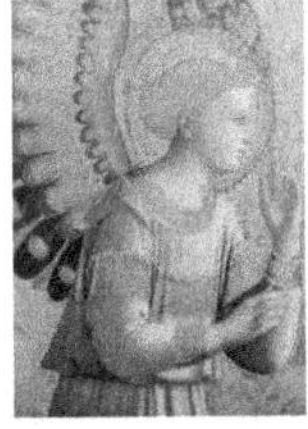
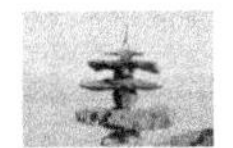
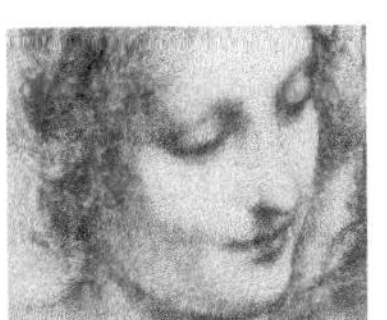
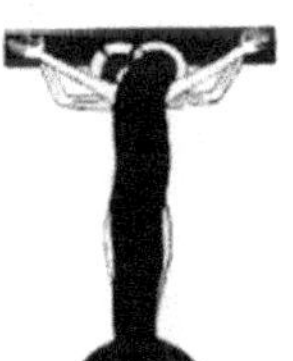
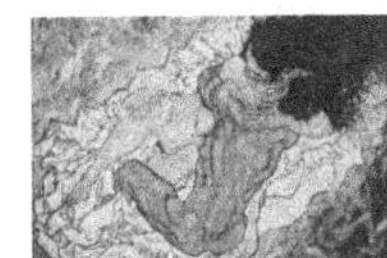

LITERATURE

J.R.R. Tolkien: The Books, The Films, The Whole Cultural Phenomenon
J.R.R. Tolkien: Pocket Guide
Tolkien's Heroic Quest
The *Earthsea* Books of Ursula Le Guin
Beauties, Beasts and Enchantment: Classic French Fairy Tales
German Popular Tales by the Brothers Grimm
Philip Ullman and *His Dark Materials*
Sexing Hardy: Thomas Hardy and Feminism
Thomas Hardy's *Tess of the d'Urbervilles*
Thomas Hardy's *Jude the Obscure*
Thomas Hardy: The Tragic Novels
Love and Tragedy: Thomas Hardy
The Poetry of Landscape in Hardy
Wessex Revisited: Thomas Hardy and John Cowper Powys
Wolfgang Iser: Essays and Interviews
Petrarch, Dante and the Troubadours
Maurice Sendak and the Art of Children's Book Illustration
Andrea Dworkin
Cixous, Irigaray, Kristeva: The *Jouissance* of French Feminism
Julia Kristeva: Art, Love, Melancholy, Philosophy, Semiotics and Psychoanalysis
Hélene Cixous I Love You: The *Jouissance* of Writing
Luce Irigaray: Lips, Kissing, and the Politics of Sexual Difference
Peter Redgrove: Here Comes the Flood
Peter Redgrove: Sex-Magic-Poetry-Cornwall
Lawrence Durrell: Between Love and Death, East and West
Love, Culture & Poetry: Lawrence Durrell
Cavafy: Anatomy of a Soul
German Romantic Poetry: Goethe, Novalis, Heine, Hölderlin
Feminism and Shakespeare
Shakespeare: Love, Poetry & Magic
The Passion of D.H. Lawrence
D.H. Lawrence: Symbolic Landscapes
D.H. Lawrence: Infinite Sensual Violence
Rimbaud: Arthur Rimbaud and the Magic of Poetry
The Ecstasies of John Cowper Powys
Sensualism and Mythology: The Wessex Novels of John Cowper Powys
Amorous Life: John Cowper Powys and the Manifestation of Affectivity (H.W. Fawkner)
Postmodern Powys: New Essays on John Cowper Powys (Joe Boulter)
Rethinking Powys: Critical Essays on John Cowper Powys
Paul Bowles & Bernardo Bertolucci
Rainer Maria Rilke
Joseph Conrad: *Heart of Darkness*
In the Dim Void: Samuel Beckett
Samuel Beckett Goes into the Silence
André Gide: Fiction and Fervour
Jackie Collins and the Blockbuster Novel
Blinded By Her Light: The Love-Poetry of Robert Graves
The Passion of Colours: Travels In Mediterranean Lands
Poetic Forms

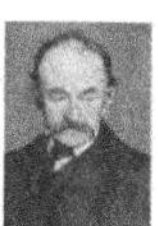
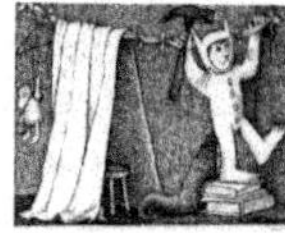
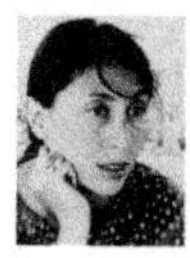
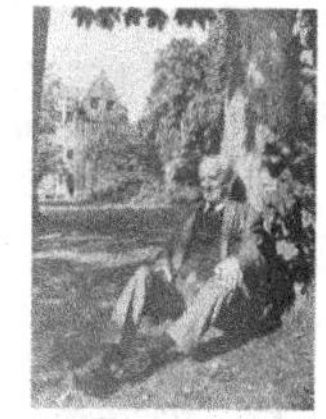
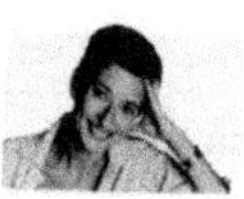
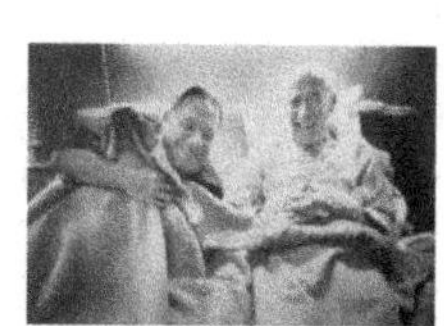
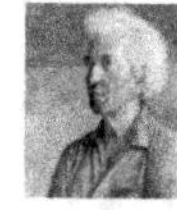
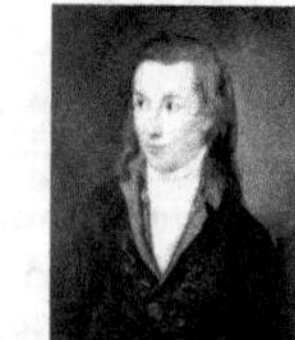

POETRY

Ursula Le Guin: Walking In Cornwall
Peter Redgrove: Here Comes The Flood

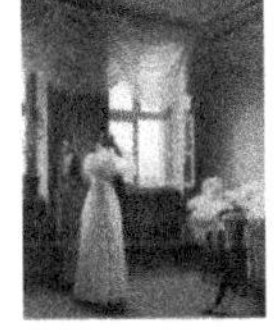

Peter Redgrove: Sex-Magic-Poetry-Cornwall
Dante: Selections From the *Vita Nuova*
Petrarch, Dante and the Troubadours
William Shakespeare: *The Sonnets*
William Shakespeare: Complete Poems
Blinded By Her Light: The Love-Poetry of Robert Graves
Emily Dickinson: Selected Poems

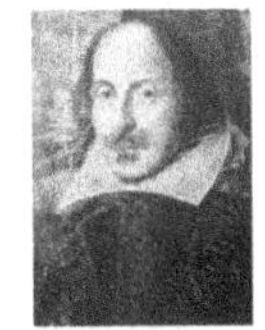

Emily Brontë: Poems
Thomas Hardy: Selected Poems
Percy Bysshe Shelley: Poems

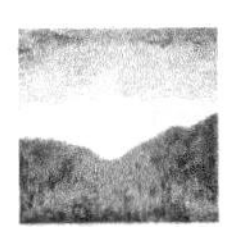

John Keats: Selected Poems
D.H. Lawrence: Selected Poems

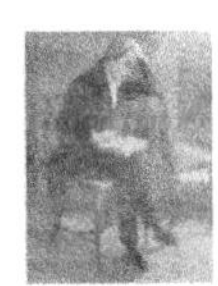

Edmund Spenser: Poems
Edmund Spenser: *Amoretti*
John Donne: Poems
Henry Vaughan: Poems
Sir Thomas Wyatt: Poems
Robert Herrick: Selected Poems
Rilke: Space, Essence and Angels in the Poetry of Rainer Maria Rilke
Rainer Maria Rilke: Selected Poems

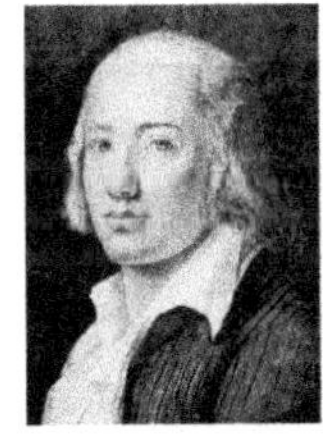

Friedrich Hölderlin: Selected Poems

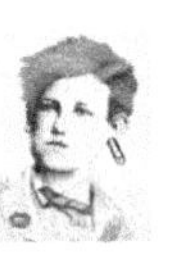

Arseny Tarkovsky: Selected Poems
Novalis: *Hymns To the Night*
Paul Verlaine: Selected Poems
Arthur Rimbaud: Selected Poems
Arthur Rimbaud: *A Season in Hell*
Arthur Rimbaud and the Magic of Poetry
D.J. Enright: By-Blows
Jeremy Reed: Brigitte's Blue Heart

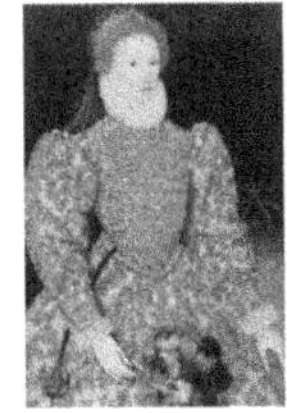

Jeremy Reed: Claudia Schiffer's Red Shoes
Gorgeous Little Orpheus
Radiance: New Poems
Crescent Moon Book of Nature Poetry
Crescent Moon Book of Love Poetry
Crescent Moon Book of Mystical Poetry
Crescent Moon Book of Elizabethan Love Poetry
Crescent Moon Book of Metaphysical Poetry
Crescent Moon Book of Romantic Poetry
Pagan America: New American Poetry

MEDIA, CINEMA, FEMINISM and CULTURAL STUDIES

J.R.R. Tolkien: The Books, The Films, The Whole Cultural Phenomenon
J.R.R. Tolkien: Pocket Guide
The *Lord of the Rings* Movies: Pocket Guide
The Cinema of Hayao Miyazaki
Hayao Miyazaki: *Princess Mononoke*: Pocket Movie Guide
Hayao Miyazaki: *Spirited Away*: Pocket Movie Guide
Tim Burton
Ken Russell
Ken Russell: *Tommy*: Pocket Movie Guide
The Ghost Dance: The Origins of Religion
The Peyote Cult

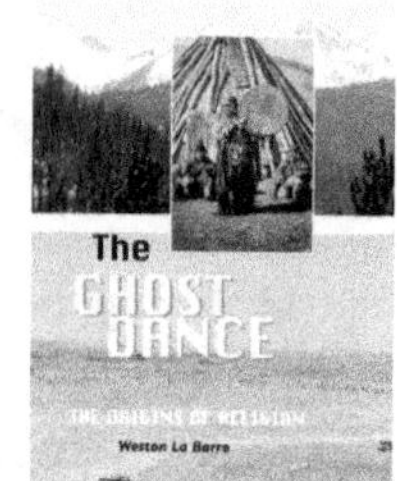

Cixous, Irigaray, Kristeva: The *Jouissance* of French Feminism
Julia Kristeva: Art, Love, Melancholy, Philosophy, Semiotics and Psychoanalysis
Luce Irigaray: Lips, Kissing, and the Politics of Sexual Difference
Hélene Cixous I Love You: The *Jouissance* of Writing
Andrea Dworkin
'Cosmo Woman': The World of Women's Magazines
Women in Pop Music
Discovering the Goddess (Geoffrey Ashe)

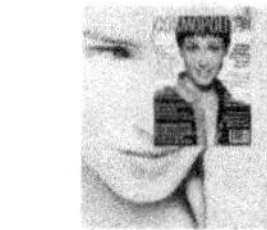

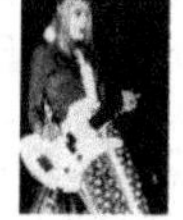

The Poetry of Cinema
The Sacred Cinema of Andrei Tarkovsky
Andrei Tarkovsky: Pocket Guide
Andrei Tarkovsky: *Mirror*: Pocket Movie Guide
Andrei Tarkovsky: *The Sacrifice*: Pocket Movie Guide
Walerian Borowczyk: Cinema of Erotic Dreams
Jean-Luc Godard: The Passion of Cinema
Jean-Luc Godard: *Hail Mary*: Pocket Movie Guide
Jean-Luc Godard: *Contempt*: Pocket Movie Guide
Jean-Luc Godard: *Pierrot le Fou*: Pocket Movie Guide

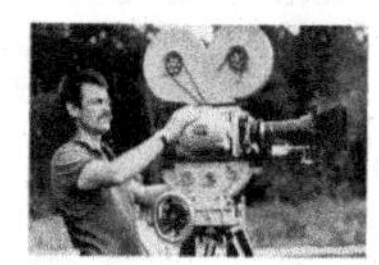

John Hughes and Eighties Cinema
Ferris Bueller's Day Off: Pocket Movie Guide
Jean-Luc Godard: Pocket Guide
The Cinema of Richard Linklater

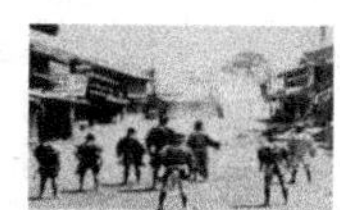

Liv Tyler: Star In Ascendance
Blade Runner and the Films of Philip K. Dick
Paul Bowles and Bernardo Bertolucci
Media Hell: Radio, TV and the Press
An Open Letter to the BBC
Detonation Britain: Nuclear War in the UK
Feminism and Shakespeare
Wild Zones: Pornography, Art and Feminism
Sex in Art: Pornography and Pleasure in Painting and Sculpture
Sexing Hardy: Thomas Hardy and Feminism

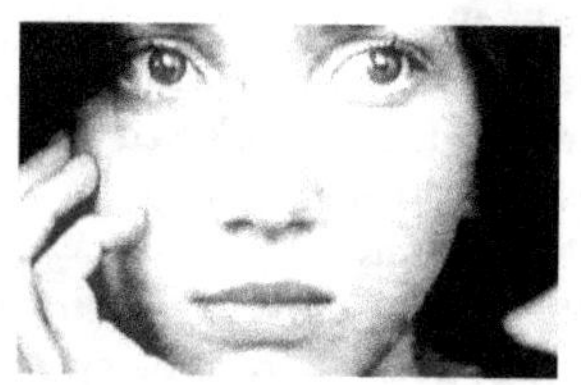

In my view *The Light Eternal* is among the very best of all the material I read on Turner. (Douglas Graham, director of the Turner Museum, Denver, Colorado)

The Light Eternal is a model monograph, an exemplary job. The subject matter of the book is beautifully organised and dead on beam. (Lawrence Durrell)

It is amazing for me to see my work treated with such passion and respect. (Andrea Dworkin)

CRESCENT MOON PUBLISHING
P.O. Box 1312, Maidstone, Kent, ME14 5XU, Great Britain. www.crmoon.com

www.ingramcontent.com/pod-product-compliance
Lightning Source LLC
LaVergne TN
LVHW020508100826
845148LV00003B/727

* 9 7 8 1 8 6 1 7 1 3 6 7 4 *